Palgrave Macmillan Studies in Banking and Financial Institutions

Series Editor: **Professor Philip Molyneux**

The Palgrave Macmillan Studies in Banking and Financial Institutions will be international in orientation and include studies of banking within particular countries or regions, and studies of particular themes such as Corporate Banking, Risk Management, Mergers and Acquisitions, etc. The books will be focused upon research and practice, and include up-to-date and innovative studies on contemporary topics in banking that will have global impact and influence.

Titles include:

Yener Altunbaş, Blaise Gadanecz and Alper Kara
SYNDICATED LOANS
A Hybrid of Relationship Lending and Publicly Traded Debt

Elena Beccalli
IT AND EUROPEAN BANK PERFORMANCE

Santiago Carbó, Edward P.M. Gardener and Philip Molyneux
FINANCIAL EXCLUSION

Violaine Cousin
BANKING IN CHINA

Franco Fiordelisi and Philip Molyneux
SHAREHOLDER VALUE IN BANKING

Munawar Iqbal and Philip Molyneux
THIRTY YEARS OF ISLAMIC BANKING
History, Performance and Prospects

Mario La Torre and Gianfranco A. Vento
MICROFINANCE

Philip Molyneux and Munawar Iqbal
BANKING AND FINANCIAL SYSTEMS IN THE ARAB WORLD

Philip Molyneux and Eleuterio Vallelado (*editors*)
FRONTIERS OF BANKS IN A GLOBAL ECONOMY

Anastasia Nesvetailova
FRAGILE FINANCE
Debt, Speculation and Crisis in the Age of Global Credit

Andrea Schertler
THE VENTURE CAPITAL INDUSTRY IN EUROPE

Alfred Slager
THE INTERNATIONALIZATION OF BANKS
Patterns, Strategies and Performance

Palgrave Macmillan Studies in Banking and Financial Institutions
Series Standing Order ISBN 1–4039–4872–0

You can receive future titles in this series as they are published by placing a standing order. Please contact your bookseller or, in case of difficulty, write to us at the address below with your name and address, the title of the series and the ISBN quoted above.

Customer Services Department, Macmillan Distribution Ltd, Houndmills, Basingstoke, Hampshire RG21 6XS, England

Frontiers of Banks in a Global Economy

Edited by

Philip Molyneux
Professor of Banking and Finance, University of Wales, Bangor, UK

and

Eleuterio Vallelado
*Vice Chancellor for Stragetic Planning and Professor of Finance,
University of Valladolid, Spain*

First published in 2008 by
PALGRAVE MACMILLAN
Houndmills, Basingstoke, Hampshire RG21 6XS and
175 Fifth Avenue, New York, N.Y. 10010
Companies and representatives throughout the world.

PALGRAVE MACMILLAN is the global academic imprint of the Palgrave
Macmillan division of St. Martin's Press, LLC and of Palgrave Macmillan Ltd.
Macmillan® is a registered trademark in the United States, United Kingdom
and other countries. Palgrave is a registered trademark in the European
Union and other countries.

ISBN-13: 978–0–230–52568–9 hardback
ISBN-10: 0–230–52568–7 hardback

This book is printed on paper suitable for recycling and made from fully
managed and sustained forest sources. Logging, pulping and manufacturing
processes are expected to conform to the environmental regulations of
the country of origin.

A catalogue record for this book is available from the British Library.

A catalog record for this book is available from the Library of Congress.

10 9 8 7 6 5 4 3 2 1
17 16 15 14 13 12 11 10 09 08

Printed and bound in Great Britain by
CPI Antony Rowe, Chippenham and Eastbourne

Contents

List of Figures

List of Tables

Acknowledgements

Chapter 6, 'Banks in the Microfinance Market' was inspired by Mario La Torre & Gianfranco Vento, Microfinance, 2006, Palgrave Macmillan.

Notes on Contributors

Dr Yener Altunbaş is a Senior Lecturer at the University of Wales, Bangor where he teaches both undergraduate and postgraduate programmes within the Bangor Business School (BBS). He has previously been Research Fellow with the Business School at South Bank University, London, and as a Research Associate at the Centre of Business Research at Cambridge University. Dr Altunbaş is currently collaborating on a research project with other European colleagues at the Bundesbank, Bank for International Settlements (BIS), the European Central Bank (ECB), Bank of Italy, and Bank of Spain.

Luisa Anderloni is Full Professor of Financial Intermediaries and Markets at the University of Milan. She is the Director of the periodical *Survey on Financial Innovation* at Newfin-Bocconi University and the Director of the PhD programme in History and Finance at the University of Milan.

Dr Rym Ayadi is the Head of Research of the Financial Institutions and Prudential Policy Unit at the Centre for European Policy Studies (CEPS) in Brussels. She also lectures on Economics and Finance on the MSc International Banking and Finance at the Isle of Man Business School. Prior to joining CEPS, she worked as an economist for the French Banking Association and the European Commission.

Dr Georgios Chortareas is a Reader in International Finance at the University of Essex and Visiting Professor of Economics at the University of Athens. He is a member of the Money Macro and Finance Research Group (MMF) Committee.

Dr Claudia Girardone is Senior Lecturer in Finance at the University of Essex where she teaches Modern Banking and Introduction to Finance. Her research focus is in the areas of bank performance and efficiency analysis.

Mario La Torre is Full Professor in Banking and Finance and Director of the MA course in Film Art Management at the University of Rome 'La Sapienza'. His main area of research is on the financial management and financial innovation of the banking and financial services industry and he has published widely in this area. Professor La Torre has directed the Research Group of the Italian National Committee for the 2005 International Year of Microcredit. He is also on the Scientific Board of various NGOs and financial institutions operating in the microfinance sector.

Dr Xijuan (Angel) Liao is a postdoctoral Research Fellow in investment and finance at University of Edinburgh (Sponsored by Martin Currie Co. Ltd).

She currently researches on hedge fund investment behaviour and performance analysis in emerging markets

Ted Lindblom is Professor and Chairman of the PhD Research Committee of Business Administration at the University of Gothenburg. His current research concerns corporate governance, risk management and financial architecture. In the banking field, he has for more than twenty years studied the pricing of payments services and market structural changes in mainly retail banking. He has authored and co-authored several articles and books on these issues.

David Marques is a Senior Economist at the European Central Bank. His research covers a range of topics such as the impact of the banking sector on the transmission mechanism of monetary policy or how changes on the European financial structure affect borrowers' financing conditions.

Philip Molyneux is Professor in Banking and Finance at Bangor University, Wales, UK. He has published widely in the banking and financial services area. His most recent co-authored texts are on: Thirty Years of Islamic Banking (Palgrave Macmillan, 2005), Shareholder Value in Banking (Palgrave Macmillan, 2006), and Introduction to Banking (FT Prentice Hall, 2006). His main research interests focus on the structural features of banking systems and bank performance.

Magnus Olsson is a PhD candidate at the School of Business, Economics and Commercial Law at Goteborg University. He works as a Researcher and as a Lecturer, mostly within courses related to the banking industry. Magnus is also the CFO of a Swedish savings bank and is involved with economic and legal issues at the Swedish Savings Banks Association.

René van der Linden studied Economics at the University of Amsterdam and is currently a Lecturer in Economics at the School of Economics INHOLLAND University Amsterdam/Diemen in the Netherlands. He previously worked for the Erasmus University Rotterdam and the Amsterdam Academy for Banking and Finance. His current research interests are in the field of International Economics, Banking and Finance, and Transition Economics.

Dr David Pelilli has recently completed his doctoral studies at University of Tor Vergata, Rome. He has published various articles on the strategic positioning of e-banking players and the adoption of internet banking by retail customers. His current research focuses on the adoption of e-money products.

Daniela Vandone is Assistant Professor of Economics of Financial Intermediaries at the University of Milan.

Dr Gianfranco Vento is a postdoctoral scholar in Microfinance at the University of Rome 'La Sapienza'. He has been a member of different research groups of the Italian National Committee for the 2005 International Year of Microcredit. Previously he was employed as an analyst in the Banking Supervision Department at Bank of Italy. He has been Visiting Professor at the University of Buenos Aires. His main research interest relates to the money market and microfinance. His research has been published by leading Italian academic journals. He is the author of *Interbank Market and Eurosystem* (Giappichelli, 2005).

Eleuterio Vallelado is Vice Chancellor for Strategic Planning and Professor of Finance at Universidad de Valladolid. Born in Valladolid, he obtained his Bachelors degree in Economics and Business and his Ph.D at the University of Valladolid and MBA from New York University. He has published widely in corporate finance and banking areas. His research interest include: Corporate finance, corporate governance in banks, and behavioral finance.

Alexia Ventouri is a PhD candidate in Finance at the University of Essex. Her research interests are in banking, finance, and efficiency measurement.

Dr Jonathan Williams is a Senior Lecturer in Banking and Finance at the Bangor Business School, University of Wales, Bangor. His research interests span developed and emerging markets and cover financial sector policies, bank efficiency and performance, corporate governance, M&A, price discovery, and volatility transmission. Dr Williams is a co-author of *The Monitoring of Structural Changes and Trends in the Internal Market for Financial Services* (EC, 2002). He has contributed to several major studies including *Credit Institutions and Banking* (EC, 1997) and the Cruickshank Report into competition in UK banking, commissioned by HM Treasury (2000).

Balzhan Zhussupova is a PhD candidate at the University of Wales, Bangor. She also holds a MBA degree with distinction (Banking and Finance) from the University of Wales, Bangor. Currently, Balzhan Zhussupova works as a Visiting Assistant Professor at the Kazakhstan Institute of Management, Economics and Strategic Research (Almaty, Kazakhstan). Her research interests include the issues of ownership and corporate governance of financial institutions, financial conglomeration, and corporate diversification.

1
Introduction

Philip Molyneux* and Eleuterio Vallelado**

Global banking systems continue to experience marked change in the light of forces that are reshaping the structure of markets and the way in which banking business is being conducted. One major trend has been the growth in both domestic and cross-border consolidation that is creating large diversified financial firms that span continents. Domestic consolidation is increasing concentration, raising competition concerns for regulators and consumers. Cross-border deals are promoting the access and coverage of foreign banks in domestic markets in both developed and emerging markets and this has implications for the competitive position of domestic banks and presents challenges for regulators – both within country but it also heightens the need for greater international collaboration. In addition, the owners of banks – namely shareholders – need to know whether such consolidation activity will increase the value of their investments or whether it will be value destroying. The potential for risk diversification and the realization of scale, scope and other economies are also of key interest.

Concurrent with the ongoing consolidation trend, banks are now subject to a new regulatory environment under Basle 2. Jurisdictions are applying different timelines for when they are to apply the new rules and there continues to be debate as to when the United States and other countries will implement the new capital adequacy regulations. It is expected that many European banks will adhere to the new rules by the end of 2007, but that only around 20 or so US banks will adopt the new regulations by then. It has been noted that 95 banking system authorities have said that they will implement the new system by 2015 – so there is some time to wait before the full global effect of the Basle 2 regulatory environment can be accurately

* Bangor Business School, Bangor University, Bangor, Gwynedd, UK. Phone: +44 1248382170, e-mail: p.molyneux@bangor.ac.uk
** Departamento de Economía Financiera y Contabilidad, Facultad de Ciencias Económicas y Empresariales, Avda. del Valle Esgueva, nº 6, 47011 Valladolid, Spain. Phone: +34 983 42 33 87, e-mail: teyo@eco.uva.es

gauged. Nevertheless, there is strong evidence that the new system will result in lower levels of regulatory capital being held by the global banking community, although it is also widely agreed that Basle 2 will enable banks to mange their credit, market and operational risks more effectively than in the past.

As banking systems become more market orientated and shareholder value focused there is growing concern from both politicians and regulators that less profitable consumer groups are being marginalized. This has led to growing interest in banks playing a more proactive role in providing banking and other financial services to un-banked consumers. The notion of financial exclusion has become mainstream and the growth in microfinance programmes (particularly in developing countries) and the offer of specialist services to migrants have gone some way to help facilitate the banking habit for marginalized banking customers. The development of such services reflects both policy initiatives and also the desire of mainstream banking firms to develop a range of services for new client groups. This reflects not only increased competition in various segments of the banking sector but also the ability of firms to provide financial innovations to meet new client demands. In more mainstream areas, banks continue to innovate both from a financial and technological perspective. There has been an explosion of new financial products dealing with a whole host of issues – internet banking and new payments media proliferate, banks now offer a myriad of tailored mortgage and deposit products, retail investors are faced with a growing number of structured and alternative investments from which they can choose.

New markets are also opening-up. Many foreign banks have developed a presence in China and other Asian banking systems aiming to take advantage of potential high-growth (mainly retail financial services) markets. As foreign banks enter new markets, domestic banks have to reassess their situation and greater competition is forcing them to improve their systems, product-offering, efficiency and productivity. Technology and other 'know-how' transfer has become an important aspect of these developments. Regulators are also not immune from these changes, they have to develop and adapt to this new environment if they are to build stable, profitable and efficient banking systems.

The aforementioned cover many of the issues that currently face the global banking community. These and various other developments are discussed in detail in this text that comprises a selection of papers that were presented at the Wolpertinger Conference of the European Association of University Teachers of Banking and Finance held at the Institute of European Studies, University of Valladolid, Valladolid, Spain, between 31 August and 1 September 2006.

The first two chapters discuss aspects relating to consolidation in banking markets. Chapter 2 by Rym Ayadi examines the performance of bank

Mergers and Acquisitions (M&A) in Europe. The European banking sector has been consolidating at a rapid pace during the 1990s. The deregulation of banking activities, the progress made towards the completion of an integrated European financial market, financial globalization, technological and financial innovations, the imperative of value creation and the introduction of the euro are some of the principal forces that fuelled the process of banking consolidation in Europe. Moreover, the adoption of most measures under the Financial Services Action Plan (FSAP) and the European Commission's White Paper on financial services policy (2005–10) towards complete integration of European financial markets is expected to act as a real impetus to accelerate banking consolidation over the coming years. This chapter introduces a new approach to examining bank M&A by considering various strategies underlying consolidation activity – namely the initial activities of the banks involved in M&As and the geographical dimension of transactions. The results show that the economic and financial performance of banking M&As depend on their underlying strategies, defined depending on the banks' initial activities and their geographical reach. The optimal combination of these two factors – defining the optimal underlying strategy – could be a factor for success or failure of an M&A.

Chapter 3 by Jon Williams and Angel Liao examines the post-1998 wave of cross-border bank mergers and acquisitions activity involving purchases of stakes in target banks in emerging market economies (EME) by acquiring banks from industrialized countries. This international consolidation of the banking industry has followed hard on the heels of extensive domestic consolidation processes, which began in the United States and Europe in the mid-1980s before spreading across EME in the 1990s and beyond. The main aim of this chapter is to see if the wave of internationalization in the banking industry has created value for bank shareholders. Using an event study methodology the authors find that returns to target bank shareholders are positive, implying that EME stockmarkets perceive cross-border bank M&A activity to be value generating. Nevertheless, the magnitude of returns to target bank shareholders tends to be larger than returns to acquiring bank shareholders. This suggests there is no evidence of wealth being transferred from EME to industrialized countries in cross-border bank M&A transactions between 1998 and 2005. An interesting finding of the Williams and Liao chapter is that the results suggest that international stockmarkets react somewhat differently than EME stockmarkets to cross-border bank M&A activity. Aside from abnormal returns being smaller, often they are significantly negative, which implies cross-border M&A is perceived to be value destructive. This is the case when international banks acquire Latin American banks, when international banks increase minority stakes or convert minority ownership into majority holdings, and when targets are acquired via open market purchase and a stock swap. On the contrary, cross-border M&A is viewed as value creating when international banks acquire stakes in CEE and Asian targets, when majority stakes are purchased or increased, and when stakes are purchased via private negotiation. The US, European (excluding Spain and the UK) and Dutch stockmarkets appear to believe that their countries' banks can generate value through cross-border M&A activity, but this belief does not extend to the Spanish and UK stockmarkets.

Chapter 4 by Ted Lindblom and Magnus Olsson focuses on Basle 2. In particular it examines how the implementation of Basle 2 is likely to affect the capital held by Nordic banks and the interest rates on their lending. The chapter starts out from the working hypothesis that the pricing of bank loans will be affected by the implementation of Basle 2 in two ways. Firstly, the improved models for assessing credit (and market) risks developed under the new capital adequacy framework may be used by banks to allocate an accurate risk premium for each individual loan or group of loans. If this premium deviates from the current one, this would lead to either lower or higher interest rates for the single borrower, simply as a result of the improved ability of banks to assess and price risks. Secondly, the Basle 2 Accord may also change the regulatory capital requirement for different types of loans. Depending on whether this would actually change the 'cost of bank capital' in practice, that is, banks will hold less or more capital than today, the interest rates to borrowers would be affected accordingly. In this chapter, Lindblom and Olsson study this empirically by making a comparative survey and analysis of the impact of the current Basle Accord on capital held by banks in the Nordic countries. The chapter examines how well the amount of capital held by banks corresponds to the variance in their earnings and profitability ratios. Overall, this chapter provides strong evidence that Basle 2 is likely to increase the loan prices of Nordic banks.

Chapter 5 by Yener Altunbaş, David Marques and Balzhan Zhussupova examines the relationship between bank corporate structure and lending for a large sample of European credit institutions over the period 1999 to 2004. The purpose of this chapter is to examine whether finance constraints exist for European credit institutions. The authors use information on bank shareholdings to analyse the behaviour of banks that have different levels of affiliation with bank and non-bank financial firms. The main result is that the loan growth of banks with a greater number and larger ownerships of financial institutions are found to be less dependent on internally generated funds for loan growth. Banks that have only a limited number of affiliations are much more dependent on internally generated funds to finance loan growth. Such banks appear financially constrained and they face market imperfections that increase the costs of banks' external finance relative to the cost of internal financing. The results generally support the hypothesis that internal capital markets created through affiliation with other financial institutions alleviate banks' financing constraints.

Chapter 6 by Mario LaTorre and Gianfranco Vento examines key features of the global microfinance business. The fight against extreme poverty has become part of a wider objective in the fight against financial exclusion where banks play a major role. The supply of products is not only confined to banking services but nowadays encompasses other financial services and is also often inextricably linked to technical assistance. The industry structure is also complex, combing traditional banks and financial firms, international donors, traditional NGOs, and unofficial providers. The chapter looks at how the entry of banks and other specialized profit-oriented institutions into the microfinance market has emphasized the trade-off between the objectives of economic and financial equilibrium on the one hand and the social goals of microfinance projects on the other hand. From this point of view, this Chapter offers a new taxonomy for modern microfinance and discusses the definitions of 'sustainability' and 'outreach', identifying the various meanings of these broad concepts. It also analyses the key variables and the operational and management choices that a commercial bank should consider in order to reconcile the aims of sustainability with those of outreach, so as to implement 'ethically profitable' microfinance programmes. The authors conclude that the development of microfinance, today, requires providers to find operational and managerial models able to yield balanced cooperation between the non-profit system and the traditional financial system. The practitioners and the institutions of microfinance have to benefit from the expertise of banks and financial intermediaries to achieve a higher level of efficiency in resource management. Financial intermediaries can, with microfinance experience, regain proximity to local territories and customer care. Together, the non-profit system and the traditional financial system must collaborate to achieve the highest level of ethicality of financial intermediation for microfinance, compatible with the objectives of sustainability and performance.

Chapter 7 by Luisa Anderloni and Daniela Vandone examine how banks and other financial providers are developing their services to meet the financial needs of migrants. In particular, this chapter discusses the potential for migrants as banking customers and analyses areas where firms have innovated in order to better serve this market segment. The first part of the chapter provides an overview of the main characteristics of this untapped market segment and follows on by introducing the issue of financial exclusion and the position of migrants as clusters at risk of financial exclusion. The authors present an interesting outline of migration phases and the financial service demands across the migrant life cycles. Particular attention is paid to the role of remittances and the wide range of such services available. The chapter also highlights various services developed by banks in Europe and North America to meet the demand for banking and financial services by migrants. Anderloni and Vandone suggest that banks may access the market best if they focus on providing a targeted offer; this means that dedicated counters are opened with suitably skilled staff and with ad hoc commercial and legal communications, but also that both specific products or product packages are prepared for the market target, and, in general, that the strategic orientation goes more towards a specific customer segment. With this approach, the strategies might go as far as making agreements or alliances with ethnic organizations.

Chapter 8 by René van der Linden examines developments in the Chinese banking system – a subject of major topical interest given the increasing exposure of international banks to that country. The first part of the chapter discusses features of the real economy and highlights the country's recent economic performance. The second part of the chapter focuses on the expanding bank-based financial system in order to understand the one-sided nature of financial intermediation in the country. In addition, the major shortcomings of the dominant banking sector, the impact of a new World Trading Organization (WTO) level playing-field and competition for new bank customers are discussed. The final part of the chapter outlines the deepening banking reforms and assesses the potential for future sustainable growth in the country. Van der Linden argues that since many of the short-comings in the bank-based financial system are interlinked, only a coordinated, transparent, system-wide reform can shape the modern financial system. The current priorities for banking reforms have focused mostly on the large commercial banks to prepare them for foreign equity listing. Since its creation in 2003, CBRC has focused on reducing and resolving the volume of bad loans and the WTO conditions have also forced some specific reforms on the banking system. The problems are all characterized by cheap corporate bank loans. In addition, these problems are closely interlinked by an underdeveloped consumer loan market, a very small bond market, a lack of domestic institutional investors, a small underdeveloped equity market, inefficient bank operations and very limited access to capital for small businesses. It is noted that priorities for the reform agenda must be to improve the allocation of capital and create a more balanced, less bank-dominated, and more efficient financial system.

Chapter 9 by Georgios E. Chortareas, Claudia Girardone and Alexia Ventouri examines the most relevant trends characterizing the Greek banking sector since the early 1990s, including the impact and run up to Economic and Monetary Union (EMU). The authors focus on studies on bank efficiency and productivity, highlighting conceptual and methodological issues associated with modelling bank performance in Greece (and elsewhere). In particular, the chapter provides an overview of the different econometric techniques used to estimate cost and profit efficiency in banking in the context of the main recent developments in efficiency and productivity analysis. Chortareas, Girardone and Ventouri discuss the implications of this literature in the context of the recent deregulation and consolidation waves as well as the catch-up process in the euro area. Finally, they assess the current challenges for Greek banks and identify potential new areas of research. One issue they highlight is that empirical studies of the Greek banking sector appear to suggest a relatively high level of inefficiency and only modest productivity – and this contrasts with the high level of profitability in the system. This, the authors suggest, deserves more research attention.

Finally, Chapter 10 by David Pelilli examines aspects of e-money usage by undertaking a detailed analysis of student's motivations for using such payments media. The chapter starts-off by analysing the factors that influence e-money use, both by considering these instruments' specific attributes and by combining the assumptions of Theory of Planned Behaviour (TPB) with Technology Acceptance Models (TAM). A survey on undergraduate students is conducted in order to identify the personal, sociological and technological variables involved in e-money use. The proposed model has been tested on students' payment habits using credit, debit and prepaid cards. Pelilli finds that personal and technological attitudes, social and control beliefs, and payment instruments features (in terms of perceived efficacy and efficiency) are linked with electronic money use. By developing research studies along similar lines the author concludes that banks and other financial firms can obtain more accurate information on the behaviour of their customer segments. As a consequence, financial intermediaries could use such information to develop more appropriate payments products.

2
Banking Mergers and Acquisitions' Performance in Europe

Rym Ayadi[*]

2.1 Introduction

The European banking sector has experienced a rapid process of mergers and acquisitions (M&A) during the 1990s.[1] The deregulation of banking activities, the progress made towards the completion of an integrated European financial market, financial globalization, technological and financial innovations, the imperative of value creation and the introduction of the euro are some of the principal forces that fuelled the process of banking consolidation. Today, it seems that (M&A) activity has picked up with various domestic and cross-border deals in the banking industry.[2] Indeed, faced with increased risks, uncertainty and enhanced competition, banking institutions must adopt the most economic strategic means to cut their costs and enhance their revenues. Moreover, the adoption of most measures under the Financial Services Action Plan (FSAP) and the European Commission's White Paper on financial services policy (2005–10) towards complete integration of European financial markets will act as a real impetus to accelerate banking consolidation in the coming years.

M&A is one of the responses that banks can use to grow externally together with alliances and partnerships. Nevertheless, many studies of the M&A wave of the 1990s have found that consolidation does not always result in improved economic performance. To explain the rationale of such a movement, the economic literature has mainly focused on examining the performance effects of M&A and then on its effects on competition in the underlying sector. Undoubtedly, economies of scale and scope have offered the main explanation source to performance change following M&A, leading to a number of empirical studies which have examined the relationship between size and costs. However, their findings were far from conclusive

* Rym Ayadi is a Research Fellow and Head of Financial Institutions Research Programme at the Centre for European Policy Studies (CEPS) Brussels, email: rym. ayadi@ceps.be

owing to the conceptual and technical limitations encountered when testing for the relevant hypotheses. Nonetheless, scale and scope economies are the foundation for newer concepts put forward nowadays to explain concentration in the banking sector. Indeed, if there is little evidence of scale and scope economies in the banking sector, it is important to question the real motivations of efficiency in this sector. Accordingly, the new justification related to X-efficiency[3] deserves particular attention. Indeed, X-efficiency is the fraction of the productive efficiency which is not explained by optimal resources allocation theory. This concept seems to offer greater predictive power in analysing performance change in banks in general and in banking M&A in particular.

Beyond scale and scope economies, and X-efficiency, M&As could be justified by revenue diversification and risks reduction, which are of particular relevance in the banking sector. Finally, another justification of M&As in banking is the one related to market power, particularly in highly concentrated banking markets and when a merger or an acquisition is targeting the same activity or region.

To test these theoretical justifications, several studies have examined the performance change of banking M&As, using either static or dynamic analyses. The former investigates the relationship between size and efficiency and the latter assesses the changes before and after an M&A.[4] Other studies have also tried to examine the impact of M&A on market power.

After displaying the findings of the US and European empirical research related to the dynamic analysis of banking M&A performance, this chapter introduces a new approach to categorize and assess banking M&A. This approach is based on a conceptual matrix[5] built on the interaction between two criteria: the activity of the banks involved in M&A and the geographical dimension of the transaction, which we consider by defining the various strategies underlying the M&A. Then, based on a subcategorization of 71 banking M&A in Europe, we assess the profitability and the efficiency (cost and profit) for the acquirers and the targets before and after deals and we compare both findings.

2.2   Theoretical background

According to the academic literature in banking and industrial economics, there is a variety of motivations driving consolidation, ranging from value maximization (including cost reduction and revenue growth) to other external and managerial goals.

The economic literature has justified banking M&A on the grounds that it enhances shareholder value. Indeed, the strengthening of the shareholders' role, the increasing importance of institutional investors in banking capital (pension funds, mutual funds and private equity), the pressures from the financial markets and new corporate governance rules have encouraged managers to orient their business objectives towards value maximization.

The traditional argument that M&A increase shareholder value is based on the assumption that the anticipated value of the entity created by the merger of two groups will exceed, in terms of potential wealth creation, the sum of the respective values of the two separate groups. That is: $1 + 1 = 3$. Two main types of synergies are achieved: operating synergies and financial synergies. The former takes the form of either revenue enhancement or cost reduction. The latter refers to the possibility that the cost of capital may be lowered by combining one or more companies.

In theory, M&A operations in the banking sector could create value by obtaining gains either in terms of efficiency or in terms of market power. Other motivations of M&A are also briefly discussed since they may partly offer a plausible explanation of certain types of transactions.

2.3   M&A and efficiency

An M&A allows the resulting company to obtain efficiency gains through cost reductions (or cost synergies), revenue increases (or revenue synergies), the exchange of best practices and/or risk diversification.

Cost synergies result from an improved organization of banking production, a better scale and/or a better combination of production factors. The core objective is to extract benefits from cost complementarities and economies of scale and scope. In practice, cost synergies might be derived from: (a) the integration of different skilled teams or information technology infrastructures; (b) the combination of different back-office and general services; or (c) the rationalization of the domestic and/or international banking networks. The more flexible the labour market, the more likely it is that the company will achieve cost synergies.

Revenue synergies also derive from a better combination of production factors. Improvements in the organization of activities, however, offer benefits from product complementarities which help to enhance revenues. In practice, revenue synergies might result from the harmonization of product ranges, the existing complementarities between activities, cross-selling and the generalization of a 'multi-distribution channel' approach to the various segments of customers.

It should be noted, however, that revenue synergies are much more difficult to obtain compared to cost synergies, because they depend not only on managers' decisions but also on customer behaviour. In this respect, several studies have estimated that some 5 per cent to 10 per cent of a bank's customers leave the bank after a merger.[6] Accordingly, M&As between banking institutions in Europe have very often targeted higher cost synergies than revenue synergies (see Table 2.1).

To achieve the goal of efficiency, two types of strategies can be pointed out. Firstly, in theory, a merger or an acquisition involving two companies with homogeneous activity profiles should lead to economies of scale by reducing the unitary production costs, as a result of an increase in activity

Table 2.1 Synergies announced in recent M&A deals in the EU

Banks	Year	Expected synergies (€ million)	Revenue synergies (%)	Cost synergies (%)
SCH-Abbey National	2004	560	20	80
Crédit Agricole-Crédit Lyonnais	2002	760	0	100
Caisses d'Epargne-CDC IXIS	2001	500	85	15
Allianz-Dresdner	2001	1080	88	12
Halifax-Bank of Scotland	2001	1113	51	49
Dexia-Artesia	2001	200	15	85
HVB-Bank Austria	2000	500	0	100
RBoS-Natwest	2000	2335	17	83
BNP-Paribas	1999	850	18	82
BBV-Argentaria	1999	511	0	100
Intesa-COMIT	1999	1000	50	50
Banco Santander-BCH	1999	630	0	100

Sources: Annual reports and financial press.

volume and a decrease in the fixed costs obtained by combining the support functions (marketing, information technology, physical infrastructures, personnel management). The final objective is to obtain a competitive advantage in the activities involved.

In Europe, expectations ride high in the reinforcement of retail banking. The strategy consists, firstly, in merging domestic banking institutions, while maintaining the existing branch network and, secondly, in implementing upstream cost synergies, that is, at the level of physical network management. The desire to achieve greater economies of scale can be seen in the recent operations of several retail banks: BHV in Germany, SCH and BBVA in Spain, CIC-Crédit Mutuel in France, Unicredit in Italy and Lloyds TSB or RBoS-Natwest in the United Kingdom.

The second strategy to achieve greater efficiency is adopted in circumstances where banking institutions are operating in heterogeneous but complementary markets. A merger or an acquisition not only allows the resulting company to widen its customers' portfolio but it also leads to a more diversified range of services and offers scope economies by optimizing the synergies between the merged activities. Here, the main objective is to increase revenues, rather than to obtain economies of scale.

For this, two possibilities could be highlighted according to the complementarities attained through diversifying activities or geographical areas. In the first case, scope economies are generally obtained through a merger or an acquisition between either commercial banks and investment banks, or banking and insurance, as illustrated by a few recent transactions in Europe: Allianz-Dresdner in Germany, BNP-Paribas and Caisses d'Epargne-CDC IXIS in France or San Paolo-IMI in Italy. Similarly, the acquisition of Bankers Trust by Deutsche Bank was completed mainly to penetrate the American market for investment banking.[7] In the second case, the principle of geographical complementarities has increased the interest on the part of Crédit Agricole to acquire Crédit Lyonnais in France. The first is firmly anchored in the provinces and in rural areas, whereas the second has a strong presence in the Ile-de-France (urban area of Paris) and other large French cities.

In sum, efficiency gains are obtained by input and output adjustments in order to reduce costs, increase revenues and/or reduce risks so as to increase the value added. Restructuring operations can also allow efficiency gains through the reorganization of teams (managers and employees) and/or the generalization of 'best practices', known as 'X-efficiency', that is the managerial ability to decide on input and output in order to minimize cost (or maximize revenues).[8] In addition to greater economies of scale and scope, efficiency can also be improved by improved diversification of risks (functional and/or geographical).[9]

Efficiency may be improved following a merger or an acquisition, if the acquiring institution is more efficient *ex ante* and brings the efficiency of the target up to its own level by spreading its superior managerial expertise, policies and procedures.[10] Simulation evidence suggests that large efficiency gains are possible if the best practices of the acquirers reform the practices of inefficient targets.[11]

The M&A event itself may also improve efficiency by awakening management to the need for improvement or to implement substantial restructuring. Alternatively, efficiency may worsen because of the costs of consummating the M&A (legal expenses, consultancy fees, severance pay) or disruptions from downsizing, difficulties in integrating corporate cultures. Efficiency from may also decline because of organizational diseconomies in operating or monitoring a more complex institution.

In practice, efficiency gains do not appear to be the only explanation for the recent M&A wave in banking. Moreover, gains obtained through increased market power seem to be a strong incentive to merge, but the relationship between market concentration and performance has only been verified partially.[12] There is thus a need to seek other explanations for the current phenomenon.[13] Studies carried out in the United States and in Europe tend to confirm that three other factors are likely to play an important role: 'managerial hubris', mimicry effect and/or defensive reaction.

2.4   M&A and market power

Theoretically, market power is defined as the capacity to fix market prices as a result of a dominant position in a certain market. The economic literature[14] concludes that prices are positively correlated to local market shares in general, but this position is not justified in the context of international markets (inter-banking activities, multinational companies). Therefore, increased market power can be gained through a merger or an acquisition of two competing institutions operating in the same local market.

Thus, value creation through market power would seem more likely to explain mergers at the local level and within the same activity (especially in retail banking), which appears to be coherent with the theoretical evidence noted above, in particular in the European Union, where the majority of the operations are within sectors and are national.[15]

In practice, banking institutions can influence supply (as a supplier) or demand prices (as a client). In the first case, the size obtained following a merger or an acquisition might create a dominant position which enables the bank to manipulate price levels in a certain market either by: (a) decreasing prices (by pre-emption and/or predation[16]) to evict some non-competitive existing banking institutions and/or new entrants; or (b) increasing prices in the absence of effective competition in the marketplace.[17] In the second case, the size obtained will enable the new group to reduce its refinancing costs thanks to reputation, size or diversification effects.

Nevertheless, some recent studies[18] have shown that the previous correlation between concentration levels and market power diminished during the 1990s. This could be attributed to the opening up of markets which has encouraged the entry of new competitors and thus increased the degree of contestability of the market.[19] Moreover, the emergence of new distribution channels such as e-banking, while contributing to the disappearance of geographical boundaries, has made the concept of 'local markets' less relevant.

Based on the hypothesis of the increase of market power, it appears that the creation of mega-banks, by altering the effective competition, does not allow for any immediate profit for consumers because of dominant position abuses[20] and consumers' surplus capture. The effects of an M&A on collective welfare, however – mainly via prices – will depend on numerous factors.

2.5   Other non-maximizing value explanations of M&A

When control and ownership are separated within the firm,[21] managers can pursue other objectives than maximizing shareholder value or increasing profit. Instead of enhancing shareholders' wealth, a manager might prefer to serve his own interests. Therefore, it is possible that a merger or an acquisition is mainly dictated by the power, prestige and/or higher remuneration that are related to the management of a larger firm. In that case, it is the desire for power[22] that is expressed, and not the direct interest of the shareholders. This situation is more likely to arise where shareholding is dispersed and passive.

M&A operations can also be triggered by mimicry effects following the consolidation process initiated by competitors in the marketplace.[23] Indeed, within a relatively concentrated sector, the actions of the major 'player(s)' might have an immediate impact on the behaviour of others, inducing in turn a homogeneous behaviour. As Keynes noted: 'Universal wisdom teaches that it is better for one's reputation to fail with the conventions than to succeed against them.'

During the last two decades, indeed, the development strategies in the banking industry were very often induced by common strategic standards, which have led to rather homogeneous behaviour. As shown in the 1980s, the commercial strategies of banking institutions were marked by a race to achieve a larger size. Similarly, in the 1990s, enhancing the profitability of shareholders' equity became the new development standard. Today, value creation represents the major strategic issue in modern banking management circles.

Moreover, the acceleration of M&A operations could also result from a defensive reaction on the part of a few actors against competitors' initiatives. Indeed, as the wave of mergers spreads, banking institutions that have remained outside the process are likely to become themselves a potential target in a hostile takeover transaction. To protect themselves from possible predators, managers can pursue an active acquisition policy in order to maintain or preserve their position.

Numerous M&As carried out recently in fact seem to have been dictated by the desire to modify the existing equilibrium and to be proactive to others' actions. Sometimes disguised as a hypothetical value creation move, a number of these operations are simply the reflection of the single market impetus, where mergers have simply become the objective rather than the result of careful strategic thinking. Most European banking institutions, reacting to the increased contestability of their national banking market, have sought to strengthen their national position, in order to improve their profitability and to protect their position from new competitive entrants.

Therefore, it seems more likely that the explanation of the recent banking consolidation process must be sought in the new rules of corporate governance. Committed to ensuring the growth of their companies while maintaining their competitiveness and forced to provide equity capital to which pressing remuneration requirements are attached, bank managers have pursued external growth through M&As as a strategic means to expand their activities.

2.6   Empirical findings on bank M&A

Several studies have tried to assess the performance of M&A in banking in the 1990s. The majority have concentrated on the impact on shareholder value and efficiency on the one hand, and on the consequences for customers – households and SMEs – via the increase of market power on the other hand.

Concerning the impact of M&As on shareholder value and efficiency, the results have been mixed. Several academic studies have been carried out mainly in the United States, using a wide range of methodologies, from the most basic (event studies or balance-sheet-based indicators) to the most sophisticated (efficiency frontiers), but their findings have not been conclusive.

The studies on the impact of mergers on consumer welfare have focused primarily on the possible market power effects without considering that under certain conditions, M&A might improve consumer surplus.

2.7 Banking M&As and value creation: still not very conclusive results

A large number of event studies have been carried out to assess the effects of M&As on stock market values. They all tend to evaluate the change in total market value of the acquiring company plus target institutions – adjusted for changes in overall stock market values – associated with an M&A announcement. This embodies the present value of expected future changes in terms of efficiency and market power. Although these effects cannot be disentangled, the change in market value may be viewed as an understatement of the expected efficiency improvement, since it is unlikely that an M&A would reduce the market power of the participants.[24]

In the US, the empirical results have been mixed.[25] On average, the combined shareholder value (i.e., the bidder and the target) is not affected by the announcement of the deal since the bidder suffers a loss that offsets the gains of the target.[26] Therefore, an M&A only implies a transfer of wealth from the shareholders of the bidder to those of the target. Compared to the 1980s, however, the evidence from the 1990s was more favourable where average abnormal returns have been higher for both bidders and targets.[27]

Other studies have examined the stock market reaction to different types of deals. Houston and Ryngaert (1994) found that the combined gains tend to be greater when the bidding firm is unusually profitable or when there is significant overlap between institutions. The first result is consistent with a market for corporate control favouring competent over incompetent managers. The second result is consistent with the market power hypothesis, according to which a higher market share leads to higher profits. DeLong (2001) found that mergers that concentrate banks geographically or in product create value, while those that diversify them do not.

On the other hand, Zhang (1995) found results consistent with the diversification hypothesis, according to which geographical diversification leads to a lower variability of income; and that out-of-market transactions create value for shareholders. Higher market concentration is likely to lead to an increase in prices for retail financial services, leading in turn to an increase in profits. It is also true, however, that firms operating in more concentrated markets are generally found to be less efficient.[28] This effect might offset the gains from an increase in market power and thus leave the market value of the bank unchanged.

In Europe, the few studies that have been carried out to assess value creation through M&As in banking have found positive abnormal combined returns. In the study conducted by Van Beek and Rad (1997), these returns were not statistically significant. In a more recent study undertaken by Cybo-Ottone and Murgia (2000), shareholder value gains were positive and significant, mostly driven by domestic bank-to-bank deals and diversification of banks into insurance. In a recent study, Beitel and Schiereck (2001) found an increase of the combined values of bidders and targets for domestic M&As but a decrease in the case of cross-border M&As. These findings were confirmed in Beitel and colleagues (2004) on a sample of 98 M&As in 1985–2000, showing that transactions focusing activities, and those on which targets are less performing, increase value.

These positive abnormal returns, however, do not necessarily mean that mergers improve efficiency; in fact, one possible explanation for the difference between the European and American markets is that weaker antitrust enforcement in some European countries allows gains in monopoly power from in-market mergers.

Globally, it seems that the large majority of M&As carried out recently, in Europe or in the United States, are far from having proved their effectiveness in terms of value creation in the short run.[29]

The empirical research based on event studies should, however, be taken with caution since the methodology suffers from several limitations. One problem is that the announcement of a deal mixes information concerning the proposed merger with information on its financing. Because investors consider the announcement of a stock issuance as 'bad news', the negative returns to the bidding bank could reflect the fact that mergers tend to be financed with stocks. Consistent with this notion, one study finds that returns to bidders are significantly higher when mergers are financed with cash relative to mergers financed with new equity.[30] Also, event studies rely heavily on investors' perception and their anticipations of the future gains when there are rumours around the transactions. This may inflict a pure speculation effect.

2.8   Banking M&As and efficiency

Various studies carried out on US banks have shown, on average, very little or no *cost efficiency* improvement from M&As in the 1980s.[31] However, more recent studies using data from the 1990s have been more mixed.[32] On the one hand, some found that mergers produce no improvement in banks' cost efficiency,[33] especially when the deals involve very large banks.[34] It was also shown that on average, smaller banking institutions tend to exhibit larger variations in X-inefficiencies than larger institutions.[35] This may be due to the organizational diseconomies of operating larger firms in relation to disruptions from the M&A process, which may offset most potential efficiency gains. And on the other hand, other studies have found cost reductions also for very large US banks.[36]

The evidence for European banks is broadly consistent with the US results. Domestic mergers among banks of equal size seem to improve cost efficiency, but these results do not hold for all countries and all banks.[37] More recent studies on Italian banks[38] or UK building societies[39] have found significant cost efficiency gains following an M&A. Moreover, simulation evidence suggests that a cross-border acquisition may be associated with a reduction in the costs of the target, while little effect is found for domestic M&As.[40] In contrast Vander Vennet (2002b) found no tangible gains in terms of cost efficiency in the case of cross-border M&As. The difficulties in improving cost efficiency may be related to the obstacles often encountered, especially in continental Europe, in reducing a bank's labour force. In fact, personnel reduction, one of the main sources of savings, is hardly an option in countries with rigid labour markets.[41]

Studies on *profit efficiency* of US banks more often found gains from M&As. The fact that cost efficiency is, on average, little improved as a result of a bank merger, does not necessarily mean that there is no improvement in profits. Profit efficiency incorporates both costs as well as revenue efficiency. Revenue efficiency can be improved by simply raising prices as market power[42] is expanded through the merger process itself. Or revenues may rise because the merged institution restructures its assets mix.

Two studies in particular have attempted to determine the profit effects of mergers. Akhavein and colleagues (1997) found little change in cost efficiency, but an improvement in profit efficiency of large US banks from 1980–90 following M&As, especially when both merger participants were relatively inefficient prior to the merger.[43] Also, after merging, banks tended to shift their portfolios to take on more loans and fewer securities. They attribute gains in profit efficiency to the benefits of risk diversification: larger banks have more diversified loan portfolios and lower equity-asset ratios. But their measure of profit efficiency does not account for changes in risk likely to result from such a portfolio switch. Berger (1998) found similar results in a study that includes all US bank mergers, both large and small, from 1990 to 1995.

In Europe, Vander Vennet (1996) found that domestic mergers of equals in European countries have a positive impact on profitability, mainly driven by improvements in operational efficiency. As regards cross-border mergers and acquisitions, he only found a partial profit efficiency improvement that may be caused by changes in the pricing behaviour of the acquired banks.[44] Focarelli and colleagues (2002) found that Italian deals that consist of the purchase of a majority (but not all) of the voting shares of the target appear to result in significant improvements, mainly due to a decrease in bad loans. For full mergers, they observe that Italian banks aim to change their business focus towards providing financial services and thus increase their non-interest income, rather than to obtain efficiency gains. After the merger, they observe an increase in profitability in the long run that is also related to a more efficient use of capital.

2.9   Banking M&As and market power

Firstly, it is necessary to distinguish between national and cross-border M&A operations. Prior studies of the pricing effects of M&As[45] found that national consolidation, by strengthening the degree of concentration, could generate substantial market power, which is likely to be harmful for households and small and medium-sized enterprises (SMEs).

However, the few existing studies on European bank mergers seem to conclude that there are often significant efficiency gains which result in better conditions for consumers. Huizinga and colleagues (2001) analysed 52 major mergers between European banks between 1994 and 1998, which were found to be largely socially beneficial. Some other studies found strong evidence of positive effects of M&As at a country level, leading to more favourable prices for consumers.[46]

Conversely, cross-border M&A operations would intensify competition in the domestic market but do not change the banks' local market shares. Consequently, the national authorities, after having encouraged the constitution of 'national champions', should promote cross-border and particularly pan-European operations. However, this hypothesis is relatively relaxed in view of the cross-border consolidation wave in Eastern European countries. Competitive concerns in these markets may arise if cross-border players would reach the concentration threshold perceived to be harmful to consumers.

Secondly, it is also essential to distinguish M&A operations according to the 'means' used – market power or efficiency gains – to create shareholder value. If the value creation occurs primarily through increased *market power*, the transaction would only constitute simple profit redistribution in favour of shareholders, but to the detriment of the customers, employees and public authorities, without a net gain in terms of collective welfare. In this case, the transaction involves a simple redistribution between the various stakeholders of the banking institution, which does not create wealth for the economy because the increase of banking profits is much lower than the welfare loss suffered by the other economic agents.

On the other hand, value creation obtained through the improvement of *efficiency* (through scale and/or scope economies, risk diversification), will benefit not only the shareholders, but also the customers (price drop and/or improvement in the quality of the services) and the public authorities (higher solvency of credit institutions). For the employees, the results remain unclear. The overall impact of the consolidation process remains ambiguous, according to whether market power or efficiency effects would prevail.

2.10 A new conceptual approach to assess banking M&A

The empirical evidence suggests that banking M&As do not significantly improve cost and profit efficiency and, on average, do not generate significant shareholder value. These results seem to contradict the motivations cited by practitioners for consolidation strategies, which are largely related to economies of scale and scope and to improvements in management quality. However, there are a few possible explanations for the divergence between the econometric evidence and bankers' beliefs.[47]

Generally

1. The lack of clear-cut results on the effects of M&A could reflect difficulties in measuring efficiency improvements.
2. Studies restricted to short post-merger periods might fail to detect value gains that can only emerge slowly, after some years. For example, studies restricted to a short post-merger period might fail to account for the efficiency gains of consolidation.[48] Long lags in the improvement of performance may reflect difficulties in refocusing lending policies, rationalizing branches, integrating data processing systems and operations, and training the personnel of the target to market the new owner's products.[49] Moreover, culture clashes may be especially harmful in banking,[50] as the relationship with customers depends heavily on soft information, which is more difficult to transfer than such objective information as balance sheet data. The resignation of key executives or the emergence of morale problems due to reassignments or employee turnover may cause a loss of information, especially when the new management has little time to develop customer information.
3. Deals done in the past might have suffered from stricter regulation that prevented firms involved in an M&A from reaping all the benefits of the deal. For example, the limitations imposed by the Glass-Steagall Act on the range of US banks' financial activities could have impeded the realization of gains from cross-selling. Similarly, restrictions on bank branching or on geographical expansion could have hampered the exploitation of scale economies. This view suggests that the deregulation of banking underway in all major countries (e.g., the Riegle-Neal Act or the Gramm-Leach-Billey Act in the US) might increase the potential for scale and scope economies. The evidence available for the 1990s in the United States is consistent with this view. Similarly, in Europe, the rigidity of labour market makes it difficult to reduce overlapping costs in the process of restructuring following M&As, which limits the potential for cost savings. Moreover, remaining obstacles[51] to an integrated European financial market hamper the exploitation of potential cost synergies.

4. The fact that mergers often occur in waves makes it hard to separate the effect of a single deal from transformations experienced by the industry as a whole.

5. Another possibility is that – in the presence of agency problems between managers and shareholders – M&As could be mainly driven by non-value maximizing motives (such as 'managerial hubris'). Non-value maximizing motivations for M&As have been analysed in recent papers that examine the relationship between executive compensation and M&A activity. According to these studies, the motivations of M&As could be traced back to managers' desire to increase their compensation (CEOs of larger institutions earn higher compensation). There is some evidence that CEOs with higher levels of stock-based compensation relative to cash-based compensation are less inclined to lead their institutions to make acquisitions.[52] Moreover, managers without a large stake in their banks are more likely to get involved in non-value maximizing mergers.[53] Thus, managerial hubris may be an important reason for the lack of conclusive evidence on the benefits of M&As among banks during the past decades.[54]

Particularly in Europe

6. The difficulties stem from the fact that the M&A phenomenon in financial services is still far too new to have produced sufficient empirical results worthy of serious academic study. As a result, the majority of the studies have mainly focused on the United States,[55] but the lessons cannot automatically be applied to the European environment since regulation and the structure of European banking markets are fundamentally different.[56]

7. Moreover, it is quite difficult to come up with general rules to assess M&As because each one depends on the particular context in which it was carried out [such as the flexibility of the labour market, the applicable takeover regulations including the broader spectrum of anti-takeover mechanisms, the liquidity of the capital market, the different sizes of the institutions involved, their original activities, their geographies, their corporate structure (private, hybrid or public) and especially the intrinsic characteristics of the operation (friendly or hostile, cash or equity financed etc.)].

Building upon the theoretical background of M&A in banking and considering the fact that the empirical literature has assessed M&A either by breaking the sample according to the geographical or activity dimension, we introduce a new approach based on a conceptual matrix built on the interaction between these two dimensions which we consider sufficient – at a first step – to characterize and define the various industrial logics or strategies underlying the M&A: the initial activities of the banks involved in the M&A and the geographical dimension of the transaction.

As we illustrate below (Table 2.2), the application of the A/G matrix can offer a useful tool for managers to decide their best strategy in terms of geographies and activities expansion when studying an M&A project. Therefore, for each institution, an optimal strategy is the one which combines optimally the levels of activities and geographies expansion.

In the banking sector, when M&A occur between banks with the aim to focus their activities locally, domestically or across borders, there is an expectation to cut costs and benefit from scale economies, while increasing market presence which does not necessarily increase market power; while, when M&A occur between banks with the aim to expand their activities locally, nationally or across borders, there is an expectation to increase revenues and benefit from scope economies.

Table 2.2   Introducing the Activity/Geography matrix (called '*AG matrix*'), we identify six industrial logics or strategies (Si)

		Geographical dimension		
		National		Cross-border (EU)
		Same city	Different cities	
Activity profile	Homogeneous	Consolidation of activities locally	Consolidation of activities nationally	Consolidation of activities cross-border
		S1	S2	S5
	Heterogeneous	Expansion of activities locally	Expansion of activities nationally	Expansion of activities cross-border
		S3	S4	S6

S1: The M&A between institutions with homogenous profiles and operating locally aims at focusing the initial activities locally – this is specific to European countries with presence of local and regional banks.

S2: The M&A between institutions with homogenous profiles and operating nationally aims at focusing the initial activities nationally.

S3: The M&A between institutions with heterogeneous profiles and operating locally aims at expanding the range of activities locally.

S4: The M&A between institutions with heterogeneous profiles and operating nationally aims at expanding the range of activities nationally.

S5: The M&A between institutions with homogenous profiles and operating across borders aims at focusing the initial activities at a cross-border level.

S6: The M&A between institutions with heterogeneous profiles and operating across borders aims at expanding the range of activities at a cross-border level.

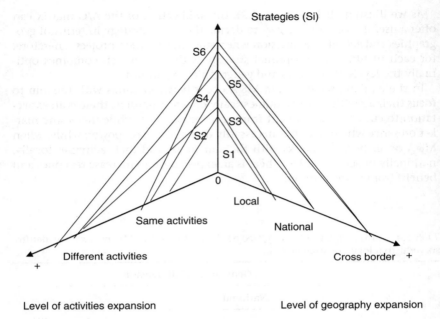

Figure 2.1 Activity/geography matrix

Opting for one or the other M&A underlying strategies would not only impact the profitability and efficiency of the banks involved in the transaction, but also would impact their future development and business model.

2.11 Analysing *banking M&A performance in Europe*

We propose to apply a new approach based on the analysis of the various strategies underlying banking M&A to assess the performance of these operations. To categorize banking M&A, we use the A/G matrix built on the interaction between the activity of the banks involved in the M&A and the geographical dimension of the transaction. Then, based on a subcategorization of M&A, we assess the profitability and the efficiency (cost and profit) for the acquirers and the targets before and after the operation. The analysis will be based on financial ratios and Data Envelopment Analysis (DEA) to assess respectively profitability and cost and profit efficiency.

2.11.1 Methodology

The profitability and efficiency analysis based on balance sheet indicators and efficiency scores consists in describing costs, revenue, risk and efficiency.

All these indicators are analysed at least one year before and three after the merger for the acquirers and the targets and compared to a control group of non-merged banks over the period 1996–2003. The three-year time period was used because it is more likely that gains will appear at least one year after the merger and then all gains should be realized within three years.

For the pre merger period, ratios for both the acquirers and the targets are examined to get an indication as to the relative performance of the acquirer and the target. In addition, ratios for the control group were examined to provide a basis for comparing performance of the merged institutions to non-merged ones that are similar in term of size, type and location.

For the post-merger period, the focus of the analysis is on the combined institutions for mergers and separate institutions for acquisitions relative to the control group. The control group was particularly valuable as it permits an assessment of whether any observed changes in the combined firm simply reflects changes in the economic environment or instead were due to the merger or acquisition.

Post-merger data were compared with the pre merger data to determine what changes occurred in performance following the merger or the acquisition.

We perform a dynamic analysis of cost and profit efficiency and profitability on a sample of 71 mergers and acquisitions cases that occurred in the period 1996–2000, broken down into domestic, cross-border transactions and into their underlying strategies, which will be defined subsequently.

2.11.2 Application of A/G matrix to assess M&A performance

In the remainder of this chapter, we focus on the banking activity *strico sensu* and on the transactions that occurred in the EU 15 plus Norway. By applying the A/G, we identify different industrial logics or strategies depending on whether the M&As are completed between banks with homogeneous versus heterogeneous activity profiles and whether they are undertaken in the same or different geographical areas (local/national versus cross-border intra EU).

The geographical dimension is defined by looking at where the bank is headquartered. Whereas, we use the banks' revenue structures to define their activity profiles.

As for the activity profiles of the merging banks, it is difficult to define with certainty the activities of European banks since disclosure requirements are such that only very few banks provide information on the type of their loan portfolios or the different types of non-interest income generated by the different business units. For our analysis, we use a pragmatic approach for the definition of homogeneous versus heterogeneous activities.[57] We rely on broad revenue and asset-based measures of diversified versus focused activities. However, we do not think this will bias our results since interest versus non interest revenue is a complete indication of whether a bank is pursuing traditional intermediation versus other financial activities.

Our preferred measures are the revenue-based measures since they capture the banks' different sources of income. We calculate the difference between interest margin from lending divided by total revenue and the difference between non-interest revenue divided by total revenue before the transaction for the acquirer and the target to define the activity profile of the banks involved in M&A. This is shown in Table 2.3.

When breaking down the revenue into interest revenue from lending and non interest revenue (revenues from commissions and trading activities), we could define the different banks' activities. The ultimate objective is to classify the activities into homogeneous and heterogeneous profiles.

- The proportion of interest revenue over total revenue is an indication of the extent to which the bank is involved in the traditional activities of deposit-taking and lending.
- The proportion of non-interest revenue over total revenue is an indication of the involvement of the banks in other activities ranging from trading and other financial services (underwriting and distributing securities, providing payments and cash-related services, etc.).

The ratios before the announcement of the transaction are calculated as shown in Table 2.4.

Table 2.3   Revenue components in bank M&A

Transaction (i)	Proportion of interest margin from lending/total revenue for the acquirer before the transaction	Proportion of interest margin from lending/total revenue for the target before the transaction	Difference	Proportion of the non interest revenue/total revenue for the acquirers beforer the transaction	Proportion of the non interest revenue/total revenue for the targets before the transaction	Difference
Transaction(1)	IRa(1)	IRt(1)	IRa(1)−IRt(1)	NIRa(1)	NIRt(1)	NIRa(1)−NIRt(1)
Transaction(i)	IRa(i)	IRt(i)	IRa(i)−IRt(i)	NIRa(i)	NIRt(i)	NIRa(i)−NIRt(i)

Table 2.4   Ratio calculations prior to announcement of a transaction

Data relative to transactions at year (X)	Before (Xb)
1996	X
1997	$((X-1)+(X))/2$
1998	$((X-2)+(X-1)+(X))/3$
1999	$((X-3)+(X-2)+(X-1)+(X))/4$
2000	$((X-4)+(X-3)+(X-2)+(X-1)+(X))/5$

Two alternatives are taken into consideration: if the values of these ratios calculated for the acquirer and target before the announcement belong to the same interval, while keeping the difference less than 20 per cent, then we consider that their profiles are similar, if not, and the difference is more than 20 per cent, then we consider that they have different profiles. The choice of the threshold of 20 per cent is somewhat arbitrary;[58] however, it was confirmed by a qualitative analysis based on other ratios in the balance sheet (such as the proportion of investment activities in total assets, the percentage of off-balance sheet in total assets ...). This choice has been necessary to conduct these analyses. More precise data is simply unavailable to allow us to draw a more precise picture on banking activities.

2.11.3 Justification of the efficiency analysis method

Several techniques – parametric or non-parametric – have been proposed in the literature to measure bank efficiency using the frontier approaches. They mainly differ in the distributional assumptions used to disentangle inefficiency differences from random errors. The parametric Stochastic Frontier Approach (SFA) and the non-parametric Data Envelopment Analysis (DEA) are the most used tools to measure efficiency, taking into account that the literature considers both techniques as equally satisfactory.[59] We choose the DEA approach as we consider it to be a more appropriate tool in our analysis since it does not require an assumption of a functional form for the frontier relating inputs and outputs, particularly when the sample used to evaluate efficiency before and after an M&A is composed of banks of different sizes, types and countries. Also, DEA does not assume any distributional form for the inefficiency term and it is easier to accommodate multiple input and output models. And finally, the banks are directly compared against a peer or combination of peers.

The DEA approach was initially developed by Charnes, Cooper and Rhodes (1978) who proposed a model that measures technical efficiency scores under constant returns to scale (CRS). The CRS assumption has however a limited scope since it is only appropriate when operating at an optimal scale. Imperfect competition and constraints on finance may cause a Decision Making Unit (DMU) not to be operating at optimal scale. Banker, Charnes and Cooper (1984) described a revised model including variable returns to scale (VRS), thus allowing the computation of pure technical efficiency and scale efficiency. The VRS specification has been the most commonly used specification in the 1990s.

The DEA model is a linear programming based method for evaluating the relative efficiency of a set of Decision Making Units (DMUs). The DEA frontier is formed as the piecewise linear combination that connects the set of 'best-practice observations' in the data set under analysis. As a consequence, the DEA efficiency score for a specific DMU is not defined by an absolute standard or 'theoretical maximum', but it is defined relative to the other DMUs in the specific data set under consideration.

DEA suffers however, from its limitations since it does not consider the existence of an error term (or 'noise') and it cannot be used to conduct conventional statistical tests of hypotheses, in particular when testing the presence of environmental variables. In that case, it seems preferable to use the Stochastic Frontier Analysis (SFA) rather than DEA.

In this chapter, we use the non-parametric DEA approach[60] to estimate cost and profit efficiency scores.[61] The frontier is obtained by means of linear combination of efficient firms contained in the sample. Although cost efficiency obtained by means of non-parametric techniques has been a widely used procedure, the estimation of profit efficiency by non-parametric techniques has rarely been done. The cost efficiency (respectively profit efficiency) measures the distance of each bank's cost (and respectively profit) and the 'best practice' in the industry when producing the same bundle of outputs. Cost efficiency provides an indication on wastes in the production process and on the optimality of the chosen mix of inputs as a function of their respective prices. Profit efficiency instead provides an indication on the optimality of the chosen mix of inputs and outputs. The comparison of cost and profit efficiency scores may give an indication on a likely market power effect.

The non-parametric DEA model uses linear programming to find the best practice bank in the sample ($i = 1, \ldots\ldots N$) that reflects minimum costs in producing the observed output vector Q, $(y_i = y_{i1}, \ldots\ldots, y_{iq}) \in \Re^{q++}$ that sell at prices $(r_i = r_{i1}, \ldots\ldots r_{iq}) \in \Re^{q++}$ given the a vector of P inputs $(x_i = x_{i1}, \ldots\ldots, x_{ip}) \in \Re^{p++}$ for which they pay prices $(w_i = w_{i1}, \ldots\ldots w_{ip}) \in \Re^{q++}$

The cost efficiency if each bank j can be by solving the following problem of linear programming:

$$Min \ \sum_p w_{pj} x_{pj}$$

$$Subject \ to \ \sum_i \lambda_i y_{iq} \geq y_{jq} \ \forall q$$

$$\sum_i \lambda_i x_{ip} \leq x_{jp} \ \forall p$$

$$\sum_i \lambda_i = 1, \lambda_i \geq o, i = 1, \ldots\ldots N$$

The solution $x_j^* = x_{j1}^*, \ldots\ldots x_{jp}^*$ corresponds to the input demand vector that minimizes the costs with the given price of inputs and is obtained from a linear combination of banks that produces at least as much of each of the inputs using the same or less amount of inputs and the cost will be $C_j^* = \sum w_{pj} x_{pj}^*$ which is by definition less than or equal to the cost of the bank j ($C_j = \sum w_{pj} x_{pj}$)

The cost efficiency[62] for bank j (CE_j) can be calculated as follows:

$$CE_j = \frac{C_j^*}{C_j} = \frac{\sum_p w_{pj} x_{pj}^*}{\sum_p w_{pj} x_{pj}}$$

Where $CE_j \leq 1$ represents the ratio between the minimum cost C_j^* associated with the use of the input vector x_j^* that minimizes the costs and the observed costs C_j for bank.

Respectively, the alternative profit efficiency[63] is empirically calculated with the following linear programming formally expressed:

$$MaxR_j - \sum_p w_{pj} x_{pj}$$
$$Subject\ to$$
$$\sum_i \lambda_i R_i \geq R_j$$
$$\sum_i \lambda_i y_{iq} \geq y_{jq}\ \forall q$$
$$\sum_i \lambda_i x_{ip} \leq x_{jp}\ \forall p$$
$$\sum_i \lambda_i = 1;\ \lambda_i \geq o;\ i = 1,\ldots\ldots N$$

The solution of the linear programming corresponds to the revenue R_j^* and input demand $x_j^* = x_{j1}^*,\ldots\ldots x_{jp}^*$ which maximizes profits given the prices of the inputs w. This solution is obtained from a linear combination of firms that produce at least as much of each of the outputs using a smaller or equal quantity of inputs and obtains at least as much revenues as bank j.

Alternative profit efficiency is then calculated as follows:

$$APE_j = \frac{P_j}{AP_j^*} = \frac{R_j - \sum_p w_{pj} x_{pj}}{R_j^* - \sum_p w_{pj} x_{pj}^*}$$

Where APE_j represents the ratio between the observed profits ($P_j = R_j - \sum_p w_{pj} x_{pj}$) and the maximum profits $AP_j^* = R_j^* - \sum_p w_{pj} x_{pj}^*$ associated with the maximum revenue and the input demand $x_j^* = x_{j1}^*,\ldots\ldots x_{jp}^*$ that maximizes profit for bank j.

In applying DEA, we adopted the intermediation approach proposed by Sealey and Lindley (1977). It assumes that the bank collects deposits to transform them, using labour and capital, into loans as opposed to the production approach which views the bank as using labour and capital to produce deposits and loans. According to the empirical literature,[64] the choice of either approaches may have an impact on the level of efficiency scores, but do not imply strong modifications in their rankings.

Two outputs are included, loans and investment assets.[65] The inputs, whose prices are used to estimate cost and alternative profit frontier, include labour, physical capital and borrowed funds.

As data on the number of employees are not available, the price of labour is measured by the ratio of personnel expenses to total assets.[66] The price of physical capital is defined as the ratio of other non-interest expenses to fixed assets. The price of borrowed funds is measured by the ratio of paid interests to all funding. Total costs are interest costs and non-interest costs. To measure total profit, we use operating gross income[67] which does not include loan provisioning as provisioning rules differ from one country to another one in Europe.

2.11.4   Balance-sheet ratios analysis[68]

Four sets of balance-sheet ratios are examined including cost, profitability, risk and activity ratios:

- The cost ratios include *cost to income ratio* which permits to examine total costs (non-interest expenses and interest expenses) to total operating revenues. This ratio reflects the ability of the bank to generate revenue from its expenditures. Furthermore, for many banks, revenues reflect income earned from the balance sheet as well from the off balance sheet.[69]

It is also of a special interest to decompose total costs to *non-interest costs* (personnel expenses, back office operations and branches, amortization expense of intangible assets) and *interest costs* (cost of financial capital) to total assets. The former should be directly affected by the cost savings that are frequently cited as resulting from horizontal bank mergers. The latter may be significantly affected by the way the bank chooses to obtain deposits. For example, a bank may choose to shift from using core deposits (predominately retail deposits) as a source of funds to using purchased money. Obtaining core deposits tends to incur high non-interest expenses from the fixed costs of running the branches and the personnel while the opposite is true for obtaining purchased money, especially when interest rates are relatively low. The advantage of using total assets as a denominator in the cost ratios is that assets reflect the earnings base of the bank and they are not highly variable from one year to another, whereas revenues tend to be more variable.

The profitability ratios include the *return on asset (ROA)* which is the ratio of gross income to average assets and the *return on equity (ROE)* which is the ratio of gross or net income to equity. Gross income[70] measure is preferred to net income[71] to avoid the differences in taxation between the European countries. ROA is a good overall indicator of a banking organization's performance that illustrates the ability of a bank to generate profits from the assets at its disposal. It has the disadvantage, however, of not accounting for the profits generated from the off-balance sheet operations. ROE is an alternative measure of profitability designed to reflect the return to owners' investment. It also has the disadvantage that the denominator may vary substantially across banks, even those of identical size, due to the discretionary choices by management as to the mix between equity and debt capital as well as the total amount of capital held by a firm.

Finally, it is also worth decomposing the total revenue into its main streams: interest and non-interest revenues to measure the diversification of income. In addition, we will measure the ability of the bank to generate revenue by the asset productivity ratio which is total revenues on total assets.

- The risk indicators are used to determine the change in the risk profile of a bank after a merger or an acquisition. For example, the *capital ratio* which is defined as equity to total assets indicates the capital strength of the bank and its ability to absorb credit and other losses. The solvency ratio measured by *loan-loss provisions to net interest revenue* provides an indication of the extent to which the bank has made provisions to cover credit losses. The higher the ratio, the larger is the amount of expected bad loans on the books, and the higher are the risks despite having been provisioned.

2.11.5 Bank M&A sample

In order to undertake our empirical analysis we identified a sample of 71 completed mergers and acquisitions executed by banks headquartered in the EU15 plus Norway. The announcement dates ranged between 01/01/1996 and 01/01/2001. The deals were obtained essentially from the Thomson Financial Securities, M&A SDC database and from press coverage. The period under scrutiny is of a particular interest because it immediately follows the regulatory changes associated with the completion of the single market programme in the EU, and it also covers the period before and after the introduction of the euro. As a breakdown is made between the domestic and the cross-border deals, both the single market programme and EMU are expected to be catalysts for cross-border M&A activity in banking.

All the deals included in our study are horizontal takeovers that can either be classified as complete mergers (involving the combination of the consolidating partners) or majority acquisitions exceeding the threshold of 49 per cent of voting rights (in which the acquiring bank buys a controlling equity stake in the target bank, and both banks remain legally separate entities), in order to take into account all the operations having generated a transfer of capital control.

The targets and the acquirers are banking institutions as defined in the EU's Second Banking Directive. Insurance and 'securities' are excluded.

Since the legal differences between the various types of institutional banks have been abolished, the sample contains commercial banks, savings institutions, cooperatives banks and public credit institutions. To explore the sample, statistical analysis on the number of transactions was performed. Full details of the sample are shown in Annex 2.

2.11.6   The control group

The control group is composed of non-merging or majority acquired European banking institutions that respect the same selection criteria as the M&A sample. Foreign branches and subsidiaries that have their parent institution outside EU15 plus Norway are excluded. We also excluded the institutions in our sample that were involved in a merger or a majority acquisition. These banks are mainly commercial, cooperative and savings banks. We excluded subsidiaries of foreign banks, specialized financial institutions and central banks. The number of banks in the control group by country is given in Annex 2.

All the data used in the empirical analysis are derived from *Bankscope*, a FitchRatings/Bureau Van Dijk international database which provides annual income and balance sheet data for banks.

2.11.7   Results on European bank M&A

The efficiency measures are the results of the implementation of a variable returns to scale (VRS) model.[72] Precisely, we perform a dynamic efficiency analysis on a sample of 71 bank-to-bank mergers and acquisitions (including 11 cross-border transactions) completed over the period 1996–2000. The construction of cost and profit frontiers was based on a large sample of approximately 587 European banks located in the same EU countries.

In addition, the control group was constituted to provide a basis for comparing performance of the merged institutions to non merged ones that are similar in term of size, type and location. This group excludes the pre-specified sample of 71 bank-to-bank mergers and majority acquisitions and more generally all the banks that were involved in a takeover during the same year. The period of observation is 1996–2003. We consider unconsolidated balance sheet data whenever possible.

2.11.8   Banking M&As and performance – cost and profit efficiency indicators

Our efficiency results indicate that **for the domestic transactions**, the banks' cost efficiency slightly improves following the merger or acquisition. See Annex 3 for the full set of empirical results. This improvement is more pronounced for the targets as they were much less efficient than the acquiring banks prior to the transaction. In other words, targets benefit more from the transaction than acquirers.[73]

This result supports two hypotheses: the first is a transfer of best practices of the acquiring bank to the target and the second, which is related to the first, is the existence of an efficient market for corporate control in European banks. This market would detect banks having a potential to improve their costs management. These findings suggest that M&A should be more successful if targets were proved to be badly cost managed.

The average cost efficiency scores displayed in domestic transactions hide interesting results when applying the AG matrix. Indeed, when M&A transactions aim at focusing activities in the same local area, acquirers and targets fail to improve their cost efficiency scores. This result contradicts the cost savings related-motive put forward by managers when justifying this type of transaction.

These findings confirm that the potential of exploiting scale economies is limited if not non-existent in this type of transaction. This could be explained by the fact that after an M&A, the new entity has reached a critical mass above which any opportunity to reduce costs is exhausted. This could also be explained by the limited scope to reduce costs owing to the rigidity of labour market[74] and the difficulties inherent to the restructuring process. Finally, this result may also be a consequence of limited opportunities to transfer best practices or a result of the manager's inability to reduce costs.

In the case where M&As aim at focusing activities in different local areas, the consolidating banks improve their cost efficiency scores. The improvement is more pronounced for the targets. However, it seems to be a high potential to improving cost efficiency scores for this type of transaction, where banks are operating in different local areas, since their cost efficiency score is below the average for domestic transactions. This finding would support the hypothesis in which scale economies and transfer of best practices could be more easily exploited in this type of transaction.[75]

When M&A transactions aim at diversifying activities in the same local area, cost efficiency scores are unchanged for the targets, while a slight deterioration is experienced by the acquirers.[76] It is important to note that the cost efficiency scores for the acquirers (and respectively the targets) in this type of transaction are substantially higher than the average cost efficiency scores for the acquirers (and the targets) in the domestic transactions. Despite the slight reduction of cost efficiency scores for the acquirers, the consolidating banks have succeeded in keeping up an above average cost efficiency level. This finding would support the hypothesis in which scale and scope economies could be more easily exploited in this type of transaction.

When M&A transactions aim at diversifying activities and geographies domestically, acquirers and targets fail to improve cost efficiency scores.[77] This finding is explained by the inability of these banks to exploit scale and scope economies, which could be a result of bad post-M&A management and all difficulties inherent to consolidating banks that operate in different activity segments.

Generally, acquirers and targets involved in the domestic transactions are more cost efficient than the banks of the control group before and after the M&A. Cost efficiency scores have slightly improved for the control group. However, this improvement is below any positive change experienced by the acquirers and the targets.

As concerns profit efficiency scores,[78] we found a positive variation for the acquiring and target banks.[79] Indeed, prior to the transaction, acquirers displayed higher scores than the targets. After the transaction, score improvement was more pronounced for the targets. This finding implies that European banks have exploited the opportunities to improve their profit efficiency either through anti-competitive pricing and/or pricing change and/or scale and scope economies and/or the advantages of a multi-specialized banking model.

The average profit efficiency score change confirms the same trend for M&A transactions focusing activities and geographies. Indeed, acquirers and targets succeeded in improving their scores. However, in this same type of transactions, cost efficiency scores dropped, this would suggest that the improvement of profit efficiency scores would be a result of an increase of revenues due to a market power manipulative effect on the local market.[80]

Similarly, with respect to M&A transaction focusing activities in different areas domestically, acquirers and targets have improved their profit efficiency scores as compared to other transaction types and to the control group. This type of transaction improved both cost and profit efficiency scores. This finding indicates that in the transactions that aim at expanding operations in different areas domestically, there is a higher incentive to improve profit and cost efficiency.

However, in the transactions aiming at diversifying activities in the same local area, acquirers experienced an increase of their profit efficiency scores,[81] whereas the opposite occurred for the targets. The latter were more profit efficient than the acquirers before the transaction. In this type of transactions, acquirers benefited from revenue synergies due to the complementarities of activities. The negative evolution of the targets' efficiency scores could be explained by the problems experienced by a few banks in the sample.

In the transactions that diversify activities and geographies, targets experienced a clear improvement of their profit efficiency scores, where a slight deterioration occurred for the acquirers. This finding indicates that targets have markedly benefited from revenue synergies due to activities and geographies extension.

For the cross-border transactions, our cost efficiency results show a deterioration of the acquirers' scores and a slight improvement for the targets' scores.[82] It is also interesting to mention that the targets involved in cross-border transactions were more efficient in terms of cost that the ones involved in domestic transactions.[83] This is an indication that the potential targets involved in the cross-border transactions are amongst the most cost efficient in the industry. For the acquirers, it is obvious that the potential of improving cost efficiency is limited due to the additional costs resulting from the difficulties to manage large and complex organizations across borders, adding to that the over-evaluation of the premium paid to the shareholders of the target.

When applying the AG matrix, cross-border transactions focusing activities fail to improve cost efficiency scores for the acquirers. The deterioration of the acquirers' scores is more pronounced in the diversifying transactions type. The targets, instead, improve their cost efficiency scores for both transactions types. The improvement is more pronounced when banks focus the same activities. Clearly, it is easier for cross-border transactions to improve cost efficiency when banks focus the same activities.

With respect to profit efficiency, acquirers and targets fail to improve their scores although they displayed higher scores as compared to the banks involved in domestic transactions and those of the control group.[84] The deterioration of profit efficiency scores is more pronounced for the acquirers.

When looking at focusing versus diversifying M&A transactions, both failed to improve profit efficiency scores for the acquirers. However, the deterioration is more pronounced in the focusing M&A transactions. For the targets, scores have slightly improved in the diversifying M&A transactions. This finding should not be generalized, however, since it is based on only one transaction, and given the fact that the target has displayed a low profit efficiency level as compared to the targets average score involved in cross-border transactions.

The findings related to cross-border transactions would suggest that despite the potential of cost and revenue synergies promised by focusing and diversifying transactions, it seems that there are some difficulties to reach this aim.

These findings confirm the conclusions of the survey conducted by the European Commission in 2004 and 2005 on a sample of 355 financial institutions under the mandate of the European Council in Scheveningenin in September 2004 (See Annex 1 for a summary of the results). These conclusions confirm that the most relevant impediment identified is **the inadequate cross-border cost and revenue synergies**. Synergies are insufficient to offset the M&A costs and fail to generate a sufficient return on investment. This lack of synergies is explained by the following drivers:

- Fragmentation of retail markets, related to the difficulties of selling similar products in different domestic markets.
- Divergent supervisory rules and practices, e.g. multiple reporting requirements, divergence of supervisory practices and complex supervisory approval processes.

- Legal impediments to corporate expansion and reorganization, for example, taxation on dividends, VAT and other forms of double taxation, employment legislation and legal structures of the companies.
- Potential reluctance of consumers or employees to takeovers and acquisitions from foreigners, especially from smaller savings or cooperative institutions.

2.11.9   Banking M&A and performance – balance sheet indicators

For all transactions, our results based on the cost to income ratio (CIR) show that the acquirers are more cost efficient than the targets and the banks of the control group (see Annex 3). After the transaction, the CIR has improved, implying a cost reduction for the acquirers and the targets. This reduction is more pronounced for the targets since they display an initial higher potential for improvement than the acquirers. It is also interesting to notice that the reduction in terms of interest costs in more important than in terms of non-interest costs.

The domestic transactions succeeded to improve the CIR and to reduce total costs. The finding confirms the potential of cost savings of this type of transaction.

The average evolution of the CIR confirms that for the transactions aiming at focusing activities in the same local area, acquirers and targets have improved their CIR and reduced total costs in their total assets. This finding supports the hypothesis of the cost savings potential of this type of transactions. Also, this improvement could be explained by a more than proportionate increase of the income (as compared to the cost reduction) due to either an increase of the activity volume resulting from the merger or acquisition or a change in pricing policy of banks after the transaction. However, the results displayed in the cost efficiency analysis are consistent with a deterioration of the acquirers' scores after the transaction. This difference is explained by the fact that the cost reduction showed by the financial indicators is insufficient to maintain or improve the cost efficiency scores. Consequently, one might think about the optimal level of cost reduction corresponding to the U-shaped cost function. Therefore, it is interesting to question about the optimum level of cost reduction from which there would be an improvement of cost efficiency. Obviously, it is important to mention that the limits inherent to the financial indicators are such that the prices of the inputs are not taken into consideration, which is not the case for the cost efficiency analysis.

For the transactions aiming at focusing activities in different local areas, the CIR has improved, while total costs, in particular interest costs, were reduced for the acquirers and more profoundly for the targets.[85] The reduction of non-interest costs seems more difficult to achieve for the reasons stated previously. Moreover, this could also relate to the existence of a number of savings banks and other proximity banks that depend strongly on their branching. The results of the cost efficiency analysis confirm these conclusions.

When M&A transactions aim at diversifying activities in the same local area, the cost efficiency analysis showed that acquirers are the most efficient, despite a slight deterioration of their scores after the transaction. The results displayed by the financial indicators analysis showed that despite an improvement of the acquirers' CIR, these banks are the least efficient as compared to the average of their counterparts in the domestic transactions. A plausible explanation would be that these banks have failed to increase their revenues while maintaining their total costs. Similarly, the fairly cost efficient targets have seen their CIR deteriorating by more than 20 per cent after the transaction. This is also an indication that the difficulties of generating additional revenues while maintaining the total costs experienced by the acquirers are transferred to the targets. Adding to the conclusions of the empirical research on the subject, these findings show that, while best practices could be transferred from the acquirers to the benefit of the targets after the transactions, the opposite scenario occurs when the acquirer is experiencing difficulties.

In the case of M&A diversifying activities and geographies, acquirers improved their CIR, despite a deterioration of their cost efficiency scores. This finding indicates that these banks generate more revenues while maintaining unchanged their total costs. For the targets, the deterioration of their cost efficiency scores could be explained by their failure to control their non-interest costs; despite the fact that they succeeded in improving their CIR thanks to an increase of revenues.

Our results based on ROA and ROE showed a slight improvement for the acquirers involved in domestic transactions, which is more pronounced for the targets, while the control group showed the opposite trend. Moreover, the decrease of interest revenues was substituted by an increase of other non-interest revenues for the acquirers and the targets. The productivity has deteriorated for the acquirers, the targets and the control group. This is an indication that the productivity of assets is a general problem for European banks.

The average trend of ROA and ROE for the banks involved in the domestic transactions showed that for the M&A focusing activities in the same local area, acquirers and targets have both improved their profitability. This improvement is more pronounced for the targets since they displayed more potential for improvement before the transaction. Productivity has also deteriorated for this type of transactions.

For M&A focusing activities in different local areas, acquirers and targets have improved their ROA and ROE. This improvement is more pronounced for the targets due to their low profitability before the transaction. Productivity has also deteriorated after the transaction.

When M&A's aim at diversifying activities in the same local area, our results show that the acquirers have slightly improved ROA's, while no improvement is registered for the targets. This finding confirms the results of the profit efficiency indicators for this type of transactions. The ROE has displayed the opposite evolution.[86] Productivity of assets has also deteriorated for this type of transactions.

When M&A transactions aim at diversifying activities and geographies domestically, acquirers and targets have both improved their profitability. The most surprising finding is that even the productivity has improved. These findings confirm the benefits of multi-specialized banking models. However, the profit efficiency analysis has shown a deterioration of the scores for the acquirers, which could indicate the incapacity of management to fully exploit the benefits of revenue synergies due to X-inefficiencies.[87]

When measuring the solvency ratio, acquirers and targets have experienced a positive change in all types of transactions. This could provide an explanation for the national prudential authorities when defending domestic transactions.

In cross-border transactions, acquirers are more cost efficient in terms of CIR than the acquirers involved in domestic transactions. However, this type of transaction has had a negative impact on the acquirers' and targets' CIR. Despite a slight reduction of total costs in the assets, these transactions do not generate sufficient revenues as compared to their expenses.

For both types of M&A (focusing-versus diversifying) transactions, the cost efficiency analysis showed a deterioration of the scores for the acquirers, despite their success in reducing total costs. For the targets, the cost efficiency analysis showed an improvement of their scores which is partly explained by the reduction of their total costs. The CIR has neither improved for the acquirers nor for the targets, not only because total costs were not controlled as expected but also because they failed to generate sufficient additional revenues while keeping the same expenses.

Our results of the profitability analysis confirm that domestic transactions are more profitable in terms of ROA and ROE than cross-border ones, despite the high profitability level of the banks involved in the cross-border transactions. Indeed, cross-border transactions have failed to improve the profitability regardless of their type. Finally, our results show the negative impact of cross-border M&As on solvency.

2.12   Conclusions

When assessing the performance of European banks involved in 71 M&A transactions during 1996–2000, we showed that the different transactions' categories including focusing versus diversifying activities and geographies would have different impacts on banking performance. Therefore, this would indicate that the activity-geography combination would be a factor of success or failure for these transactions.

On average, our results confirm the conclusions of the previous empirical research in which domestic transactions have a higher chance to reduce costs, increase profits and achieve higher cost and profit efficiency.

However, M&A transactions that focus activities in the same local area could raise an anti-competitive concern since the improvement of profit efficiency is shown to be driven by an increase of revenues, suggestive of changes in pricing policy rather than improvements in cost efficiency. This result should, however, be interpreted with caution owing to the limitation of data collection by banking activity segment and also the unavailability of output prices.

Furthermore, it seems that the cost reduction potential in M&A transactions aimed at achieving multi-specialization are limited. This result confirms that it is more difficult to reach a critical mass when a bank is running several activities and therefore the opportunities to exploit scale economies are reduced. However, this may suggest that there are opportunities to exploit scope economies.

Finally, in our sample, cross-border transactions have failed to improve performance both in terms of costs and profits. These results could be clearly explicable in view of the obstacles that impede cross-border cost and revenue synergies. Therefore, to achieve an efficient, competitive and integrated European banking market, policy makers should continue their efforts to tackle the most relevant obstacles identified by the European Commission's survey in 2005.

Annex 1 Findings of the European Commission's survey (2005)[88]

	Intensity	Especially relevant for:
I. Elements that lower the economic value of cross-border acquisitions	+++	
30. Non-overlapping fixed costs*	+++	Across the board
I.1 Difficulties in selling the same products across countries	+++	Smaller institutions
29. Different product mixes	+++	
21. Discriminatory tax treatments	+++	
20. Specific domestic tax breaks	+++	
15. Uncertainty on VAT regime	++	
11. Divergent consumer protection rules	++	
13. Differences in private law	+	
I.2 Implications of supervision for cross-border institutions	++	Large and very large institutions
27. Multiple reporting requirements	+++	
26. Divergences in supervisory practices	++	
25. Supervisory approval processes	++	

Continued

Annex 1   Continued

	Intensity	Especially relevant for:
I.3 Legal impediments to corporate expansion and reorganisation	++	
22. Taxation on dividends	+++	Large institutions, with
9. Employment legislation	++	cross-border M&A
3. Legal structures	++	experience or having
18. Inter-group VAT	+	tried cross-border M&A
16. Exit tax on capital gains	+	(except for dividends taxation which was raised by all types of institutions)
II. Elements contributing to an unfavourable/disabling environment	++	
35. Political interference	+++	Share capital companies,
39. Political concessions	+	large and very large
24. Misuse of supervisory powers	++	institutions, with cross-
4. Limits or controls on foreign participations	++	border M&A experience
2. Opaque decision making processes	+	or having tried cross-
5. Defence mechanisms	+	border M&A
6. Impediments to effective control	+	
III. Consequences of individual perception of EU foreign entities	++	
36. Employees' reluctance	+++	Smaller institutions,
40. Consumer mistrust in foreign entities	++	cooperative and savings institutions

Note: * The number next to each item corresponds to the numbering of the background paper that served as a reference for the online survey.

Annex 2   M&A Sample

Table A: Number of transactions by year and country of target

Country	1996	1997	1998	1999	2000	Total	%
Portugal	1	2	1	1	1	6	8
Denmark	0	0	1	1	1	3	4
Finland	0	1	0	0	0	1	1
Sweden	2	0	0	0	0	2	3
Spain	0	6	5	5	1	17	24
Germany	0	2	2	1	0	5	7
France	3	4	1	3	1	12	17
Italy	0	7	10	5	3	25	35
Total	6	22	20	16	7	71	100
%	8	31	28	23	10	100	

Table B: Acquirers and targets by country

Country	Acquirers	Targets	Total
Portugal	6	8	14
Denmark	2	3	5
Finland	1	1	2
Sweden	3	2	5
Spain	10	15	25
Germany	5	4	9
Austria	0	1	1
France	10	12	22
Italy	19	25	44
Luxembourg	1	0	1
Total	57	71	128

Table C: The number of transactions per strategies per country

Country	S1	S2	S3	S4	S5	S6	Total
Portugal	2	3	0	1	0	0	6
Denmark	0	0	2	0	1	0	3
Finland	0	0	0	0	1	0	1
Sweden	1	0	1	0	0	0	2
Spain	1	10	0	0	5	1	17
Germany	1	0	1	1	2	0	5
France	6	2	2	1	0	1	12
Italy	5	18	1	1	0	0	25
Total	16	33	7	4	9	2	71
%	23	46	10	6	13	3	100

Table D: Transactions by strategy and year

Strategy	1996	1997	1998	1999	2000	total	%
S1	2	9	3	1	1	16	23
S2	0	8	12	8	5	33	46
S3	2	0	2	2	1	7	10
S4	1	1	1	1	0	4	6
S5	0	3	2	4	0	9	13
S6	1	1	0	0	0	2	3
Total	6	22	20	16	7	71	100

Table E: Control group by country

Country	Total
Austria	38
Belgium	22
Denmark	26
Finland	3
France	106
Germany	126
Greece	7
Italy	131
Netherlands	20
Portugal	10
Spain	29
Sweden	9
UK	42
Norway	18
Total	587

Annex 3:   Results – Efficiency analysis & Balance Sheet Indicators

a) Cost and profit efficiency indicators

		Cost efficiency indicators						
		Acquirers			Control group			
Transaction type	Number	Before (1) %	After (2) %	Difference (A=(2)−(1)) %	Before (1) %	After (2) %	Difference (B=(2)−(1)) %	Difference (A)−(B) %
Total	63	67.39	66.61	−0.78	36.69	39.90	3.21	−3.99
National	54	65.89	66.15	0.27	36.72	39.89	3.17	−2.90
Cross border	9	78.20	69.88	−8.32	36.60	39.88	3.27	−11.59
S1	14	78.15	75.77	−2.37	36.92	39.46	2.54	−4.92
S2	31	58.27	62.06	3.79	36.62	40.04	3.42	0.37
S3	5	81.99	81.77	−0.22	36.36	40.56	4.20	−4.42
S4	4	57.86	43.51	−14.36	37.09	39.60	2.51	−16.87
S5	8	76.42	69.37	−7.04	36.53	39.99	3.46	−10.50
S6	1	92.50	73.93	−18.57	37.19	38.99	1.79	−20.36

		Cost efficiency indicators						
		Targets			Control group			
Transaction type	Number	Before (1) %	After (2) %	Difference (A=(2)−(1)) %	Before (1) %	After (2) %	Difference (B=(2)−(1)) %	Difference (A)−(B) %
Total	65	50.94	55.72	4.78	36.65	39.94	3.29	1.49
National	55	51.02	57.78	6.76	36.67	39.93	3.25	3.51
Cross border	10	50.49	54.99	4.50	36.54	40.00	3.45	1.05
S1	14	68.88	69.68	0.80	36.92	39.46	2.54	−1.74
S2	33	41.99	53.38	11.39	36.58	40.10	3.52	7.87
S3	4	69.34	69.33	−0.01	36.17	40.46	4.29	−4.30
S4	4	44.69	40.85	−3.84	37.09	39.60	2.51	−6.35
S5	9	52.52	57.28	4.76	36.47	40.11	3.64	1.12
S6	1	32.20	34.43	2.23	37.19	38.99	1.79	0.44

		Profit efficiency indicators						
		Acquirers			Control group			
Transaction type	Number	Before (1) %	After (2) %	Difference (A=(2)−(1)) %	Before (1) %	After (2) %	Difference (B=(2)−(1)) %	Difference (A)−(B) %
Total	63	33.19	40.19	7.00	10.16	16.22	6.06	0.93
National	54	28.94	39.07	10.13	10.19	16.21	6.03	4.10
Cross border	9	55.95	44.22	−11.73	10.12	16.07	5.95	−17.68
S1	14	37.95	44.27	6.32	10.67	15.38	4.71	1.61
S2	31	27.32	40.30	12.98	10.00	16.57	6.57	6.41
S3	5	21.85	34.19	12.34	9.47	17.57	8.11	4.23
S4	4	25.06	23.56	−1.50	10.51	15.12	4.61	−6.11
S5	8	58.70	46.92	−11.77	9.98	16.28	6.30	−18.07
S6	1	34.00	22.63	−11.37	11.28	14.41	3.13	−14.49

		Profit efficiency indicators						
		Targets			Control group			
Transaction type	Number	Before (1) %	After (2) %	Difference (A=(2)−(1)) %	Before (1) %	After (2) %	Difference (B=(2)−(1)) %	Difference (A)−(B) %
Total	65	19.75	30.72	10.97	10.10	16.27	6.17	4.80
National	55	18.94	32.47	13.53	10.12	16.27	6.15	7.38
Cross border	10	24.20	22.76	−1.44	10.01	16.29	6.28	−7.72
S1	14	26.82	40.75	13.94	10.67	15.38	4.71	9.22
S2	33	13.12	30.60	17.48	9.94	16.67	6.73	10.74
S3	4	46.23	30.59	−15.64	9.25	17.18	7.93	−23.56
S4	4	12.13	20.86	8.74	10.51	15.12	4.61	4.13
S5	9	26.50	24.81	−1.69	9.87	16.50	6.63	−8.32
S6	1	3.50	4.33	0.83	11.28	14.41	3.13	−2.29

Results-Balance-sheet indicators:

		Cost Income Ratio (CIR)						
		Acquirers			Control group			
Transaction type	Number	Before (1) %	After (2) %	Difference (A=(2)−(1)) %	Before (1) %	After (2) %	Difference (B=(2)−(1)) %	Difference (A)−(B) %
Total	71	63.37	60.30	−3.06	63.96	66.66	2.71	−5.77
National	60	64.59	60.30	−4.29	63.95	66.66	2.72	−7.01
Cross border	11	56.72	60.36	3.64	63.99	66.65	2.66	0.98
S1	16	64.18	60.43	−3.75	63.96	65.69	1.74	−5.48
S2	33	62.81	58.20	−4.61	63.94	67.12	3.18	−7.79
S3	7	71.40	70.18	−1.22	63.99	66.99	3.00	−4.22
S4	4	68.94	59.77	−9.18	63.93	66.23	2.30	−11.47
S5	9	57.28	61.09	3.81	63.99	67.07	3.08	0.72
S6	2	54.18	57.06	2.88	64.02	64.75	0.74	2.15

		Targets			Control group			
	Number	Before (1) %	After (2) %	Difference (A=(2)−(1)) %	Before (1) %	After (2) %	Difference (B=(2)−(1)) %	Difference A−B %
Total	69	73.08	70.05	−3.02	63.95	66.63	2.67	−5.70
National	59	72.81	68.30	−4.51	63.94	66.62	2.68	−7.19
Cross border	10	74.63	80.38	5.75	64.05	66.66	2.62	3.13
S1	16	69.22	65.06	−4.17	63.96	65.69	1.74	−5.90
S2	33	78.10	68.46	−9.63	63.94	67.12	3.18	−12.81
S3	7	45.53	65.85	20.32	54.77	57.12	2.34	17.98
S4	4	73.10	67.14	−5.97	63.93	66.23	2.30	−8.26
S5	8	76.07	82.55	6.48	64.05	67.14	3.09	3.39
S6	2	68.86	71.68	2.82	64.02	64.75	0.74	2.09

		Non-interest costs/Total assets						
		Acquirers			Control group			
	Number	Before (1) %	After (2) %	Difference (A=(2)−(1)) %	Before (1) %	After (2) %	Difference (B=(2)−(1)) %	Difference A−B %
Total	71	2.24	2.05	−0.19	1.59	1.59	0.00	−0.18
National	60	2.16	2.06	−0.10	1.59	1.59	0.00	−0.10
Cross border	11	2.63	2.00	−0.62	1.60	1.59	−0.01	−0.61
S1	16	2.01	1.82	−0.19	1.61	1.56	−0.05	−0.14
S2	33	2.52	2.45	−0.06	1.58	1.60	0.02	−0.08
S3	7	1.10	0.99	−0.11	1.58	1.60	0.02	−0.13
S4	4	1.71	1.62	−0.09	1.60	1.58	−0.02	−0.07
S5	9	2.39	2.04	−0.35	1.59	1.60	0.01	−0.36
S6	2	3.68	1.82	−1.85	1.62	1.53	−0.09	−1.76

Continued

Continued

	Number	Targets Before (1) %	After (2) %	Difference (A=(2)−(1)) %	Control group Before (1) %	After (2) %	Difference (B=(2)−(1)) %	Difference A−B %
Total	71	3.16	2.71	−0.45	1.57	1.56	0.00	−0.45
National	60	3.24	2.87	−0.37	1.56	1.56	0.00	−0.37
Cross border	11	2.75	1.86	−0.89	1.60	1.59	−0.01	−0.88
S1	16	2.44	1.68	−0.75	1.61	1.56	−0.05	−0.70
S2	33	3.29	3.19	−0.10	1.54	1.55	0.02	−0.11
S3	7	5.55	4.14	−1.41	1.58	1.60	0.02	−1.43
S4	4	1.97	2.67	0.70	1.60	1.58	−0.02	0.72
S5	9	2.82	1.91	−0.91	1.59	1.60	0.01	−0.92
S6	2	2.45	1.64	−0.81	1.62	1.53	−0.09	−0.72

Interest costs/Total assets

Transactions	Number	Acquirers Before (1) %	After (2) %	Difference (A=(2)−(1)) %	Control group Before (1) %	After (2) %	Difference (B=(2)−(1)) %	Difference A−B %
Total	71	4.30	3.22	−1.08	3.94	3.48	−0.46	−0.62
National	60	4.25	3.12	−1.13	3.94	3.48	−0.46	−0.67
Cross border	11	4.55	3.75	−0.80	3.98	3.53	−0.45	−0.35
S1	16	4.35	3.59	−0.76	4.00	3.54	−0.46	−0.30
S2	33	4.09	2.64	−1.46	3.90	3.44	−0.46	−1.00
S3	7	4.45	3.56	−0.89	3.91	3.45	−0.46	−0.42
S4	4	4.88	4.54	−0.35	3.99	3.54	−0.45	0.10
S5	9	4.19	3.23	−0.95	3.96	3.51	−0.45	−0.50
S6	2	6.18	6.07	−0.10	4.07	3.61	−0.46	0.36

	Number	Targets Before (1) %	After (2) %	Difference (A=(2)−(1)) %	Control group Before (1) %	After (2) %	Difference (B=(2)−(1)) %	Difference A−B %
Total	68	4.68	3.20	−1.48	3.94	3.48	−0.46	−1.02
National	59	4.73	3.24	−1.49	3.94	3.48	−0.46	−1.03
Cross border	9	4.39	2.97	−1.42	3.98	3.53	−0.45	−0.97
S1	16	5.58	3.84	−1.74	4.00	3.54	−0.46	−1.28
S2	33	4.14	2.57	−1.57	3.90	3.44	−0.46	−1.11
S3	6	4.99	4.73	−0.26	3.91	3.45	−0.46	0.20
S4	4	5.78	3.81	−1.97	3.99	3.54	−0.45	−1.52
S5	8	3.91	2.96	−0.95	3.96	3.51	−0.45	−0.50
S6	1	6.55	3.02	−3.53	4.07	3.61	−0.46	−3.07

		ROA						
		Acquirers			Control group			
	Number	Before (1) %	After (2) %	Difference (A=(2)−(1)) %	Before (1) %	After (2) %	Difference (B=(2)−(1)) %	Difference A−B %
Total	71	0.95	0.99	0.05	0.73	0.69	−0.04	0.09
National	60	0.95	1.03	0.08	0.73	0.69	−0.04	0.13
Cross border	11	0.95	0.79	−0.16	0.73	0.70	−0.03	−0.13
S1	16	0.85	0.97	0.13	0.73	0.73	0.00	0.12
S2	33	1.12	1.16	0.04	0.73	0.67	−0.06	0.10
S3	7	0.63	0.72	0.09	0.73	0.67	−0.07	0.16
S4	4	0.49	0.77	0.27	0.73	0.71	−0.02	0.29
S5	9	1.03	0.83	−0.20	0.73	0.69	−0.05	−0.15
S6	2	0.57	0.59	0.02	0.72	0.76	0.03	−0.02

		Targets			Control group			
	Number	Before (1) %	After (2) %	Difference (A=(2)−(1)) %	Before (1) %	After (2) %	Difference (B=(2)−(1)) %	Difference A−B %
Total	71	0.77	1.04	0.27	0.73	0.69	−0.04	0.31
National	60	0.58	0.91	0.33	0.73	0.69	−0.04	0.37
Cross border	11	1.81	1.73	−0.08	0.73	0.70	−0.03	−0.05
S1	16	−0.18	0.86	1.03	0.73	0.73	0.00	1.03
S2	33	0.77	1.02	0.24	0.73	0.67	−0.06	0.30
S3	7	1.52	0.63	−0.89	0.73	0.67	−0.07	−0.82
S4	4	0.41	0.78	0.37	0.73	0.71	−0.02	0.39
S5	9	2.06	1.99	−0.07	0.73	0.69	−0.05	−0.02
S6	2	0.72	0.58	−0.14	0.72	0.76	0.03	−0.17

		ROE						
		Acquirers			Control group			
	Number	Before (1) %	After (2) %	Difference (A=(2)−(1)) %	Before (1) %	After (2) %	Difference (B=(2)−(1)) %	Difference A−B %
Total	71	13.43	14.14	0.71	13.83	13.34	−0.27	0.98
National	60	12.53	13.66	1.12	13.84	13.32	−0.26	1.38
Cross border	11	18.33	16.78	−1.54	13.80	13.47	−0.33	−1.22
S1	16	10.06	13.57	3.51	13.69	14.12	0.43	3.08
S2	33	13.96	14.25	0.29	13.91	12.98	−0.93	1.21
S3	7	13.33	11.49	−1.84	13.91	12.84	1.22	−3.06
S4	4	9.20	12.88	3.69	13.76	13.69	−0.06	3.75
S5	9	18.38	16.98	−1.41	13.85	13.21	−0.64	−0.76
S6	2	18.08	15.91	−2.16	13.56	14.65	1.09	−3.25

Continued

Continued

	Number	Targets			Control group			Difference A−B %
		Before (1) %	After (2) %	Difference (A=(2)−(1)) %	Before (1) %	After (2) %	Difference (B=(2)−(1)) %	
Total	71	3.79	10.30	6.51	13.83	13.34	−0.27	6.78
National	60	2.85	10.97	8.12	13.84	13.32	−0.26	8.38
Cross border	11	8.92	6.66	−2.26	13.80	13.47	−0.33	−1.93
S1	16	1.97	11.93	9.96	13.69	14.12	0.43	9.54
S2	33	6.92	10.94	4.02	13.91	12.98	−0.93	4.95
S3	7	−14.76	8.25	23.01	13.91	12.84	1.22	21.79
S4	4	3.60	12.12	8.52	13.76	13.69	−0.06	8.58
S5	9	8.10	4.64	−3.45	13.85	13.21	−0.64	−2.81
S6	2	12.65	15.76	3.11	13.56	14.65	1.09	2.02

Interest revenue/Total revenue

	Number	Acquirers			Control group			Difference A−B %
		Before (1) %	After (2) %	Difference (A=(2)−(1)) %	Before (1) %	After (2) %	Difference (B=(2)−(1)) %	
Total	71	69.72	63.79	−5.93	83.10	77.64	−5.46	−0.46
National	60	69.30	63.92	−5.38	83.06	77.61	−5.45	0.07
Cross border	11	72.00	63.07	−8.93	83.34	77.79	−5.55	−3.38
S1	16	73.24	67.26	−5.99	83.65	78.41	−5.24	−0.75
S2	33	69.86	64.18	−5.68	82.78	77.16	−5.62	−0.06
S3	7	54.99	54.33	−0.66	82.82	77.62	−5.20	4.54
S4	4	73.92	65.25	−8.67	83.47	78.22	−5.26	−3.41
S5	9	73.13	62.09	−11.04	83.15	77.38	−5.77	−5.27
S6	2	66.93	67.49	0.56	84.21	79.65	−4.56	5.12

	Number	Targets			Control group			Difference A−B %
		Before (1) %	After (2) %	Difference (A=(2)−(1)) %	Before (1) %	After (2) %	Difference (B=(2)−(1)) %	
Total	71	72.25	65.93	−6.32	83.10	77.64	−5.46	−0.85
National	60	72.38	66.63	−5.75	83.06	77.61	−5.45	−0.30
Cross border	11	71.54	62.14	−9.40	83.34	77.79	−5.55	−3.85
S1	16	73.15	68.24	−4.92	83.65	78.41	−5.24	0.32
S2	33	69.69	65.04	−4.65	82.78	77.16	−5.62	0.97
S3	7	77.31	69.75	−7.57	82.82	77.62	−5.20	−2.37
S4	4	82.84	67.87	−14.96	83.47	78.22	−5.26	−9.71
S5	9	75.51	66.51	−9.00	83.15	77.38	−5.77	−3.23
S6	2	53.69	42.48	−11.21	84.21	79.65	−4.56	−6.65

		Non interest revenue/Total revenue						
		Acquirers			Control group			
	Number	Before (1) %	After (2) %	Difference (A=(2)−(1)) %	Before (1) %	After (2) %	Difference (B=(2)−(1)) %	Difference A−B %
Total	71	29.28	35.00	5.72	16.88	22.34	5.46	0.26
National	60	29.51	34.65	5.13	16.92	22.36	5.44	−0.31
Cross border	11	28.00	36.93	8.93	16.66	22.21	5.55	3.38
S1	16	26.76	32.74	5.99	16.35	21.59	5.24	0.75
S2	33	30.14	35.82	5.68	17.19	22.80	5.61	0.07
S3	7	34.83	33.38	−1.45	17.18	22.38	5.20	−6.65
S4	4	26.08	34.75	8.67	16.53	21.78	5.26	3.41
S5	9	26.87	37.91	11.04	16.85	22.62	5.77	5.27
S6	2	33.07	32.51	−0.56	15.79	20.35	4.56	−5.12

		Targets			Control group			
	Number	Before (1) %	After (2) %	Difference (A=(2)−(1)) %	Before (1) %	After (2) %	Difference (B=(2)−(1)) %	Difference A−B %
Total	71	27.75	34.07	6.32	16.88	22.34	5.46	0.86
National	60	27.62	33.37	5.75	16.92	22.36	5.44	0.31
Cross border	11	28.46	37.86	9.40	16.66	22.21	5.55	3.85
S1	16	26.85	31.76	4.92	16.35	21.59	5.24	−0.32
S2	33	30.31	34.96	4.65	17.19	22.80	5.61	−0.95
S3	7	22.69	30.25	7.57	17.18	22.38	5.20	2.37
S4	4	17.16	32.13	14.96	16.53	21.78	5.26	9.71
S5	9	24.49	33.49	9.00	16.85	22.62	5.77	3.23
S6	2	46.31	57.52	11.21	15.79	20.35	4.56	6.65

		Total revenue/Total assets						
		Acquirers			Control group			
Transactions	Number	Before (1) %	After (2) %	Difference (A=(2)−(1)) %	Before (1) %	After (2) %	Difference (B=(2)−(1)) %	Difference A−B %
Total	71	7.37	6.12	−1.25	6.49	5.89	−0.60	−0.65
National	60	7.36	5.95	−1.41	6.48	5.88	−0.60	−0.81
Cross border	11	7.43	7.04	−0.39	6.54	5.94	−0.60	0.21
S1	16	7.44	5.92	−1.51	6.58	5.97	−0.61	−0.90
S2	33	7.51	5.68	−1.84	6.44	5.84	−0.59	−1.24
S3	7	6.06	5.22	−0.85	6.45	5.85	−0.60	−0.25
S4	4	8.03	9.60	1.57	6.55	5.96	−0.59	2.16
S5	9	7.39	6.94	−0.45	6.51	5.92	−0.59	0.13
S6	2	7.63	7.53	−0.10	6.67	6.05	−0.62	0.52

Continued

	Number	Targets			Control group			Difference A−B %
		Before (1) %	After (2) %	Difference (A=(2)−(1)) %	Before (1) %	After (2) %	Difference (B=(2)−(1)) %	
Total	71	8.25	6.85	−1.40	6.49	5.89	−0.60	−0.81
National	60	8.40	7.15	−1.25	6.48	5.88	−0.60	−0.65
Cross border	11	7.44	5.18	−2.26	6.54	5.94	−0.60	−1.66
S1	16	8.60	5.91	−2.69	6.58	5.97	−0.61	−2.08
S2	33	8.32	7.60	−0.72	6.44	5.84	−0.59	−0.12
S3	7	8.13	7,20	−0.94	6.45	5.85	−0.60	−0.34
S4	4	8.79	8.40	−0.40	6.55	5.96	−0.59	0.20
S5	9	6.97	5.25	−1.71	6.51	5.92	−0.59	−1.12
S6	2	9.57	4.85	−4.72	6.67	6.05	−0.62	−4.09

		Capital ratio						
		Acquirers			Control group			Difference A−B %
Transactions	Number	Before (1) %	After (2) %	Difference (A=(2)−(1)) %	Before (1) %	After (2) %	Difference (B=(2)−(1)) %	
Total	71	7.12	8.46	1.33	5.28	5.18	−0.11	1.44
National	60	7.47	9.06	1.58	5.28	5.18	−0.10	1.69
Cross border	11	5.22	5.19	−0.03	5.29	5.18	−0.11	0.08
S1	16	6.88	10.39	3.51	5.30	5.16	−0.13	3.64
S2	33	8.45	9.58	1.13	5.27	5.18	−0.09	1.22
S3	7	5.34	5.24	−0.10	5.27	5.18	−0.09	0.00
S4	4	5.55	6.12	0.57	5.30	5.18	−0.12	0.69
S5	9	5.60	5.61	0.01	5.29	5.19	−0.10	0.11
S6	2	3.49	3.26	−0.22	5.32	5.16	−0.16	−0.06

		Targets			Control group			Difference A−B %
Transactions	Number	Before (1) %	After (2) %	Difference (A=(2)−(1)) %	Before (1) %	After (2) %	Difference (B=(2)−(1)) %	
Total	71	9.80	8.96	−0.84	5.28	5.18	−0.11	−0.74
National	60	9.07	8.23	−0.84	5.28	5.18	−0.10	−0.73
Cross border	11	13.78	12.93	−0.85	5.29	5.18	−0.11	−0.74
S1	16	7.90	8.78	0.88	5.30	5.16	−0.13	1.01
S2	33	8.01	8.74	0.73	5.27	5.18	−0.09	0.82
S3	7	17.27	5.44	−11.84	5.27	5.18	−0.09	−11.75
S4	4	8.10	6.70	−1.40	5.30	5.18	−0.12	−1.28
S5	9	15.30	14.85	−0.45	5.29	5.19	−0.10	−0.35
S6	2	6.92	4.25	−2.66	5.32	5.16	−0.16	−2.51

		Solvency ratio						
		Acquirers			Control group			
Transactions	Number	Before (1) %	After (2) %	Difference (A=(2)−(1)) %	Before (1) %	After (2) %	Difference (B=(2)−(1)) %	Difference A−B %
Total	71	17.71	13.11	−4.60	15.03	16.57	1.54	−6.14
National	60	18.55	12.73	−5.82	15.02	16.58	1.56	−7.38
Cross border	11	13.13	15.19	2.06	15.06	16.49	1.43	0.62
S1	16	28.53	16.81	−11.72	14.77	15.63	0.87	−12.58
S2	33	16.38	14.88	−1.50	15.12	16.96	1.84	−3.34
S3	7	12.53	9.19	−3.34	15.13	17.23	2.10	−5.44
S4	4	7.09	−15.07	−22.16	14.96	16.12	1.16	−23.32
S5	9	13.53	14.80	1.27	15.17	16.80	1.63	−0.36
S6	2	11.34	16.94	5.60	14.57	15.12	0.56	5.04

		Targets			Control group			
	Number	Before (1) %	After (2) %	Difference (A=(2)−(1)) %	Before (1) %	After (2) %	Difference (B=(2)−(1)) %	Difference A−B %
Total	71	22.19	17.91	−4.29	15.03	16.54	1.51	−5.80
National	50	22.74	16.89	−5.85	15.01	16.50	1.49	−7.34
Cross border	11	18.63	24.58	5.95	15.13	16.77	1.64	4.31
S1	16	36.38	22.62	−13.76	14.77	15.63	0.87	−14.62
S2	33	12.54	13.55	1.01	15.12	16.96	1.84	−0.82
S3	7	38.26	18.28	−19.98	15.09	16.55	1.46	−21.44
S4	4	29.00	19.35	−9.65	14.96	16.12	1.16	−10.81
S5	9	17.94	26.02	8.08	15.20	17.01	1.81	6.26
S6	2	24.15	13.11	−11.03	14.57	14.83	0.27	−11.30

Notes

1. Ayadi and Pujals (2004, 2005).
2. PwC (2006) and ECB (2005).
3. Leibenstein (1966).
4. Berger, Demsetz Strahan (1999).
5. Ayadi and Pujals (2004).
6. See Burger (2001).
7. One might also mention in this context UBS and PaineWebber or Crédit Suisse Group and DLJ in 2000, and Dresdner Bank and Wasserstein Perella in 2001.

8. Originally the concept of X-inefficiency was introduced by Leibenstein (1966) who noted that, for a variety of reasons, people and organizations normally work neither as hard nor as effectively as they could. In technical terms, X-efficiency refers to the deviations from the production efficient frontier that depicts the maximum attainable output for a given level of output.

9. According to Méon and Weill (2001), a comparison of the annual growth rate of real GDP suggests that the economic cycles of many European countries are not perfectly correlated. Consequently, geographical diversification could enable European banks to significantly reduce their risks.

10. Generally, the acquiring bank in a merger is more cost efficient and more profitable than the institution being acquired. As noted in a recent survey (Berger, Demsetz and Strahan 1999), this holds for the US (Berger and Humphrey, 1992; Pilloff and Santomero, 1997; Peristiani, 1997; Cummins, Sharon and Weiss, 1999; and Fried, Lovell and Yaisawarng, 1999) as well as for Europe (Vander Vennet, 1996; Focarelli, Panetta and Salleo, 2002). The expectation is that the more efficient and profitable acquiring bank will restructure the target institution and implement policies and procedures to improve its performance.

11. Shaffer (1993).

12. Rhoades (1998).

13. Deutsche Bundesbank (2001).

14. Hannan (1991) and Berger and Hannan (1989, 1997).

15. Vander Vennet (1996).

16. *Pre-emption* implies that the price fixed by the bank is lower than the average cost while *predation* involves fixing the price at a level lower than the marginal cost.

17. Market power could be gauged by looking at the transmission of market interest rates to bank retail rates.

18. Hannan (1997) and Radecki (1998).

19. A contestable market is one with low barriers to entry and exit (Baumol and al., 1982). In such a situation, potential competitors may engage in hit-and-run behaviour to take advantage of the super-normal profit situation of the market. Contestability hinges on the absence of exit costs (called 'sunk costs'), which are the costs that cannot be recovered by transferring assets to other uses or by selling them. Entry to the financial services sector requires substantial investment that tends to be sunk to a high degree.

20. The possibility of a cartel in banking is not purely theoretical and can be prejudicial for effective competition, as shown by the 'Cruickshank' report (2000) in the UK and in the Canoy and Onderstal (2003) in the Netherlands.

21. 'Agency relation' of Jensen and Meckling (1976).

22. 'Managerial' theory (Berle and Means, 1932; Williamson, 1964).

23. 'Follow the leader' strategy.

24. Berger (2003).

25. Rhoades (1994) and Pilloff and Santomero (1997) provide a survey of event studies. Some studies of US banking M&As found increases in the combined value around the time of the M&As' announcement (Cornett and Tehranian, 1992; Zhang, 1995); others found no improvement in combined value (Hannan and Wolken, 1989; Houston and Ryngaert, 1994; Pilloff, 1996; Kwan and Eisenbeis, 1999); while still others found that the measured effects depended upon the characteristics of the M&A (Houston and Ryngaert, 1997). A study of domestic and cross-border M&A involving US banks found more value created by the cross-border M&A (DeLong, 1999).

26. Stock market event studies of bank mergers have shown that merger announce-ments typically result in a fall in the equity value of the acquiring firm and no significant gain in the combined value of the two firms together. This result suggests that the market believes that, on average, there are unlikely to be sub-stantial gains realized from bank mergers. And since the value of the acquiring firm typically falls, the market also believes that acquiring firms tend to overpay for acquisitions in anticipation of merger benefits that are not likely to be realized. This is a common finding and is not limited to bank mergers, which points in the direction of a more general problem associated with the corporate governance of M&As.
27. Becher (2000), Houston, James and Ryngaert (2001).
28. Berger and Hannan (1998).
29. According to A. T. Kearney (1999): '58% of the M&As announced and completed are unfortunately a failure. Indeed, the stock market value of the merged entity two years after the operation is lower than the sum of both separated partners three months before. Similarly, Arthur D. Little's study (1999) has shown that: 'Two years following the announcement of the operation, the stock market performance of 60% of the companies having merged has been lower than the average of their sector.' Finally, according to a KPMG survey (2001): '30% of the M&As have increased the shareholders' value, 39% haven't brought any consider-able change and almost 31% have destroyed value.' In other words, 70% of mergers were unsuccessful in producing any business benefit as regards share-holder value.
30. Houston and Ryngaert (1997).
31. Berger and Humphrey (1992), Srinivasan (1992) and Pilloff (1996).
32. One limitation applies to this literature, indeed, the efficiency gains or losses associated to M&A activity may take a very long period to materialize, but these studies only focus on a short period of time before and after each M&A, Berger (2003).
33. Peristiani (1997), Berger (1998) and Rhoades (1998).
34. Akhavein, Berger and Humphrey (1997) and Berger (2000).
35. X-inefficiencies have been broadly investigated in the US, but without giving a final answer. Indeed, the first cause is linked to the size; on average, operating costs of larger banks are found to be closer to the optimal frontier curve than those of smaller banks to their respective cost frontier (Kwan and Eisenbeis (1996)). This could be explained by the fact that larger banks which operate in metropolitan markets are more likely to face stronger competition than smaller banks which are morel likely to operate in suburban or rural areas. The second rea-son is linked to risk taking, inefficient institutions are found to take in a higher level of risk (Gorten and Rosen (1995)). It is indeed very likely that managers of inefficient banks are more inclined to compensate for the operating inefficiency by taking on more risk which may reward them with a higher yield. Finally, the third reason is the financial condition which is linked to the percentage of prob-lem loans and other illiquid positions in the balance and off-balance sheet. The correlation between poor asset quality and inefficiency may be an indication of poor management.
36. Houston, James and Ryngaert (2001).
37. Vander Vennet (1996).
38. Resti (1998).
39. Haynes and Thompson (1999).

40. Altunbaş, Molyneux and Thornton (1997).
41. Focarelli, Panetta and Salleo (2002).
42. Many studies of market structure, price conduct and profit performance have found that higher bank concentration is significantly associated with lower prices for deposits, but the relationship between higher concentration and higher profits is often mixed, being sometimes significant and sometimes not. A recent study has found that cost efficiency tends to be lower in markets where concentration is higher (Berger and Hannan, 1998). Indeed, higher concentration (market power) may lead to higher prices and revenues but, with less competition, the incentive to reduce costs to their minimum levels is blunted. So, the higher revenues are largely absorbed in higher costs rather than contributing fully to expanded profits. From this perspective, market concentration seems to have a greater negative effect on cost efficiency than it does on prices.
43. Other relevant studies include Berger, Hancock and Humphrey (1993) and Berger, Humphrey and Pulley (1996), Berger and Mester (1997), Clark and Siems (1997), Cummins, Sharon and Weiss (1999) and Berger (2000).
44. Vander Vennet (2002b).
45. Berger, Saunders et al. (1998), Berger, Demsetz and Strahan (1999).
46. A number of further studies exist at the country level. For example, Focarelli and Panetta (2002), by distinguishing between short-run and long-run effects of M&A, have found strong evidence that these effects are different. Precisely, they showed that national mergers leading to deposit rate changes are unfavourable to consumers in the short run, but in the long run if banks succeed in reducing costs, efficiency gains from mergers prevail over the market power effects, so that consumers benefit. Hence, the adverse price changes generated through consolidation are by all means temporary. Thus, studies restricted to a short post-merger period might fail to register the efficiency gains and as a consequence overestimate the adverse price changes.
47. Amel, Barnes et al. (2002).
48. In an analysis of the effects of M&A in the market for bank deposits, Focarelli & Panetta (2002) find that in the short run the costs of restructuring the consolidated bank cancel out the gains, which cannot fully emerge for years. In the long run, however, the efficiency gains dominate over the market power effect, leading to more favourable prices for consumers.
49. Berger, Saunders et al. (1998) and Calomiris & Karceski (1998) mention three years as the gestation period needed to restructure the merged bank. This was consistent with the results of the interviews conducted by the Federal Reserve Board staff with officials of banks involved in mergers (Rhoades, 1998). In a study of US bank mergers, Houston, James and Ryngaert (2001) find that cost savings and revenue gains take two to four years.
50. Practitioners indicate that 'differences in corporate cultures' are one of the main obstacles to the completion of bank mergers in all the major industrial countries (see BIS, 2001).
51. Identified in the European Commission's survey in 2005, see Annex 1.
52. See De Vincenzo, Doria and Salleo (2006), Bliss and Rosen (2001). Similar results on the existence of agency problems in the banking industry can be found in Gorton and Rosen (1995) and Ryan (1999).
53. Palia (1993).
54. Pilloff & Santomero (1997).
55. DeLong and DeYoung (2004) have advanced the 'learning by observing' hypothesis which supposes that the mergers of the mid- or late 1990s would have been

more likely to create value than the mergers of the 1980s and this is due to the fact that bank managers would have benefited from observing a large number of mergers before starting one. This is typically linked to the information spillover hypothesis. It also suggests that the stock market would have been a more accurate predictor of the long-term performance of banking mergers announced during the 1990s than those announced during the 1980s.

56. Dietsch and Oung (2001).
57. Same methodology used in Baele, De Jonghe and Vander Vennet (2006).
58. The same methodology has been tested in Baele, De Jonghe and Vander Vennet (2006).
59. Weill (2004).
60. Berger and Mester (1997), Maudos and Pastor (2003).
61. The efficiency of a firm consist of two components: *technical efficiency*, which reflects the ability of a firm to obtain maximal output from a given set of inputs, and *allocative efficiency*, which reflects the ability of a firm to use the inputs in optimal proportions, given their respective prices.
62. Radial cost efficiency, Banker, Charnes and Cooper (1984).
63. Berger and Mester (1997), Rogers (1998).
64. Wheelock and Wilson (1995), Berger, Leusner and Mingo (1997).
65. This item includes the 'other earning assets' in the FitchRatings terminology, which are the earning assets other than loans.
66. Dietsch and Weill (2001), Altunbaş, Gardener and al. (2001), Maudos, Pastor et al. (2002).
67. Which is profit before provisions and taxes.
68. Rhoades (1998).
69. Among the large banks, derivatives are important off-balance sheet item that may be larger as measured by notional value than total asset. For many other banks, unused commitments such as credit cards, and home equity lines of credit represent major off-balance sheet items that are sometimes larger in value than assets. Standby and commercial letters of credit represent an important although much smaller source of off-balance sheet items for mostly larger banks. Off-balance sheet activities result in expenses and also revenues.
70. Which is the income before taxes.
71. Which is the income after taxes.
72. In our empirical analysis computer routines are carried out using DEAP 2.1 (Coelli, 1996).
73. These results are confirmed in Vander Vennet (1996), Altunbaş and Ibanez (2004), Ayadi and Pujals (2005).
74. Focarelli, Panetta and Salleo (2002).
75. This result confirms the findings of Beitel et al. (2004) in Europe, DeLong (2001) and Cornett et Hovakimian et al. (2000) in the US.
76. This result confirms the findings of Beitel et al. (2004) in Europe, DeLong (2001) and Cornett et Hovakimian et al. (2000) in the US.
77. This result confirms the findings of Beitel et al. (2004) in Europe, DeLong (2001) and Cornett et Hovakimian et al. (2000) in the US.
78. These results should be interpreted with caution owing to a number of limits of the DEA methodology, particularly the non availability of output prices.
79. Results confirmed by Vander Vennet (1996), Altunbaş and Ibanez (2004), Ayadi and Pujals (2005) for European banks; and Houston, James and Ryngaert (2001) for US banks; and Focarelli and Panetta (2002) for Italian banks.

80. This type of transactions could potentially lead to a concentration increase in a given local market. The conclusions of Berger and Hannan (1998) confirmed that higher concentration would result in a price increase and thus revenue increase. Moreover, in a less competitive market, motivations to reduce costs to minimum levels are limited.
81. Findings confirmed by Vander Vennet (1996).
82. These findings are confirmed in Vander Vennet (2002a) and Ayadi and Pujals (2005), also in Beitel et al. (2004) for European banks and Houston and Ryngaert (1997) for US banks, who concluded that transactions focusing geographies are more successful that the one diversifying geographies.
83. See note 82.
84. These findings are confirmed by Vander Vennet (1996, 2002a); Altunbaş and Ibanez (2004); Ayadi and Pujals (2005).
85. Could be also explained by fact that in1996–2000, interest rates were relatively low, pushing banks to seek re-finance in the inter-bank market.
86. The targets of this type of transaction exhibited a low profitability level in terms of ROA and ROE.
87. Confirmation of the hypothesis of Leibenstein (1966).
88. This document provides an overview of the issues raised by the Commission Staff Working Document SEC (2005) 1398, 'Cross-border consolidation in the EU financial sector', available on the Commission website at: http://europa.eu.int/comm/internal_market/finances/cross-sector/index_en.htm#obstacles

References

Akhavein, J. D., A. N. Berger and D. B. Humphrey (1997). 'The effects of megamergers on efficiency and prices: Evidence from a bank profit function', *Review of Industrial Organization* 12(1), 95–139.

Allen, L. and A. Rai (1996), 'Operational efficiency in banking: An international comparison', *Journal of Banking and Finance*, No. 20(4), pp. 655–672.

Altunbaş, Y. and D. Marquez Ibanez (2004). 'Mergers and acquisitions and bank performance in Europe: The role of strategic similaritites', *ECB*, Working paper series no 398, October.

Altunbaş, Y., E. P. M. Gardener, P. Molyneux and B. Moore (2001). 'Efficiency in European banking', *European Economic Review* 45(10), 1931–55.

Altunbaş, Y., P. Molyneux and J. Thornton (1997). 'Big-bank mergers in Europe: An analysis of the cost implications', *Economica* 64(254), 317–29.

Amel, D., C. Barnes, F. Panetta and C. Salleo (2002). 'Consolidation and efficiency in the financial sector: A review of the international evidence', *Temi di discussione*, Banca d'Italia, No. 464, December.

Arthur D. Little (1998). *Successful Post-Merger Integration: Realising the Synergies*, New York: Arthur D. Little.

Ayadi, R. (2001), 'Etude du mouvement de Fusions et acquisitions bancaires en Europe sur la période 1994–2000', Journées AFSE, Economie des intermédiaires financiers, 17–18 May.

Ayadi, R. (2006), 'Les fusions et Acquisitions bancaires européennes et leurs performances', Thèse de Doctorat, Université Paris Dauphine, Septembre.

Ayadi, R., and G. Pujals (2004). 'Banking consolidation in the EU: Overview and prospects', Research Report in Banking and Finance, No. 34, April, Centre for European Policy Studies, Brussels.

Ayadi, R. and G. Pujals (2005). 'Mergers and acquisitions in European banking: Overview, Assessment and Prospects', SUERF Study, July.

Ayadi, R., P. De Lima and G. Pujals (2002), 'Les restructurations bancaires en Europe', Revue de L'OFCE, Hors Série: 'La mondialisation de l'Europe', Mars.

Baele, L., O. De Jonghe, and R. Vander Vennet (2006). 'Does the stock market value bank diversification?', Paper presented in the Banking Symposium in Bocconi, Italy.

Bank for International Settlements (2001). 'Report on Consolidation in the Financial Sector', *Group of Ten*, January.

Banker, R., A. Charnes and W. Cooper (1984). 'Some models for estimating technical and scale inefficiencies in DEA', *Management Science* 30(9), 1078–92.

Bauer, P.W., A. N. Berger et D.B. Humphrey (1993). 'Efficiency and productivity growth in US banking', in H. O. Fried, C.A.K. Lovell et S. S. Schmidt, eds, '*The measurement of productive efficiency: Techniques and Applications*' (Oxford: Oxford University Press), pp. 386–413.

Baumol, W. J., J. C. Panzar and R. D. Willig (1982). *Contestable Markets and The Theory of Industry Structure*, New York: Harcourt Brace Jovanovich.

Becher, D. A. (2000). 'The valuation effects of bank mergers', *Journal of Corporate Finance* 6, 189–214.

Beitel, P. and D. Schiereck (2001). 'Value creation at the ongoing consolidation of the European banking market' Institute for Mergers and Acquisitions Working papers.

Beitel P., D. Schiereck and M. Wahrenburg (2004). 'Explaining M&A Success in European Banks', *European Financial Management* 10(1), 109–139.

Bell, F.W. et N.B. Murphy (1968). 'Costs in commercial banking: A quantitative analysis of bank behavior and its relation to bank regulation', Research report N° 41, Federal Reserve Bank of Boston.

Benston, G. (1965). 'Economies of Scale and marginal costs in banking operations', *National Banking Review*, June, pp. 312–341.

Berle, A. A. and G. C. Means (1932). *The Modern Corporation and Private Property*, New York: Macmillan Publishing Co.

Berger, A. N. (1998). 'The efficiency effects of bank mergers and acquisitions: A preliminary look at the 1990s data', in Y. Amihud and G. Miller (eds), *Bank Mergers and Acquisitions*, Boston: Kluwer Academic, 79–111.

Berger, A. N. (2000). 'The integration of the financial services industry: Where are the efficiencies?', *North American Actuarial Journal* (4).

Berger, A. N. (2003). 'The efficiency effects of a single market for financial services in Europe', *European Journal of Operational Research* (150).

Berger, A. N. and T. H. Hannan (1989). 'The price-concentration relationship in banking', *Review of Economics and Statistics* 71, 291–9.

Berger, A. N. and T. H. Hannan (1997). 'Using measures of firm efficiency to distinguish among alternative explanations of the structure-performance relationship', *Managerial Finance* 23, 6–31.

Berger, A. N. and T. H. Hannan (1998). 'The efficiency cost of market power in the banking industry: A test of "quiet life" and related hypotheses', *Review of Economics and Statistics* 80(3), 154–65.

Berger, A. N. and D. B. Humphrey (1992). 'The megamergers in banking and the use of cost efficiency as an antitrust device', *Journal of Financial Economics* 50, 187–229.

Berger, A. N. and D. B. Humphrey (1997), 'Efficiency of financial institutions: International survey and directions for future research', *European Journal of Operational Research*, No. 98.

Berger, A. N. and L. J. Mester (1997). 'Inside the black box: What explains the differences in the efficiencies of financial institutions?', *Journal of Banking and Finance* 21, 895–947.

Berger, N. Allen et David B. Humphrey (1993). 'Economies d'échelles, fusions, concentration et efficacité: l'expérience banque américaine', *Revue d'Economie Financière* 27 (Hiver 1993), 123–54.

Berger, A. N., R. S. Demsetz and P. E. Strahan (1999). 'Consolidation of the financial services industry: Causes, consequences and implications for the future', *Journal of Banking and Finance* (23).

Berger, A. N., D. Hancock and D. B. Humphrey (1993), 'Bank efficiency derived from the profit function', *Journal of Banking and Finance*, No. 17, pp. 317–347.

Berger, A. N., D. B. Humphrey and L. B. Pulley (1996), 'Do consumers pay for one-stop banking? Evidence from an alternative revenue function', *Journal of Banking and Finance*, No. 20(9), pp. 1601–1621.

Berger, A. N., W. C. Hunter and S. G. Timme (1993). 'The efficiency of financial institutions: the review and preview of research past, present and future', *Journal of Banking and Finance*, 17, pp. 221–249.

Berger, A. N., J. Leusner and J. Mingo (1997). 'The efficiency of bank branches', *Journal of Monetary Economics* 40(1), 141–62.

Berger, A. N., A. Saunders, J. M. Scalise and G. J. Udell (1998), 'The effects of bank mergers and acquisitions on small business lending', *Journal of Financial Economics*, No. 50, pp. 187–229.

Bliss, R. and R. Rosen (2001). 'CEO compensation and bank mergers', *Journal of Financial Economics* 61, 107–138.

Burger, Y. (2001). 'European Banking consolidation: Time out?', *Standard & Poor's*, October.

Calomiris, C. W. and J. Karceski (1999). 'Is the bank merger wave of the 1990s efficient? Lessons from nine case studies', in S. N. Kaplan (ed.), *Mergers and Productivity*, Chicago: University of Chicago Press/NBER, 93–178.

Canoy, M. and S. Onderstal (2003). 'Tight oligopolies: In search of proportionate remedies', CPB Document, No. 29, Central Planning Bureau, The Hague.

Charnes, A. W. W. Cooper and E. Rhodes (1978). 'Measuring the efficiency of Decision-Making-Units', *European Journal of Operational Research* 2, 429–44.

Chtourou, I. (2005), 'Les métiers des banques européenes', Revue d'économie financière, n 78, pp. 65–78.

Clark, J. A. and T. F. Siems (1997). 'Rethinking bank efficiency and regulation: How off-balance sheet activities make a difference', *Financial Industry Studies*, December, 1–12.

Coelli, T. J. (1996). 'A guide to DEAP Version 2.1.: A Data Envelopment Analysis (Computer) Program', CEPA Working Paper, Centre for Efficiency and Productivity Analysis, University of New England, Armidale, Australia.

Contamin, R. and H. P. Melone (2002). 'Les fusions et acquisitions en Europe: Un enjeu de taille', Flash Eco, Crédit Agricole SA, No. 15.

Cornett, M. M. and H. Tehranian (1992). 'Changes in corporate performance associated with bank acquisitions', *Journal of Financial Economics* 31(2), 211–34.

Cornett, M. M., G. Hovakimian, D. Palia and H. Tehranian (2003). 'The impact of the manager–shareholder conflict on acquiring bank returns', *Journal of Banking and Finance* 27, 103–131.

Cruickshank, D. (2000). *The Banking Review* (a UK Treasury-sponsored study), March.

Cummins, J. D., L. T. Sharon and M. A. Weiss (1999). 'Consolidation and efficiency in the US life insurance industry', *Journal of Banking and Finance* 23, 325–57.

Cybo-Ottone, A. and M. Murgia (2000). 'Mergers and shareholder wealth in European banking', *Journal of Banking and Finance* 24(6), 831–59.

Deutsche Bundesbank (2001). Activity Report, Frankfurt.

De Long, G. and R. De Young (2004). 'Learning by observing: Information spillovers in the execution and valuation of commercial bank M&As', WP 2004/17 Federal Reserve Bank of Chicago.

De Long, G. L. (1999). 'Domestic and international bank mergers shareholder gains from focusing versus diversifying', Baruch College.

De Long, G. L. (2001). 'Stockholder gains from focusing versus diversifying bank mergers', *Journal of Financial Economics*, 59(2), 221–52.

De Vincenzo, A., C. Doria and C. Salleo (2006). 'Efficiency versus agency motivations for bank takeovers', forthcoming, working papers Bank of Italy.

Dietsch, M. and L. Weill (2001). 'The evolution of cost and profit efficiency in European banking', in *Research in Banking and Finance* (Ed. I. Hassan and W. Hunter), Vol.1, Amsterdam: Elsevier.

Dietsch, M. and V. Oung (2001). 'L'efficacité économique des restructurations bancaires en France au cours des années 1990'. *Bulletin de la Commission Bancaire* 24, April.

Focarelli, D. and F. Panetta (2002). 'Are mergers beneficial to consumers? Evidence from the market for bank deposits', Temi di discussione, Banca d'Italia, No. 448, July.

Focarelli, D., F. Panetta and C. Salleo (2002). 'Why do banks merge?', *Journal of Money, Credit and Banking* 34(4), November, 1047–66.

Fried, H. O., C. A. K. Lovell and S. Yaisawarng (1999). 'The impact of mergers on credit union service provision', *Journal of Banking and Finance* 23, 367–86.

Gorton, G. and R. Rosen (1995). 'Corporate control, portfolio choice and the decline of banking', *Journal of Finance* 50, 1377–420.

Hannan, T. H. (1991). 'Bank commercial loans markets and the role of market structure: Evidence from surveys of commercial lending', *Journal of Banking and Finance* (15).

Hannan, T. H. (1997). 'Market share inequality, the number of competitors, and HHI: An examination of bank pricing', *Review of Industrial Organisation* (12).

Hannan, T. H. and J. D. Wolken (1989). 'Returns to bidders and targets in the acquisition process: Evidence from the banking industry', *Journal of Financial Services Research* 3(1), 5–16.

Haynes, M. and S. Thompson (1999). 'The productivity effects of bank mergers: Evidence from the UK building societies', *Journal of Banking and Finance* 23(5), 825–46.

Houston, J. F. and M. D. Ryngaert (1994). 'The overall gains from large bank mergers', *Journal of Banking and Finance* 18(6), 1155–76.

Houston, J. F. and M. D. Ryngaert (1997). 'Equity issuance and adverse selection: A direct test using conditional stock offers', *Journal of Finance* 52(1), 197–219.

Houston, J. F., C. M. James and M. D. Ryngaert (1999). '"Why are value enhancing mergers in banking so hard to find?", A discussion of "Is the bank merger wave of the 90's efficient?" Lessons from nine case studies', in S. N. Kaplan (ed.), *Mergers and Productivity*, Chicago: University of Chicago Press/NBER.

Houston, J. F., C. M. James and M. D. Ryngaert (2001). 'Where do merger gains come from? Bank mergers from the perspective of insiders and outsiders', *Journal of Financial Economics* 60, 285–331.

Huizinga, H. P., J. H. M. Nelissen and R. Vander Vennet (2001). 'Efficiency effects of bank mergers and acquisitions in Europe', Discussion Paper, Ti-2001 088/3, Tinbergen Institute.

Jensen, M. C. and W. H. Meckling (1976). 'Theory of the firm: Managerial behavior, agency costs and ownership structure', *Journal of Financial Economics*, October, 3(4), 305–360.

Kearney, A. T. (1999). *Corporate Marriage: Blight or Bliss? A Monograph on Post-Merger Integration*, April, New York: A. T. Kearney.

Kohers, T., M. Huang and N. Kohers (2000). 'Market perception of efficiency in bank holding company mergers: The roles of the DEA and SFA models in capturing merger potential', *Review of Financial Economics*, No. 9, pp. 101–120.

Kwan, S. H. and R. A. Eisenbeis (1999). 'Mergers of publicly traded banking organisations revisited', Federal Reserve Bank of Atlanta, *Economic Review*, 84/4, 26–37.

Leibenstein, H. (1966). 'Allocation efficiency and X-efficiency', *American Economic Review* (56).

Lintner, J. (1965). 'Security prices, risk and maximal gains from diversification', *Journal of Finance*, Vol. 20, No. 4, December.

Markowitz, H.M. (1952). 'Portfolio selection', *Journal of Finance*, 7 (1) March pp. 77–91.

Markowitz, H.M. (1959). Portfolio selection: Efficient diversification of investments, Yale University Press, 197, Second Edition, Basis Blackwell, 1991.

Maudos, J. and J. M. Pastor (2003). 'Cost and profit efficiency in the Spanish banking sector (1985–1996): a non-parametric approach', *Applied Financial Economics*, 13, January, 1–12.

Maudos, J., J. M. Pastor, F. Perez and J. Quesada (2002). 'Cost and profit efficiency in European banks', *Journal of International Financial Markets, Institutions and Money* 12(1), 33–58.

Méon, P. G. and L. Weill (2001). 'Can mergers in Europe help banks hedge against macroeconomic risk?', Communications aux journées de l'AFSE, 17–18 May, Orléans.

Mester, L. J. (1987b). 'A multi-product cost study of saving and loans', *Journal of Finance*, No. 42.

Mester, L. J. (1987a). 'Efficient production of financial services: Scale and scope', *Business Review*, Federal Reserve Bank of Philadelphia, January/February.

Mitchell, K. and N. Onvural (1996). 'Economies of scale and scope at large commercial banks: Evidence from the Fourier flexible functional form', *Journal of Money, Credit and Banking* (28).

Molyneux, P., Y. Altunbaş and E. Gardener (1996). *Efficiency in European Banking*, Chichester: John Wiley.

Palia, D. (1993). 'Recent evidence on bank mergers', *Financial Markets, Institutions, and Instruments*, December, 36–59.

Peristiani, S. (1997). 'Do mergers improve the X-efficiency and scale efficiency of US banks? Evidence from the 80s', *Journal of Money, Credit and Banking* 29(3), 326–37.

Piloff, S. J. (1996). 'Performance changes and shareholder wealth creation associated with mergers of publicly traded banking institutions', *Journal of Money, Credit and Banking* 28(3), 59–78.

Piloff, S. J. and A. M. Santomero (1997). 'The value effect of bank mergers and acquisitions', Working Paper, 97(7), The Wharton Financial Institutions Centre, October.

Radecki, L. J. (1998). 'Small expanding geographic reach of retail banking markets', Federal Reserve Bank of New York Policy Review, No. 4.

Resti, A (1997), 'Evaluating the cost efficiency of the Italian banking system: what can be learned from the joint application of parametric and non parametric techniques', *Journal of Banking and Finance*, 21, 221–250.

Resti, A. (1998). 'Regulation can foster mergers: Can mergers foster efficiency?', *Journal of Economics and Business* 50(2) 157–69.

Rhoades, S. A. (1994). 'A summary of merger performance studies in banking, 1980–93, and an assessment of the operating performance and event study methodologies', Federal Reserve Board Staff Study, No. 167.

Rhoades, S. A. (1998). 'The efficiency effects of bank mergers: An overview of case studies of 9 mergers', *Journal of Banking and Finance* 22(3), 273–91.

Rogers, K. E. (1998). 'Non-traditional activities and the efficiency of US commercial banks', *Journal of Banking and Finance* 22, 467–82

Ryan, S. J. (1999). 'Finding value in bank mergers', in the Proceedings of the 35th Annual Conference on Bank Structure and Competition, Federal Reserve Board of Chicago, 548–52.

Scherer, F. M. and D. Ross (1990). *Industrial market structure and economic performance*, 3rd Edition, Boston: Houghton Mifflin Company.

Sealey, C. W. and J. T. Lindley (1977). 'Inputs, outputs and theory of production and cost at depository financial institutions', *Journal of Finance* 32(4), 1251–66.

Shaffer, S. (1993). 'Can mega-mergers improve bank efficiency?', *Journal of Banking and Finance* (17).

Sharpe, W. F. (1963). 'A simplified model for portfolio analysis', *Management Science* 9, 277–93.

Sharpe, W. F. (1964). 'Capital asset prices: A theory of market equilibrium under conditions of risk', *Journal of Finance* 19(4), 425–42.

Srinivasan, A. (1992). 'Are there cost savings from bank mergers?', *Economic Review*, Federal Reserve Bank of Atlanta 77(2), 17–28.

Van Beek, L. and A. T. Rad (1997). 'Market valuation of bank mergers in Europe', *Financial Services*, Amsterdam.

Vander Vennet, R. (1994). 'Economies of scale and scope in EC banking institutions', *Cahiers Economiques de Bruxelles* 144, 507–48.

Vander Vennet, R. (1996). 'The effects of mergers and acquisitions on the efficiency and profitability of EC credit institutions', *Journal of Banking and Finance* 20, 1531–58.

Vander Vennet, R. (2002a). 'Cost and profit efficiency of financial conglomerates and universal banking in Europe', *Journal of Money, Credit and Banking* 34(1), 254–82, February.

Vander Vennet, R. (2002b). 'Cross-border mergers in European banking and bank efficiency', University of Ghent, Working paper series, No. 152.

Weill, L. (2004). 'The evolution of efficiency in European banking during the 1990s', Communications at GDR (Groupement de recherche 'Economie monétaire et financière') 10–11 June 2004, Nice.

Wheelock, D. and P. Willson (1995). 'Evaluating the efficiency of commercial banks: Does our view of what banks do matter?', *Review of Federal Reserve Bank of Saint-Louis* 77(4), 39–52.

Williamson, O. E. (1964). *The Economics of Discretionary Behavior: Managerial Objectives in a Theory of the Firm*, Englewood Cliffs, NJ: Prentice-Hall.

Zhang, H. (1995). 'Wealth effects of US bank takeovers', *Applied Financial Economics* 5(5), 32.

3
Cross-Border Bank M&A in Emerging Markets – Value Creation or Destruction?

Jonathan Williams[*] and Angel Liao[**]

3.1 Introduction

This chapter considers the post-1998 wave of cross-border bank mergers and acquisitions (M&A) activity involving purchases of stakes in target banks in emerging market economies (EME) by acquiring banks from industrialized countries (international banks). This international consolidation of the banking industry has followed hard on the heels of extensive domestic consolidation processes, which began in the United States and Europe in the mid-1980s before spreading across EME in the 1990s and beyond (see Berger, Demsetz and Strahan, 1999; Berger, DeYoung et al., 2000).[1] Banking sector consolidation is one outcome of financial liberalization and technological developments over the past quarter-century. However, there are salient differences between the consolidation processes in industrial markets and EME: (1) cross-border M&A is a more important source of consolidation in EME; (2) consolidation is used to restructure EME banking sectors following episodes of financial crisis rather than to eliminate excess capacity; (3) governments in EME are active participants in the consolidation process (Gelos and Roldós, 2004).

Financial liberalization – and technological developments – has stimulated cross-border M&A activity by changing public policy towards foreign bank entry and foreign ownership of domestic banks. From the early 1990s onwards, international banks have acquired ownership stakes in EME banks at an increasing pace. It is suggested that the international consolidation process reflects two events neatly dovetailing to equate market forces: (1) the intensification of competition in industrialized banking markets which

[*] Bangor Business School, Bangor University
[**] Edinburgh Management School, Edinburgh University

forced international banks to look further afield geographically for opportunities to diversify risks and generate profits; (2) EME governments' deregulation of domestic banking sectors including the repeal of restrictions on foreign investment and foreign bank activities, and privatization of state-owned financial institutions. The rising incidence of financial crises in EME in the mid- to late 1990s highlighted a shortfall in domestic capital and the need to encourage foreign participation to recapitalize and consolidate domestic banking sectors. Thus, international banks had *demand* for access into new markets which EME could *supply*, and EME banking systems had *demand* for additional capital which international banks could *supply* (Cardias Williams and Williams, 2007).

Our principal objective is to empirically validate whether the present wave of internationalization in the banking industry has created value for bank shareholders. Specifically, we carry out an event study analysis around the dates on which cross-border M&A transactions are announced, and calculate cumulative abnormal returns to shareholders. In so doing, we estimate how M&A transactions are valued by stockmarkets both in industrialized countries and EME, and also for the combined bank (joint abnormal returns are weighted by the market capitalizations of the acquiring and target banks). It is important not only to see if M&A create value, but also how value is distributed between the two groups of shareholders. In previous studies of M&A in industrial banking markets, and in accordance with expectations, target bank shareholders received the greater proportion of the distribution of value. However, and worryingly from a public policy perspective, empirical evidence from the non-financial sector found that whereas the acquisition of majority control in EME firms created value for shareholders, the value gains were unevenly distributed in favour of shareholders of acquiring firms in industrialized countries (Chari, Ouimet and Tesar, 2004). This implies a transfer of wealth from EME to already richer countries, and it will be informative to see if this characteristic is also a feature of cross-border M&A in banking.[2]

Whether the announcement of cross-border bank M&A transactions generates value is an empirical issue. For this purpose, we have identified 74 M&A transactions involving the acquisition of stakes in 46 listed target banks in EME between 1998 and 2005, using M&A transactions reported in *Acquisitions Monthly*, with additional information about transactions and participating banks sourced from Thomson Analytics Banker One, Datastream, and BankScope. The transactions take place in three regions: Latin America, Central and Eastern Europe, and Asia. In total, $1,057,515 million of EME bank assets were sold for $38,172 million (at 2000 prices). Over 56 per cent of EME bank assets were sold in Asia but at a lower cost to acquiring banks compared to Latin America and CEE. The acquisition of stakes in Latin American banks accounted for more than 72 per cent of the total value of M&A transactions with Latin bank assets the most expensive to buy.[3]

The remainder of the chapter is organized as follows. Section 2 reviews the internationalization of the banking industry and considers issues pertaining to broader foreign bank penetration in EME. Section 3.3 presents the event study methodology. The construction of the sample and analysis of the data are discussed in Section 3.4. Section 3.5 discusses the abnormal returns to shareholders estimated using the event study methodology whilst Section 6 concludes.

3.2   International consolidation in banking

There is a substantial literature discussing why banks go abroad (see Heffernan, 2005). Traditionally, international banks have sought to exploit their comparative advantages over domestic counterparts in specific financial activities, or they have established branches to circumvent restrictions. The motives for M&A in terms of the present internationalization of banking may be summarized as follows: (a) banks follow customers to new markets; (b) to increase earnings and diversify risk; (c) to exploit growth potential in host countries; (d) to circumvent limited growth opportunities in highly concentrated home markets; and (e) to realize efficiency gains (Slager, 2004). Point (e) is highlighted by several authors who claim that large banks originating from competitive, well-regulated domestic markets are more likely to expand overseas (Berger, DeYoung et al., 2000; Focarelli and Pozzolo, 2001). Indeed, cost efficiency is suggested to be more important than the overall degree of economic integration in explaining the internationalization of the banking industry. A related stand of literature considers which EME are more likely to receive investment from international banks: large, relatively poor countries are targets for international banks using cross-border M&A to reach widely spaced populations; cross-border M&A is related positively to shared language and geographical proximity (Guillén and Tschoegl, 1999; Sebastián and Hernansanz, 2000; Buch and DeLong, 2001); and, finally, relatively more open EME can be expected to receive a higher share of cross-border M&A activity (Buch and DeLong, 2001; Focarelli and Pozzolo, 2001).

During the 1990s, foreign direct investment became the largest single source of external finance for many EME (Goldberg, 2004). Prompted by financial liberalization – bank privatization[4] and a relaxed treatment of foreign ownership – and the expansion into EME markets by corporate clientele, international banks increasingly penetrated EME. Survey evidence reports that this penetration by international banks has been achieved by the acquisition of ownership stakes in target banks rather than via establishment of a branch or subsidiary (BIS, 2004).[5]

The pattern of foreign bank entry, however, is uneven and reflects intertemporal differences in regulatory reforms across EME: Latin American and Central and Eastern Europe (CEE) EME have allowed and received the most foreign bank entry (Clarke, Cull et al., 2003). Foreign bank shares of total banking system assets has rapidly increased over time with foreigners controlling the majority of banking assets in some Latin and CEE markets (see Barth, Caprio and Levine, 2001; Clarke, Cull et al., 2003; Bonin, Hasan and Wachtel, 2005).[6] The resolution of EME financial crises involved the implementation of policies that – at the very least – have offered a more liberal treatment of foreign ownership that has stimulated an increase in cross-border M&A transactions. This is most certainly the case in Asia. In 1996, the degree of financial openness varied across South East Asia. The most restrictive rules on foreign bank activity were found in Korea, Malaysia and Thailand. Following the 1997 financial crisis, national banking laws have been amended to liberalize the treatment of foreign banks to such an extent that there are no longer any restrictions on foreign acquisition of majority stakes in domestic banks in Indonesia, Korea, and Thailand.[7]

It is informative to consider why the acquisition of ownership stakes in EME target banks by international banks would influence stockmarkets' valuation of returns, first, for the acquiring bank, and, second, the target bank. As noted above, greater competitive pressure in industrialized banking systems has forced banks to seek out new, profitable investment strategies in other markets (BIS, 2004). EME, although they tend to be perceived as higher-risk, higher expected return investments, offer considerable opportunities for expanding bank credit and sourcing of relatively cheap customer deposits. EME entry can diversify earnings streams and risks for acquiring banks. However, stockmarket valuations of M&A transactions consider the expected future profitability of the investment. Indeed, there is evidence that the decision to retreat from international markets is valued more highly by stockmarkets than lowly profitable international investments (Slager, 2004). To make valuation more complex, evaluations of expected profitability are influenced by perceptions of country risk – especially political risk – expectations of the acquiring bank's future strategy in the EME, and the structure of the host banking system.[8]

Some empirical evidence finds foreign banks are more efficient than domestic banks in EME with foreign bank entry conditioning the behaviour of domestic banks; in other words, foreign competition leads to lower margins, profits and overhead costs at domestic-owned banks (Claessens, Demirgüç-Kunt and Huizinga, 2001). It is uncertain how stockmarkets would value an increase in competitive conditions in EME banking systems given international banks' strategic goals of exploiting arbitrage opportunities and specializing in market segments where they hold comparative advantage over domestic banks. The implementation of international best practice and technology is expected to raise efficiency in the target bank and it is reasonable to assume investors' value improving bank efficiency. However, we note several important caveats. First, there are suggestions that foreign ownership stakes need to be very large (over 70 per cent) if a target bank is to be successfully restructured and achieve improvements in cost efficiency (Claessens and Jansen, 2000). Second, Berger and colleagues (2000) emphasize the existence of diseconomies arising from operating a subsidiary at distance, which may prevent foreign-owned banks from operating efficiently.[9] Berger and colleagues note that such diseconomies are more likely to be overcome by acquiring banks that originate in highly competitive and well-regulated environments.

There may be hostility in EME markets towards foreign ownership of domestic banks. Market reaction could reflect sentiments towards the sale of national champions which may be perceived as a loss of cultural identity; there could be concerns about the future strategy for the target bank; foreign banks are often thought to lack loyalty to the host EME and exit in times of financial distress; domestic banks may lose market share because they cannot compete effectively against better resourced foreign-owned banks. On the contrary, the market may value so-called reputation effects if the acquiring bank is a renowned financial institution, and the re-branding of [often formerly troubled] domestic banks. Foreign bank entry is associated with an improvement in the range and quality of financial products and services, and an improvement in the regulatory and supervisory environment in the EME (see Clarke, Cull et al., 2003).

3.3   Event study methodology

The established literature on bank M&A has three strands. First, event studies ascertain if M&A deals generate value (abnormal returns) for bank shareholders around announcement date; studies investigate intra-financial industry deals, cross-border deals, and pre- and post-risk valuation (see Cybo-Ottone and Murgia, 2000; DeLong, 2001; Amihud, DeLong and Saunders 2002). Generally speaking, there is mixed evidence from the United States (see Pilloff and Santomero, 1998). The evidence suggests value gains are distributed in favour of target bank shareholders at the expense of acquiring bank shareholders (Berger, Demsetz and Strahan, 1999), but gains accruing to target bank shareholders are offset by value destruction for acquiring bank shareholders, which means there are insignificant joint returns to the combined bank (Houston and Ryngaert, 1994). Whilst the number of European studies is limited, they do offer a cross-border perspective. Contrary to US experience, the empirical record states that M&A transactions in Europe add significant value. Gains accrue to target bank shareholders with no significant value destruction for acquiring bank shareholders (Cybo-Ottone and Murgia, 2000; Beitel and Schiereck, 2001).

In the second strand of literature, bank operating performance (measured by ratios or estimated efficiency) is compared pre- and post-merger (see, for instance, Altunbaş and Marqués Ibáñez, 2004; Humphrey and Vale, 2004). A review of several studies reports that on average there are no cost efficiency gains accruing from M&A, although cost-efficient banks with superior management are expected to raise efficiency in acquired banks (Berger and Humphrey, 1997). However, sizeable profit efficiency gains do accrue when large banks merge (Akhavein, Berger and Humphrey, 1997). Neither of the two strands explains the motives underlying bank M&A. This issue is considered by a third literature which uses discrete outcome methods to model the probability of M&A given a set of covariates (see Cardias Williams and Williams, 2007, for an overview of this literature). Since our objective is to quantify whether the announcement of cross-border M&A transactions creates value, the current study belongs to the first category. The methodology for the event study is described in the following paragraphs.

The calculation of abnormal share price returns implies we consider only listed banks in our sample of cross-border M&A transactions. (It should be noted at this point that a number of cross-border M&A deals have involved non-listed banks.) Whilst this is a limitation of the event study methodology – especially in comparison with dynamic efficiency studies – nevertheless, the exercise and its objectives remain vitally important as an analysis of market behaviour and wealth generation effects. Share price returns are calculated as the logarithmic difference between the share price index at day t and day $t-1$. The market model – see equation (1) – is used to estimate alpha and beta over an estimation period which spans -392 days to -130 days before the M&A announcement is made (on day 0). Although the choice of estimation period is arbitrary, we select a period commencing 18 months and ending six months before the announcement date in order not to bias the estimates of alpha and beta with expectations of an impending M&A transaction. Abnormal returns to bank shareholders are measured as the difference between actual returns and predicted returns; the latter is derived using (constant) estimates of alpha and beta from OLS estimation of the market model (see Brown and Warner, 1985). Following convention, abnormal returns to target bank shareholders and acquiring bank shareholders are calculated.

The market model (1) is estimated for each target bank and acquiring bank. We select national stockmarket indexes as measures of the market but note that other authors have used national banking sector indexes and even the world banking sector index.

$$AR_{it} = R_{it} - \left[\hat{\alpha}_i + \hat{\beta}_i * R_{mt} \right] \tag{1}$$

where AR_{it} is the abnormal return and R_{it} the raw return to bank i at time t; R_{mt} is the return to the stockmarket m at time t; $\hat{\alpha}_i$ is the estimated intercept and $\hat{\beta}_{it}$ the estimated beta which shows the sensitivity of the returns to each bank to stockmarket returns.

The Brown and Warner (1980) t test statistic is used to determine if cumulative average abnormal returns are statistically significant. For day 0 the test statistic is given by:

$$\frac{\dfrac{1}{N}\sum_{i=1}^{N}AR_{i0}}{\dfrac{1}{N}\left(\sum_{i=1}^{N}\left[\dfrac{1}{261}\sum_{t=-392}^{-130}\left(AR_{it}-\left(\dfrac{1}{262}\sum_{t=-392}^{-130}AR_{it}\right)\right)^{2}\right]\right)^{\frac{1}{2}}}$$

A measure of joint returns to the combined bank is constructed by summing the weighted abnormal returns to target and acquiring bank shareholders; returns are weighted by the respective shares in combined market capitalization. In order to better approximate returns to international investors, returns are denominated in US dollars (except in a few cases where returns denominated in domestic currency are used. In all cases, market capitalization is dollar-denominated). Cumulative average abnormal returns are calculated across different event windows: symmetric and non-symmetric window lengths account for features such as thin trading in EME stock markets and leakage effects prior to official announcements. *A priori*, a positive abnormal return implies stockmarkets expect value to be created by M&A activity whilst negative returns imply value destruction. Given that the size of acquiring banks tends to be considerably greater than the target banks, we expect joint returns will be driven by abnormal returns to acquiring banks.

3.4 Construction of sample and data

We compiled the sample of M&A transactions after searching *Acquisitions Monthly* and identifying cross-border transactions involving acquiring international banks and target banks from EME. The 74 transactions precipitated an exchange of ownership rights in 46 EME banks. To supplement our analysis, we sourced information about each transaction from Thomson One Banker Analytics which contains the SDC Mergers and Acquisitions database. We collected data on the value of the transaction, the percentage stake acquired in each transaction – which enabled us to establish a cumulative stake and classify the five types of acquisition with a dummy variable. Additional information was collected on the dollar price paid per share and the method of acquisition (open market purchase, tender offer, privately negotiated purchase, divestitures, stock swap, privatization, other).

The individual M&A transactions are listed in Table 3.1. Columns 1 and 2 show the name and country of the target banks with comparative information for the acquiring banks in columns 3 and 4. Column 5 shows the size of ownership stakes following the transactions; the reader should understand that in several instances acquiring banks already held a stake in target banks, and that the acquisition we consider represents an additional purchase of

Table 3.1   Sample of targets and acquiring banks, 1998–2005

Target	Country	Acquirer	Country	Stake %	>1	Value $m
Latin America						
Banco Rio de la Plata	Argentina	Merrill Lynch	US	18.54	No	261.20
Banco Rio de la Plata	Argentina	BSCH	Spain	79.83	Yes	783.00
Banco Frances	Argentina	BBVA	Spain	100.00	Yes	1,138.64
Banespa	Brazil	BSCH	Spain	97.10	Yes	4,847.60
Banco Sudameris Brazil	Brazil	ABN AMRO	Netherlands	94.57	No	712.30
Banco Real	Brazil	ABN AMRO	Netherlands	80.00	Yes	2,833.48
Banco Santander Chile	Chile	BSCH	Spain	78.90	No	671.52
BHIF	Chile	BBVA	Spain	62.96	Yes	387.37
Sud Americano	Chile	ScotiaBank	Canada	60.20	No	118.22
Ganadero	Colombia	BBVA	Spain	95.16	Yes	477.49
Banco Santander Colombia	Colombia	BSCH	Spain	88.50	No	74.10
Banamex	Mexico	Citigroup	US	99.86	No	12,520.63
Serfin	Mexico	JP Morgan	US	8.60	No	70.49
BITAL	Mexico	HSBC	UK	99.59	No	1,089.10
BITAL	Mexico	BSCH	Spain	26.60	No	81.58
Bancomer	Mexico	BBVA	Spain	30.00	No	1,400.00
Banco Provincial	Venezuela	BBVA	Spain	49.50	No	106.97
Central and Eastern Europe						
Ceska Sporitelna	Czech	Erste	Austria	87.90	Yes	1,158.50
Zivnostenska banka	Czech	BankGes	Germany	100.00	Yes	31.60
Komercni Banka	Czech	SocGen	France	60.35	No	996.10
Inter-Europa Bank	Hungary	IMI San Paolo	Italy	85.26	No	23.80
Bank Slaski	Poland	ING	Netherlands	87.70	Yes	345.80
Bank Handlowy	Poland	Citigroup	US	87.83	Yes	969.50
Bank Amerykanski	Poland	DZ Bank	Germany	58.00	No	37.52
BPH Bank	Poland	Hypo Bank	Germany	81.46	Yes	956.19
Kredyt Bank	Poland	KBC	Belgium	76.46	Yes	340.97
Bank Wspolpracy Reg.	Poland	Deutsche Bank	Germany	89.20	No	58.85
SKB Bank	Slovenia	SocGen	France	96.46	No	130.47
Asia						
Ping An	China	HSBC	UK	19.90	No	929.70
Shanghai Pudong Dev.	China	Citigroup	US	5.00	No	69.49
Uti Bank	India	Citigroup	US	16.67	No	32.45
Uti Bank	India	HSBC	UK	14.62	No	64.53
Vysya Bank	India	ING	Netherlands	43.99	Yes	67.91
HDFC Bank	India	Deutsche Bank	Germany	3.75	No	146.87
Pan Bank	Indonesia	ANZ	Australia	4.90	No	3.07
Bank Buana Indonesia	Indonesia	UOB Bank	Singapore	23.00	No	105.41
Bank Permata	Indonesia	Std. Chartered	UK	62.20	No	64.90
Bank Lippo	Indonesia	Swiss First	Switzerland	52.05	No	131.99
Korea Exchange Bank	Korea	Commerzbank	Germany	32.50	Yes	432.74
Kookmin Bank	Korea	Goldmans	US	17.00	No	479.91
Shinhan Financial Group	Korea	BNP Paribas	France	4.00	No	118.65
KorAm	Korea	Citigroup	US	97.50	No	1,500.84
KorAm	Korea	Std. Chartered	UK	9.76	No	144.87
H&CB	Korea	ING	Netherlands	10.00	No	286.81
Far East Bank & Trust	Philippine	DBS Bank	Singapore	7.40	No	92.68
Asia Plus Securities	Thailand	ABN AMRO	Netherlands	100.00	No	93.41
Bank of Asia	Thailand	UOB Bank	Singapore	96.10	Yes	778.52

Source: Thomson Banker One Analytics.

ownership rights. Frequently, international banks have acquired stakes in their targets via multiple acquisitions, and this is indicated by the Yes/No classification in column 6. Finally, the value of the transactions in US $ millions at 2000 prices is shown in column 7.

The data are segmented by the three EME regions under consideration. Some general points emerge: the increasing penetration of Latin and CEE banking sectors by international banks; the relatively recent penetration of Asia; the considerable difference in value expended by international banks in acquiring ownership stakes in Latin American banks in comparison to CEE and Asian banks; the entry of Spanish banks into Latin America (consistent with the shared language and culture hypothesis); the entry of Western European banks into CEE markets (consistent with the proximity hypothesis); and few truly international players: between 1998 and 2005, only four international banks acquired stakes in banks in more than one EME region: a US bank (Citibank), a UK bank (HSBC), and two Dutch banks (ABN Amro and ING).

The distribution of M&A transactions is shown in Table 3.2. The data are constructed to show acquisitions by European, North American and developed Asian banks in the three EME regions: Latin America, Central and Eastern Europe, and Asia. The following features emerge: European banks have been more active purchasers of emerging market bank assets using M&A as a point of entry into these markets. European banks acquired 34 EME banks over 58 separate transactions for $21,565 million whilst US banks acquired 9 banks over 11 deals for $16,480 million. This partly reflects strategic decisions by some US banks with existing presence in emerging markets to concentrate on organic growth rather than engaging in M&A.

European (excluding Spanish) banks have acquired stakes in CEE targets, whilst Spanish banks acquired stakes in Latin America (Argentina, Chile, Colombia, Mexico and Venezuela). The Spanish acquisitions accounted for

Table 3.2 Distribution of M&A transactions by region, 1998–2005

	No. of deals	No. of targets	Value $m	Share of value %	Average value $m
EUR-CEE	18	10	4,144.00	10.86	230.22
EUR-LAT	26	12	14,601.80	38.25	561.61
EUR-ASIA	14	12	2,819.00	7.39	201.36
Asia-Asia	5	3	852.80	2.23	170.56
NA-CEE	3	1	969.50	2.54	323.17
NA-LAT	4	4	13,265.90	34.75	3,316.48
NA-ASIA	4	4	2,244.30	5.88	561.08
Total EME	74	46	38,171.65	100.00	515.83

Source: Thomson Banker One Analytics.

Table 3.3   Distribution of M&A transactions by ownership stake, 1998–2005

Holding	Value $ m	% share	Average $ m	Deals
D1 – acquire majority (> 50%)	81,608	7.72	6,278	13
D2 – acquire minority (< 50%)	520,438	49.21	30,614	17
D3 – increase minority (from n < 50% to < 50%)	114,202	10.80	11,420	10
D4 – minority to majority (from < 50% to > 50%)	152,557	14.43	10,170	15
D5 – increase majority (from n > 50%)	188,710	17.84	9,932	19

Source: Thomson Banker One Analytics.

36 per cent of the value of all M&A transactions in Latin America, whereas the acquisition of stakes in two Mexican banks by two US banks accounted for 47 per cent. The data suggest European, US, and developed-Asian nation banks are establishing a presence in Asian markets. European banks have acquired stakes in 12 Asian banks whilst US banks and banks from developed Asia acquired stakes in four banks each. More than 56 per cent of the total value of Asian M&A transactions has been spent on acquiring stakes in Korean banks. Although there are restrictions on foreign ownership, international banks have started to acquire stakes in Chinese and Indian targets: we suspect further stakes will be acquired by other banks and stakes will increase when current restrictions are lowered.

The data are organized according to the size of ownership holdings in Table 3.3. It shows how international banks enter emerging market banking sectors. Based on the percentage stake acquired in each transaction and the cumulative stake held, we suggest international banks follow five modes of entry: (1) acquisition of majority stake (13 cases); (2) acquisition of minority stake (17 cases); (3) increasing existing minority stake (10 cases); (4) increasing minority stake to majority stake (15 cases); and (5) increasing majority stake (19 cases). Banks increasingly penetrated Latin American and CEE banking systems between 1998 and 2005; cumulatively, they acquired majority control, increased from minority to majority control, or increased majority stakes in 90.48 per cent and 70 per cent of transactions with Latin American and CEE targets, respectively. On the contrary, international banks acquired minority stakes in 52.17 per cent of M&A transactions with Asian targets; the acquisition of majority control was made only in 17.39 per cent of transactions.

3.5   Results

We present the estimated cumulative abnormal returns according to several criteria: by EME region; size of ownership stake; method of acquisition; and the nationality of the acquiring bank. Returns to target, acquirer and combined bank shareholders are shown for seven different sized event windows. As expected and consistent with theoretical expectations, abnormal returns to target bank shareholders are higher than returns to acquiring bank shareholders. However, due to the fact that the acquiring international banks are considerably larger than their targets, it is the returns of the former which drive joint weighted returns. How do the abnormal returns to EME banks and their acquirers compare with those found elsewhere in the literature? Generally speaking, the size of abnormal returns to US and European targets tend to be higher than the returns to target banks in EME which we have calculated. For instance, Beitel and Schiereck (2001) report cumulative abnormal returns to European targets of 11.38 per cent, 13.54 per cent and 14.39 per cent for the following event windows [−2, 0], [−2, +2] and [−10, +10]. Similar sized returns have been found in studies of US M&A. In terms of cumulative returns to acquiring banks, our results are consistent with the US and European results; returns are small and often negative. There is mixed evidence of value gains and losses to combined banks from the United States whilst European evidence points to significant value gains. Whereas the evidence from EME is more consistent with US results, we note that joint returns to combined EME/international banks are driven by returns to considerably larger acquiring banks.

Cumulative abnormal returns are presented by region (see Table 3.4). Returns to target bank shareholders are considerably greater in Latin

Table 3.4 Cumulative average abnormal returns by region (per cent)

Region	Latin America	CEE	Asia	All regions
Returns to Target banks				
CAR[−2,0]	4.1956***	0.2663	1.1356**	2.1294***
CAR[−2,1]	3.4930***	1.7890***	1.9309***	2.5239***
CAR[−2,2]	4.5312***	2.9803***	1.7866***	3.2380***
CAR[−10,−1]	3.7582***	0.4946***	0.0152	1.6687***
CAR[−10,2]	7.0863***	2.8545	1.3803	4.1119***
CAR[−10,10]	6.6369***	0.6378***	−0.1898	2.8126***
CAR[−15,15]	4.8556***	0.6680***	−2.6770***	1.3260***
Returns to Acquiring banks				
CAR[−2,0]	−0.2316***	0.4707**	0.1612	0.0898
CAR[−2,1]	−0.4768***	0.3019	0.6866***	0.1058
CAR[−2,2]	−1.3955***	0.3554**	0.6850***	−0.2520***
CAR[−10,−1]	−0.5872***	1.1775***	0.3413***	0.2022***
CAR[−10,2]	−1.9476***	1.5660	0.8849	−0.0701
CAR[−10,10]	−1.4748***	1.2006***	0.2923***	−0.1663***
CAR[−15,15]	−0.4500***	1.4461***	0.3624***	0.3406***

Continued

Table 3.4 Continued

Region	Latin America	CEE	Asia	All regions
Returns to Combined banks				
CAR[−2,0]	−0.0939	0.2461	0.5987***	0.2178**
CAR[−2,1]	−0.3465***	0.1346	1.0795***	0.2333***
CAR[−2,2]	−1.1443***	0.1598	1.0582***	−0.0897
CAR[−10,−1]	−0.5852***	1.3829***	0.6440***	0.3554***
CAR[−10,2]	−1.7145***	1.6281	1.2344	0.1506
CAR[−10,10]	−1.2377***	0.7292***	0.3775***	−0.1775***
CAR[−15,15]	−0.5178***	0.9203***	−0.1769***	−0.0037

Notes: ***, **, * statistically significant at 1%, 5% and 10%, respectively.

America compared with the CEE and Asia. Latin returns are significantly large across all window lengths whereas returns are significant only for shorter window lengths for Asian banks and CEE banks. Although Latin stockmarkets expect value to be created from cross-border bank M&A activity, international stockmarkets appear not to share this sentiment since we observe significant value destruction. On the contrary, international stockmarkets anticipate M&A activity involving CEE and Asian banks much more favourably: returns to acquiring bank shareholders are significantly positive, in the main, for CEE and Asian banks; returns are less than 1 per cent for acquisitions of stakes in Asian banks, and range between 1 and 1.5 per cent at CEE banks (for longer window lengths only). We find significant joint returns to combined banks of around 1 per cent for transactions involving CEE banks (at longer window lengths), whilst smaller, yet significant joint returns from 0.5 to around 1 per cent are found for deals involving Asian targets (at shorter window lengths).

The returns data are expressed according to the size of stake acquired by international banks (see Table 3.5). The largest returns to target banks are found when international banks acquire majority control (D1 – but only in the longer windows) and when they increase an existing minority stake (D3 – but only in the shorter windows). However, and somewhat surprisingly, the purchase of stakes which convert international banks' minority holding to a majority yields significant negative returns in all but two windows. This might reflect sentiment at the loss of 'national' assets or former champions. The returns to acquiring banks tentatively suggests that stockmarkets positively value both acquisition of majority control (D1) and increase in existing majority holdings (D5) in the case of EME bank investments. This produces a joint return of more than 1 per cent when existing majority stakes are increased, whilst acquisition of majority control yields mainly insignificant returns.

Table 3.5 Cumulative average abnormal returns by ownership stake (per cent)

Ownership stake	D1	D2	D3	D4	D5
Returns to Target banks					
CAR[−2,0]	2.4169***	2.7961***	6.9518***	−2.3316***	2.5587***
CAR[−2,1]	2.9182***	4.9108***	7.1732***	−4.1859***	3.1925***
CAR[−2,2]	3.6316***	5.1096***	6.1181***	−2.2720***	4.2592***
CAR[−10, −1]	2.4801***	1.9561***	−1.2313***	3.6303***	0.6386***
CAR[−10,2]	6.4345**	5.3357*	3.6286	1.8554	3.3160
CAR[−10,10]	6.0599***	2.3688***	2.7149***	−0.5075***	3.4845***
CAR[−15,15]	5.7613***	1.0143***	0.3096*	−4.7002***	3.5758***
Returns to Acquiring banks					
CAR[−2,0]	0.2023	−0.6311***	−0.0381	0.8081***	0.1454
CAR[−2,1]	0.0838	−0.4491**	0.1679	0.4167**	0.3437**
CAR[−2,2]	0.3756**	−0.5785***	0.1667	−1.1572***	0.0940
CAR[−10, −1]	0.5860***	−0.7914***	−0.0146	−0.7747***	1.6822***
CAR[−10,2]	1.3470	−1.1116	0.1472	−2.7378**	1.8207
CAR[−10,10]	0.8597***	−1.1161***	0.1583	−2.3595***	1.5050***
CAR[−15,15]	1.9112***	−0.4949***	1.8381***	−3.7975***	2.4883***
Returns to Combined banks					
CAR[−2,0]	−0.3105	0.2524	0.2462	0.7831***	0.1165
CAR[−2,1]	−0.5026**	0.4670**	0.5189**	0.4549**	0.2561
CAR[−2,2]	−0.3011*	0.3401**	0.6188***	−0.9871***	0.0544
CAR[−10, −1]	0.6242***	−0.1616	−0.3410**	−0.2245*	1.4075***
CAR[−10,2]	0.6737	0.0671	0.0053	−1.9045	1.5312
CAR[−10,10]	0.0006	−0.0063	0.1027	−2.3346***	1.1083***
CAR[−15,15]	0.5172***	0.1789***	1.9470***	−4.0382***	1.7103***

Notes: D1 indicates the acquisition of majority control; D2 indicates the acquisition of a minority stake; D3 indicates the increase of an existing minority stake; D4 indicates increased ownership from minority to majority; D5 indicates increasing an existing majority stake.

***, **, * statistically significant at 1%, 5% and 10%, respectively.

Tables 3.6 and 3.7 examine returns by the method of acquisition and nationality of acquiring bank. Target returns similar in size to those reported by Beitel and Schiereck (2001) for European banks (see above) are found when emerging market banks are acquired via a tender offer. Returns to targets are relatively large when the method of acquisition is a stock swap, and privately negotiated purchase albeit to a lesser extent. Surprisingly, open market purchases of bank stock leads to very large, negative returns; privatization also yields negative returns. The data show that only privately negotiated purchases produce a positive and mostly significant gain to

Table 3.6 Cumulative average abnormal returns by type of acquisition (per cent)

Type of acquisition	Open market	Tender offer	Private neg	Stock swap	Privatization	Other
Returns to Target banks						
CAR[−2,0]	−2.0118***	4.6940***	2.2928***	7.7097***	−1.5879**	−1.3096**
CAR[−2,1]	−4.5644***	7.8447***	3.5198***	6.8984***	−1.3480**	−4.2166***
CAR[−2,2]	−6.4300***	10.7396***	3.5606***	7.0092***	−0.4255	−4.5170***
CAR[−10,−1]	−2.9657***	3.3416***	0.6299***	0.4390	−4.2846***	9.0138***
CAR[−10,2]	−9.4030**	13.3619***	3.3040	7.2275*	−3.5229	3.9823
CAR[−10,10]	−9.8522***	11.0897***	2.9383***	8.7419***	−4.5922***	2.3351***
CAR[−15,15]	−12.6598***	10.0020***	0.7579***	8.2070***	−2.9548***	0.5432***
Returns to Acquiring banks						
CAR[−2,0]	0.4633**	0.0016	0.0730	−0.7475**	−0.1092	0.4784
CAR[−2,1]	0.3112*	−0.4783***	0.2909**	−1.3366***	−1.3942***	1.4877***
CAR[−2,2]	−1.0926***	−1.0114***	0.4461***	−2.6575***	−2.9978***	1.8375***
CAR[−10,−1]	−1.3066***	0.5443***	0.8591***	−0.7567***	−0.1404	−0.6956***
CAR[−10,2]	−2.8093**	−0.3054	1.1716	−3.4109*	−4.4129	1.4388
CAR[−10,10]	−3.8709***	0.9899***	0.9698***	−1.8820***	0.5683***	−0.2147*
CAR[−15,15]	−5.3909***	1.7810***	0.7895***	−2.8470***	3.3347***	1.5013***
Returns to Combined banks						
CAR[−2,0]	0.4449**	0.0410	0.5820***	−0.6549**	−0.8367*	0.3096
CAR[−2,1]	0.0913	−0.2526	0.8588***	−1.2904***	−2.2647***	1.2497***
CAR[−2,2]	−1.1817***	−0.6017***	0.9669***	−2.5193***	−3.7747***	1.3945***
CAR[−10,−1]	−1.5184***	0.9406***	0.9998***	−0.5711***	−0.5247**	−0.1497
CAR[−10,2]	−3.1646**	0.4778	1.6615	−2.9163	−5.2094*	1.2178
CAR[−10,10]	−4.6591***	1.0722***	1.3550***	−1.7893***	0.2993*	0.0280
CAR[−15,15]	−6.3224***	1.9977***	0.7282***	−2.6438***	2.9261***	0.6432***

Notes: ***, **, * statistically significant at 1%, 5% and 10%, respectively.

acquiring banks and this generates a joint return of around 1 per cent across the different window lengths (see Table 3.6).

Finally, returns are presented according to the nationality of the acquiring bank in Table 3.7. Win-win situations are found when US banks and Dutch banks acquire an emerging market target (but not in all windows). There is a contrast in the joint returns: returns are positive and high for longer window lengths for US banks but negative for Dutch banks: yet, returns across the shorter windows are positive and significant for Dutch banks. Whereas UK bank and Spanish bank purchases yield significant returns to target banks, the joint returns are significantly negative due to unfavourable stockmarket reactions in Spain and the UK.

Table 3.7 Cumulative average abnormal returns by nationality of acquirer (per cent)

Nationality of acquirers	US	European	Dutch	Spain	UK
Returns to Target banks					
CAR[−2,0]	2.1186***	−0.7347**	3.7503***	2.7291***	5.9066***
CAR[−2,1]	1.5013***	0.3104	6.3440***	2.2118***	4.1524***
CAR[−2,2]	1.2516***	0.9241***	6.9481***	3.7130***	5.2814***
CAR[−10,−1]	3.9580***	0.3125	−3.3150***	2.6099***	5.0400***
CAR[−10,2]	4.3399	1.4086	2.7302	4.7721**	9.9604
CAR[−10,10]	6.2277***	−1.9934***	2.8828***	3.9360***	8.2538***
CAR[−15,15]	3.1551***	−0.3803***	−2.2800***	2.0635***	7.9943***
Returns to Acquiring banks					
CAR[−2,0]	−0.3344	0.2222	0.9572***	0.0693	−0.7539***
CAR[−2,1]	−0.0713	−0.0656	1.9295***	−0.3842**	−1.0611***
CAR[−2,2]	0.0285	0.0142	1.7617***	−1.5606***	−0.8849***
CAR[−10,−1]	1.3583***	1.1437***	0.1932	−1.1833***	0.0605
CAR[−10,2]	1.6947	1.2388	1.3968	−2.8478***	−1.3408
CAR[−10,10]	0.9634***	1.3205***	−0.2687***	−2.1750***	−0.6513***
CAR[−15,15]	1.6219***	1.9707***	0.0161	−1.1362***	−0.8978***
Returns to Combined banks					
CAR[−2,0]	−0.2599	−0.0157	0.5234**	0.1433	−0.5483**
CAR[−2,1]	0.0045	−0.2529	1.3928***	−0.3234**	−0.8090***
CAR[−2,2]	0.1900	−0.2234	1.1576***	−1.3506***	−0.6294***
CAR[−10,−1]	1.3454***	1.4302***	−0.0939	−1.3664***	0.1900
CAR[−10,2]	1.8303	1.2315	0.6351	−2.7923***	−1.0466
CAR[−10,10]	1.1589***	0.9609***	−1.5693***	−1.9487***	−0.8071***
CAR[−15,15]	1.9586***	1.4266***	−1.6333***	−1.2832***	−0.7689***

Notes: European excludes transactions involving Dutch, Spanish, and British banks.
***, **, * statistically significant at 1%, 5% and 10%, respectively.

3.6 Conclusion

We construct a sample of cross-border bank M&A transactions between international banks and target banks in EME covering 74 transactions involving 46 targets between 1998 and 2005. The transactions involved a small number of acquiring European and US banks, and targets from Latin America, CEE and Asia. The chapter contributes to the literature on the internationalization of banking by analysing stockmarket reactions to cross-border bank M&A involving banks from EME and industrialized countries.

Our analysis of cumulative average abnormal returns shows some consistency with results obtained from the US and Europe, as well as with theoretical expectations. Generally, returns to target bank shareholders are positive implying that EME stockmarkets perceive cross-border bank M&A activity to be value generating. There are exceptions when negative abnormal returns are found. These findings, however, may be explained by specific characteristics of M&A transactions such as the conversion from minority foreign ownership to majority and the privatization of EME banks. Nevertheless, the magnitude of returns to target bank shareholders tends to be larger than returns to acquiring bank shareholders. This suggests there is no evidence of wealth being transferred from EME to industrialized countries in cross-border bank M&A transactions between 1998 and 2005. In other words, our results are opposite to those of Chari and colleagues (2004) for the non-financial sector.

The results suggest that international stockmarkets react somewhat differently than EME stockmarkets to cross-border bank M&A activity. Aside from abnormal returns being smaller, often they are significantly negative, which implies cross-border M&A is perceived to be value destructive. This is the case when international banks acquire Latin American banks, when international banks increase minority stakes or convert minority ownership into majority holdings, and when targets are acquired via open market purchase and a stock swap. On the contrary, cross-border M&A is viewed as value creating when international banks acquire stakes in CEE and Asian targets, when majority stakes are purchased or increased, and when stakes are purchased via private negotiation. The US, European (excluding Spain and the UK) and Dutch stockmarkets appear to believe that their countries' banks can generate value through cross-border M&A activity, but this belief does not extend to the Spanish and UK stockmarkets.

Due to the sizeable discrepancies in market values between EME banks and international banks, it is abnormal returns to international banks that drive joint returns to the combined bank. Nevertheless, inter-regional differences in joint returns are observed: acquisitions of Asian banks and CEE are considered value generating for combined shareholders. Similarly, value is generated when international banks' increase existing majority holdings in EME targets and deals are privately negotiated. Joint returns are highest for transactions involving acquiring international banks from the United States and Europe (over longer window lengths).

The results presented in this chapter suggest stockmarkets are reasonably sophisticated in determining the value generating properties of cross-border bank M&A activity. We observe both similarities and differences in perception between EME and international stockmarkets. This is expected because there are information asymmetries associated with valuing opaque EME bank assets, and uncertainties associated with investing in banks in financial systems that have been under stress in recent times. In a small number of transactions, ownership rights are limited by regulations. Nevertheless, we expect the internationalization of banking to continue as regulations on foreign ownership of domestic banks are changed. Similarly, increasingly competitive markets in US and Europe may force banks to seek out shareholder value in EME that offer potential for expansion and diversification.

Notes

1. The causes of the consolidation of US and European banking as well as the possible outcomes are discussed by various authors including Berger et al. (1999), Berger (2000), Berger et al. (2000), Berger et al. (2001), Berger and DeYoung (2001, 2002), and Berger et al. (2003).
2. Although the volume of cross-border bank M&A activity in EME is not as extensive as in the non-financial sector – due partly to regulatory restrictions and information asymmetries/the opacity of bank value (Focarelli and Pozzolo, 2001) – the pace of M&A is increasing due to regulatory reforms and technological developments.
3. The assets of target banks, the value of deals, and cost per unit of asset for each region are as follows: Latin America ($278,994m, $27,578m, $0.0988); CEE ($189,574m, $5,049m, $0.0266); Asia ($588,947m, $5,545m, $0.0094). Source: own calculations from Thomson and BankScope data.
4. See Megginson (2005) for a review of the bank privatization literature and a list of privatized banks.
5. Purchasing an established branch network is one mode through which acquiring banks access underdeveloped, but potentially large, retail banking markets that exist in EME. Other investment options include taking a minority stake in a target bank and increasing it over time, or entering into a joint venture agreement. We note that hostile takeovers in banking are very rare and foreign bank takeovers are subject to regulations which vary between countries.
6. Barth et al. (2001) provide an exhaustive source for the proportion of banking system assets held by foreigners in nearly 100 countries.
7. For a fuller discussion of the resolution strategies adopted in SE Asia we refer the interested reader to references cited in Williams and Nguyen (2005), whereas for a review of recent developments in Asian banking we draw readers' attention to Nguyen and Williams (2007).
8. This type of evaluation is a complex task owing to informational asymmetries and data availability.
9. Operational diseconomies associated with distance are heightened by barriers relating to the following: culture, language, currency, the host regulatory and supervisory structure, and explicit and/or implicit rules against foreign banks (Berger et al., 2000).

References

Akhavein, J. D., A. N. Berger and D. B. Humphrey (1997). 'The effects of megamergers on efficiency and prices: Evidence from a bank profit function', *Review of Industrial Organisation* 12, 95–130.

Altunbaş, Y., and D. Marqués Ibáñez (2004). 'Mergers and acquisitions and bank performance in Europe: The role of strategic similarities'. European Central Bank Working Paper, series no. 398, October.

Amihud, Y., G. L. DeLong and A. Saunders (2002). 'The effects of cross-border bank mergers on bank risk and value', *Journal of International Money and Finance* 21, 857–77.

Barth, J. R., J. Caprio and R. Levine (2001). 'Bank regulation and supervision: What works best? A new database', World Bank Policy Research Paper, no. 2588.

Beitel, P., and D. Schiereck (2001). 'Value creation at the ongoing consolidation of the European banking market', Institute for Mergers and Acquisitions (IMA), Working Paper No. 05/01.

Berger, A. N. (2000). 'The integration of the financial services industry: Where are the efficiencies?', *North American Actuarial Journal* 4, July, 25–45.

Berger, A., and R. DeYoung (2001). 'The effects of geographic expansion on bank efficiency', *Journal of Financial Services Research* 19, 163–84.

Berger, A., and R. DeYoung (2002). 'Technological progress and the expansion of the banking industry', Working Paper Series WP-02-07. Federal Reserve Bank of Chicago.

Berger, A. N., and D. B. Humphrey (1997). 'Efficiency of financial institutions: International survey and directions for future research', *European Journal of Operational Research* 98, 175–212.

Berger, A. N., R. S. Demsetz and P. E. Strahan (1999). 'The consolidation of the financial services industry: Causes, consequences, and implications for the future', *Journal of Banking and Finance* 23, 153–94.

Berger, A. N., R. DeYoung and G. F. Udell (2001). 'Efficiency barriers to the consolidation of the European financial services industry', *European Financial Management* 7(1), 117–30.

Berger A. N., Q. Dai, S. Ongena and D. C. Smith (2003). 'To what extent will the banking industry be globalized?', in Courchene, T. J. and E. H. Neave (eds), *Framing Financial Structure in an Information Environment* (John Deutsch Institute – Queens University), 221–58.

Berger, A. N., R. DeYoung, H. Genay and G. F. Udell (2000). 'Globalisation of financial institutions: Evidence from cross-border banking performance', Brookings-Wharton Papers on Financial Services 3, 23–158.

BIS (2004). 'Foreign direct investment in the financial sector of emerging market economies', Committee on the Global Financial System, Bank for International Settlements, March.

Bonin, J. P., I. Hasan and P. Wachtel (2005). 'Bank performance, efficiency and ownership in transition countries', *Journal of Banking and Finance* 29, 31–53.

Brown, S. J., and J. B. Warner (1980). 'Measuring security price performance', *Journal of Financial Economics* 8, 205–58.

Brown, S. J., and J. B. Warner (1985). 'Using daily stock returns: The case of event studies', *Journal of Financial Economics* 14, 3–31.

Buch, C. M., and G. L. DeLong (2001). 'Cross-border bank mergers: What lures the rare animal?', Kiel Institute of World Economics, Working Paper, no. 1070.

Cardias Williams, F., and J. Williams (2007). 'Does ownership explain bank M&A? The case of domestic banks and foreign banks in Brazil', in P. Arestis and L. F. de Paula (eds), *Financial Liberalization and Economic Performance in Emerging Countries*, Basingstoke: Palgrave Macmillan (forthcoming).

Chari, A., P. P. Ouimet and L. Tesar (2004). 'Acquiring control in emerging markets: Evidence from the stock market', NBER Working Paper, no. 10872, November.

Claessens, S., and M. Jansen (2000). 'Internationalisation of Financial Services, WTO – World Bank (2000)', *Kluwer Law International*, London: Kluwer, ch. 1.

Claessens, S., A. Demirgüç-Kunt and H. Huizinga (2001). 'How does foreign entry affect domestic banking markets', *Journal of Banking and Finance* 25, 891–911.

Clarke, G., R. Cull, M. S. Martinez Peria and S. M. Sánchez (2003). 'Foreign bank entry: Experience, implications for developing economies, and agenda for further research', *The World Bank Research Observer* 18(1), 25–59.

Cybo-Ottone, A., and M. Murgia (2000). 'Mergers and shareholder wealth in European banking', *Journal of Banking and Finance* 24, 831–59.

DeLong, G. L. (2001). 'Stockholder gains from focusing versus diversifying bank mergers', *Journal of Financial Economics* 59, 221–52.

Focarelli, D., and A. F. Pozzolo (2001). 'The patterns of cross-border bank mergers and shareholdings in OECD countries', *Journal of Banking and Finance* 25, 2305–37.

Gelos, R. G., and J. Roldós (2004). 'Consolidation and market structure in emerging market banking systems', *Emerging Markets Review* 5, 39–59.

Goldberg, L. (2004). 'Financial-sector FDI and host countries: New and old lessons', NBER Working Paper, no. 10441, April.

Guillén, M., and A. E. Tschoegl (1999). 'At last the internationalization of retail banking? The case of Spanish banks in Latin America', Wharton Financial Institutions Center, Working Paper, 99–141.

Heffernan, S. (2005). *Modern Banking*, Chichester: John Wiley and Sons.

Houston, J. F., and M. D. Ryngaert (1994). 'The overall gains from large bank mergers', *Journal of Banking and Finance* 18, 1155–76.

Humphrey, D. B., and B. Vale (2004). 'Scale economies, bank mergers, and electronic payments: A spline function approach', *Journal of Banking and Finance* 28, 1671–96.

Megginson, W. L. (2005). 'The economics of bank privatisation', *Journal of Banking and Finance* 29, 1931–80.

Nguyen, N., and J. Williams (2007). 'The financial system in Asia and Australia', *Papeles de Economia Espanola* 110, 116–44.

Piloff, S. J., and A. M. Santomero (1998). 'The value effects of bank mergers', in Y. Amihud and G. Miller (eds), *Bank Mergers and Acquisitions*, Dordrecht: Kluwer Academic Publishers.

Sebastián, M., and C. Hernansanz (2000). 'The Spanish banks strategy in Latin America', SUERF Working Paper, no. 9, Paris.

Slager, A. M. H. (2004). 'Banking across borders: Internationalisation of the world's largest banks between 1980 and 2000'. Erasmus Research Institute of Management.

Williams, J., and N. Nguyen (2005). 'Financial liberalisation, crisis and restructuring: A comparative study of bank performance and bank governance in South East Asia', *Journal of Banking and Finance* 29(8–9), 2119–54.

4

Bank Capital and Loan Pricing: Implications of Basle II

*Ted Lindblom and Magnus Olsson**

4.1 Introduction

For a long period of time, the regulation of banking activities was top-down and highly centralized. Major decisions were in principle determined independently by regulators, with little involvement by bank management. After deregulation, which occurred in the 1980s in most European countries, regulations were relaxed and even abolished in many areas. The overall aim was to open up for decentralized decision-making in a competitive environment. Conservative regulation should be replaced with good management and sound risk appetite in banks by creating a competitive arena, directed towards both customers as well as investors. However, not all bank regulations were removed. On the contrary, at the end of the 1980s the first Basle Capital Accord, Basle I, was launched by the Bank for International Settlement (BIS).

Basle I stipulates the minimum amount of capital required by the regulator to be held by a bank. The basic idea is that each bank should hold at least 8 per cent 'qualified' capital in relation to a risk-weighted asset base. Basle I has been widely recognized and has been implemented in most European countries through national legislation. The Accord is intended particularly to serve as a protection for uninsured creditors, that is, households or organizations with depository claims on the bank, in times of unexpected losses. It is, however, also aiming at harmonizing domestic regulation of banking activities in order to facilitate bank competition across country borders. Capital adequacy requirements have implications for the pricing of bank loans as it may affect the 'cost of bank capital' (Barfield, 2004; Carey and Flynn, 2005; Pitschke and Bone-Winkel, 2006).

In Basle I qualified capital is divided into two major types or categories (e.g., Saunders and Cornett, 2004). The first type (labelled Tier I) is defined as core capital. It consists of common equity, minority interests, and perpetual preferred stock up to one-quarter of Tier 1. The second type, or Tier II, is

* School of Business, Economics and Law, University of Gothenburg, Sweden.

referred to as supplementary capital. It includes the remaining perpetual stock (not included in Tier 1), loan loss reserves (up to 1.25 per cent of the risk adjusted asset base) and a variety of convertible and subordinated debt instruments (often with an upper limit with respect to Tier I capital). The supplementary capital may not exceed the amount of core capital, that is, Tier I $\geq$ Tier II.

The risk-weighted asset base is given by the sum of the product of each specific asset and its corresponding risk-weight. There are four different risk categories defined in Basle I and, accordingly, there are four risk-weights: 0 per cent, 20 per cent, 50 per cent and 100 per cent. Not surprisingly, government securities are usually regarded as 'risk free' and consequently given a 0 per cent risk-weight, which means that a bank's lending to the government will not require any qualified capital at all according to Basle I. Loans to domestic banks are often classified as low-risk assets and are accordingly given a low risk-weight of only 20 per cent, thus requiring 1.6 per cent of qualified capital to the total loan amount. The next bucket, in increasing capital demand order, includes claims of a moderate risk, like loans in the form of mortgages up to the real value of the underlying property. Such assets require 4 per cent qualified capital (i.e., the risk-weight is 50 per cent). The risk-weight of most corporate lending, along with other retail lending, is 100 per cent. These loans are regarded as standard-risk assets requiring a minimum of 8 per cent qualified capital. (Off-balance sheet items are classified into these four risk categories accordingly.)

The first Basle Capital Accord has been subjected to increasing criticism during the past decade (Hendricks and Hirtle, 1997; Garside and Bech, 2003; Bergendahl and Lindblom, 2007). It is mostly the broad buckets of the risk-weights or the 'one size fits all approach' that has been the primary target of criticism (Avery and Berger, 1991; Jones, 2000; Calem and LaCour-Little, 2004). The Basle Committee has responded with the development of a second Accord, Basle II, which also considers the growing importance of operational risks in banking activities.[1] The Basle II Accord is presently scheduled to be implemented in many countries through national legislation in January 2007.

Basle II rests on a three pillar concept. The first pillar is the part that has most similarities to the current Accord, keeping the definitions of qualified capital and the eight per cent risk-weighted capital ratio, but it requires that risk-weights are more carefully determined and calculated in accordance with the underlying risk of each specific asset (Bergendahl and Lindblom, 2007). There are three main approaches to risk-weight calculations that banks may choose among: The Standardized approach, which mainly rests on external ratings and regulatory benchmarks (see Table 4.1 below), and two Internal Ratings Based (IRB) approaches – the Foundation and the Advanced IRB approach – allowing banks to use their own internal ratings and risk models. In addition to the changed treatment of credit risks and

Table 4.1   Risk-weights within the Standardized approach

	%
Real-estate mortgage:	35
Retail portfolio:	75
Corporate lending with an external rating between AAA to AA−:	20
Corporate lending with an external rating between A+ to A−:	50
Corporate lending with an external rating between BBB+ to B − :	100*
Corporate lending with an external rating less than B−:	150
Other corporate exposures	100

* According to one alternative, this bucket could be divided into two buckets, that is, BBB+ to BBB− may be moved up to the 50 per cent bucket.

market risks, the new Accord stipulates that banks should also hold qualified capital to cover operational risks. The second pillar may be regarded as a complement to the first pillar. It is a supervisory review process ensuring the quality of the bank's approach to estimating risk and capital requirements. In short it puts an explicit demand on the management of the bank to prove its ability to calculate an appropriate amount of capital to be held within the bank to absorb unexpected losses. In addition to these pillars, a third pillar concerns the transparency of the bank's risk measurement and risk management practices, thus adhering to the increasing public demand for disclosure of banks' risk profiles and risk exposures not only to the supervisory authority but also to other stakeholders.

Certainly, Basle II will have a major impact on the European financial system as it will be adopted by financial supervisory authorities all over the European Union.[2] What it will mean for the individual bank and its bank customers is not equally clear. One interesting study, from the customer point of view, made by Repullo and Suarez (2004) on the loan-pricing effect of Basle II capital requirements, has reached the conclusion that low-risk firms will be able to lower their debt costs by lendings from a bank using an IRB approach. The high-risk firms, on the other hand, are concluded as having constant debt costs between the regulations, by lendings from a bank adopting the Standardized approach. The authors also conclude that a bank would benefit from specializing in lending to either low-risk or high-risk firms.

Although research has been conducted on the topic during the past decade, additional research is still required to fully grasp the possible effects of the new Accord. In this chapter, we aim to analyse the effect of Basle II on banks' interest rates to borrowers in order to increase our knowledge and general understanding of how banks are pricing loans with respect to capital adequacy requirements. Focusing on credit risks, our working hypothesis is that the loan pricing of banks may be affected in two ways, which are not mutually exclusive. On the one hand, banks may improve their skills in assessing and pricing risks. On the other hand, they may hold less or more capital than currently. The lending rates would be affected directly in the first case, and indirectly in the second one. This chapter investigates this hypothesis by making a comparative survey and analysis of what impact the current Basle Accord (Basle I) is having and has had on the capital held by banks in the Nordic countries. This analysis is based on accounting data from Bankscope. Thereafter, the expected effects of Basle II are explored by a questionnaire study and two interview-based case studies. Both the questionnaire study and the case studies are conducted on Swedish independent savings banks (ISBs). These banks are retail oriented and relatively small, implying that the new Accord will significantly effect their regulatory capital and their lending rates to customers. Before we turn to these empirical studies, we will in the following two sections first demonstrate how the implementation of the new Accord will be likely to affect the qualified capital held by banks in general, and then elaborate on its implications for banks' loan pricing.

4.2   Implications of Basle II on bank capital

The implementation of Basle II will not only change the way of determining capital adequacy requirements for banks, the new Accord may also considerably affect the amount of capital held by banks. The magnitude of this effect is expected to depend on which of the approaches the individual bank adopts. The more sophisticated the approach, the less the qualified capital required. Table 4.1 shows the (credit) risk-weights that should be applied when using the Standardized approach.[3]

In comparison to the current Accord, the Standardized approach will mean lower risk-weights for mortgage loans, retail loans (on a portfolio basis), and loans to corporations with a high external credit rating. The riskier corporate customers will, however, be given a higher risk-weight.

The third quantitative impact study made by BIS (2003), covering 365 banks in 43 countries, indicates that the average bank will face an increase in capital requirements if it adopts the Standardized approach. This is particularly the case for larger banks. These banks are more or less obliged to adopt one of the sophisticated IRB approaches, and then, preferably, the advanced IRB approach (see Table 4.2).

Table 4.2   Estimated effects of Basle II on capital adequacy requirements

	Standardised			IRB Foundation			IRB Advanced		
	Average %	Max %	Min %	Average %	Max %	Min %	Average %	Max %	Min %
G 10 Group 1	11	84	−15	3	55	−32	−2	46	−36
Group 2	3	81	−23	−19	41	−58			
EU Group 1	6	31	−7	−4	55	−32	−6	26	−31
Group 2	1	81	−67	−20	41	−58			
Other Group 1&2	12	103	−17	4	75	−33			

Source: BIS (2003: 3).

Table 4.3 Contributions to change in capital when adopting the IRB Foundation approach

	G 10		EU		Other
Portfolio	Group 1 %	Group 2 %	Group 1 %	Group 2 %	Groups 1&2 %
Corporate	−2	−4	−5	−5	−1
Sovereign	2	0	2	1	1
Bank	2	−1	2	−1	1
Retail	−9	−17	−9	−18	−8
SME	−2	−4	−3	−5	1
Securitised assets	0	−1	0	−1	1
General provisions	−1	−3	−2	−2	−2
Other portfolios	4	3	3	5	5
Overall credit risk	−7	−27	−13	−27	−3
Operational risk	10	7	9	6	7
Overall change	3	−19	−4	−20	4

Source: BIS (2003: 5).

Group 1 contains larger, often internationally active, banks with Tier 1 capital greater than €3bn, whereas the banks in the second group are smaller or medium-sized banks. These banks are mainly retail oriented, which explains why they seem to be better off (on average) after the implementation of the new Accord. As was shown in Table 4.1, Basle II will lower the (credit) risk-weights for the retail portfolio. This effect is even more evident in Table 4.3, which shows the expected average percentage changes in capital adequacy requirements, broken down into the contributions of different asset portfolios when adopting the IRB Foundation approach.[4]

As the IRB Foundation approach is based on the bank's internal ratings system, banks using this approach should be likely to allocate a more accurate risk premium for each individual loan or group of loans. Moreover, the internal ratings system and models applied by the banks must be approved and validated from a regulatory point of view. The following internal components should be included:

- *Group of assets.* The assets should be divided into more than 14 classes with similar risk characteristics.
- *Probability of default (PD).* The banks own calculations of probability of default, based on internal ratings and/or scorecards for counterparts.
- *Exposure at default (EAD).* This parameter is given by the authorities and varies over different types of loans and mortgages. It aims to capture the part of the current exposure towards a borrower being exposed to the event of a default.

- *Loss given default (LGD)*. This parameter is also provided by the authorities and varies between 0 per cent and 100 per cent. The parameter aims to capture the part of the exposure actually being lost in the event of a credit situation.
- *Maturity (M)*. This parameter is given by the authorities and is 2.5 years for most of the exposures.

These parameters are used to calculate the required risk-weight for each group of assets. Table 4.4 shows information provided by the Basle committee on the risk-weights to be used under the IRB Foundation approach.

Table 4.4 clearly implies that the strong companies will call for a lower amount of capital to be held within the banks. If one holds in mind that the *expected losses* (i.e., the PD, the LGD and the EAD) are already priced when using an adequate pricing of credit risks, an important question is whether the capital structure in banks to meet *unexpected losses* will affect the interest rates offered on corporate lending.

Table 4.4 Risk-weights according to the Basle II proposition as a function of the probability of default (PD)

Corporate exposures		
LGD	45%	45%
M	2.5	Years
Turnover(€)	50m	5m
PD		
0.03%	14.44%	11.30%
0.05%	19.65%	15.39%
0.10%	29.65%	23.30%
0.25%	49.47%	39.01%
0.40%	62.72%	49.49%
0.50%	69.61%	54.91%
0.75%	82.78%	65.14%
1.00%	92.32%	72.40%
1.30%	100.95%	78.77%
1.50%	105.59%	82.11%
2.00%	114.86%	88.55%
2.50%	122.16%	93.43%
3.00%	128.44%	97.58%
4.00%	139.58%	105.04%
5.00%	149.86%	112.27%
6.00%	159.61%	119.48%
10.00%	193.09%	146.51%
15.00%	221.54%	171.91%
20.00%	238.23%	188.42%

Source: Bank for International Settlement (2005).

4.3   Implications of Basle II on loan pricing

According to the findings presented by BIS (2003), a small retail-oriented bank that manages to implement an internal ratings-based approach will be subject to a substantial reduction of the regulatory capital required by the supervisory authority. This is expected to be the case even after considering that operational risks will have the opposite effect on regulatory capital.[5] These findings are verified by estimates made by Garside and Bech (2003). They also comment on the expected effect on the risk-weighted assets (RWAs) of banks in specific countries: 'The Nordic region, with a high concentration in retail lending and relatively low risk, will experience a substantial drop in overall RWAs under the IRB approaches' (Garside and Bech, 2003, p. 29). This implies that the bank may significantly reduce its interest rates on retail loans, that is, provided that the bank is not currently operating with a capital-to-loan ratio more in accordance with its economic capital than the regulatory capital required by Basle I.[6] Whether or not this is true remains to be explored, though.

Grünert and colleagues (2002) divide the lending rate ('kreditzinssatz') offered by banks into four components (see Figure 4.1).

Capital adequacy requirements are explicitly related to the component displayed in the shaded box ('eigenkapitalkostensatz'). Provided that a change in the regulatory capital requirement for different types of loans will actually change the amount of capital held by the bank, the interest rate to borrowers should be adjusted in accordance with the 'eigenkapitalkostensatz', that is, the cost of equity. The other components (i.e., the market rate, the administration cost and the specific risk premium for covering expected losses) should 'in principle' be expected to remain unchanged. Note that we have inserted 'in principle' as many banks might assess risks poorly today (cf. Cartwright and Sarrat, 2005). With such circumstances, the bank could be adopting an improved model for assessing credit (and market) risks developed under the new capital adequacy framework, which leads to a more

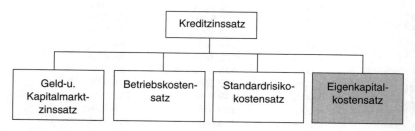

Figure 4.1   Components of a bank's lending rate
Source: Grünert, Kleff et al. (2002: 1048).

accurate risk premium for an individual loan or group of loans, that is, if this premium deviates from the current one it should be expected to affect the specific risk premium ('standardrisikokostensatz'). This would thus lead to either lower or higher interest rates for the single borrower, simply as a result of the improved ability of the bank to assess and price risks for covering expected losses.

4.4   Data and risk definitions

We have collected accounting data for the largest banks in Sweden, Norway, Finland, Iceland, and Denmark from Bankscope for the years 1999–2004. Since there have been some mergers and acquisitions during this time period, the names of the banks do sometimes refer to one or more banks at an earlier state.

The findings from the empirical survey of how the banks have been affected by the current Basle Accord are presented in the following sections. This survey concerns the larger commercial banks within each country.

For some of the banks, data concerning some year(s) are missing. Those banks have been included in the analysis as long as not more than two years of data are missing. When three or more years are missing, the bank has been excluded from that part of the analysis.

The questionnaire study to the Swedish ISBs is focused on the 72 largest ones of the total 81 banks for which data is available. The questions were as follows:

1. Will your bank use interest added for capital (IAC) under the new Capital Accord?
2. If yes, how much do you expect IAC to increase interest rate at risk-weight (RW) = 100 per cent?
3. Does your bank use IAC under the old Basle framework?
4. If yes, how much does this increase interest rate at RW = 100 per cent?

To guarantee anonymity, which is presumed to increase the response rates, the ISBs have only been divided into two groups. The ISBs as well as the reason for the division of the banks into two groups will be described and commented upon more in detail when presenting the findings. The interviews with representatives for two different types of ISBs were conducted by phone.

We have used the following definitions of risk:

• *Total risk.* Partly as a consequence of data availability, we have chosen to use the standard deviation of the ratio between earnings before tax and total assets for each bank in each year. A stable ratio signals that the bank, during the years that are studied, has had a low total risk, which implies a low demand for qualified capital in relation to total assets.

- *The risk of unexpected losses in the credit portfolio.* In this study we have used the standard deviation of the loan loss provision as a percentage of total assets to calculate the risk of unexpected losses. The usage of total assets instead of total loans should be commented upon. As long as the banks have the same ratio between loan and total asset, the choice will have no effect. However, if the bank holds other assets, such as non-earning assets to provide different banking services, for example corporate governance services, the risk involved in credit transactions will decline, simply as a result of loans having smaller impact on the bank with a large percentage of other assets. By choosing total assets rather than total loans, the risk of impact on the bank as a whole is estimated. A stable ratio signals that the bank, during the years that we study, has a low risk of unexpected losses due to either a small percentage of loans to total assets or as a result of non-volatile losses, which in both cases imply a low demand for capital to total asset ratio due to unexpected losses in the credit portfolio.

4.5   The relationship between risk and bank capital held under Basle I

One major improvement of the new Accord is that it should better match the actual risk-taking of individual banks. This implies that it should give a more accurate indication of capital at risk, thus leading to a higher reliability in the allocation process of capital for unexpected losses. Moreover, the new Accord will, through the second pillar, force the management of the banks to demonstrate their ability to make an explicit estimation of the capital requirement, in accordance with the regulatory capital calculated through the first pillar. In this section, we will examine the amount of capital held by banks in the selected countries under the current Accord, that is, Basle I. In order to establish the correlation between overall risk and capital employed in the banking industry of the selected countries, the amount of capital held by the banks is compared to their exposures to credit risk as well as to total risk. The riskier the banking business, measured as the standard deviation of the ratio of profit to total assets, the more capital is expected to be held by the bank in order to avoid default (or costs from the possibility of default) in times of high unexpected losses. Table 4.5 shows the correlation between credit losses and net profit for each bank in the sample.

As could be expected, most banks show a negative correlation between loan loss provisions to total assets and profit before tax to total assets (i.e., when credit losses are high, the net profit as a percentage of total assets are low). Since this Accord has mainly been focusing on credit risk, it should be expected to force bank managers to allocate capital for unexpected credit

Table 4.5 Correlation between loan loss provisions to total assets and profit before tax to total assets for each bank in the survey

Bank of Aland	Finland	0.03
Amagerbanken	Denmark	−0.87
Arbejdernes Landsbank	Denmark	−0.12
Danske Bank	Denmark	0.27
FB Bank Copenhagen	Denmark	−0.29
Fionia Bank	Denmark	−0.04
Fokus Bank	Norway	−0.85
Glitnir Bank	Iceland	0.12
Jyske Bank	Denmark	0.67
National Bank of Iceland	Iceland	−0.25
Nordea	Sweden	−0.01
OKO Bank	Finland	−0.54
Roskilde Bank	Denmark	−0.16
Sampo Bank	Finland	−0.97
Skandia Banken	Sweden	0.50
SEB	Sweden	−0.33
Spar Nord Bank	Denmark	−0.79
Sparbank Vest	Denmark	−0.13
Svenska Handelsbanken	Sweden	−0.56
Sydbank	Denmark	−0.54
Swedbank	Sweden	−0.57
Vestjysk Bank	Denmark	−0.05

Source: BankScope

losses. Even though the credit losses have been fairly low during the period, several banks show a high correlation between the variables. The lack of correlation for some banks, however, exposes the importance of widening the risk concept in the banking business.

A major aim of Basle I is to secure the capital held by banks. Table 4.6 provides information about the capital held by banks during the period.

The correlation between the ability of the banks to absorb unexpected losses (seen as the capital to asset ratio) and the total risk (seen as the standard deviation in net profit before taxes to total assets ratio) is shown in Table 4.7.

Table 4.7 shows that the correlation between capital to asset and total risk is positive ($\rho = 0.63$), implying that the total risk during the period in some way has affected the capital held by banks.

Since Basle I is expected to force riskier banks to withhold more capital than less risky banks, our findings are not unexpected. However, an interesting question is whether this effect has been accomplished solely by the current Accord or if the banks have allocated capital to cover their risk-taking regardless of the minimum qualified capital required by the regulatory

Table 4.6   Nordic banks: descriptive statistics about the capital to total asset ratio

Capital to asset ratio	Country	Median %	Max %	Min %	Standard deviation %
Bank of Aland	Finland	5.8	6.0	5.3	0.3
Amagerbanken	Denmark	10.3	12.9	9.0	1.5
Arbejdernes Landsbank	Denmark	10.0	11.0	9.0	0.8
Danske Bank	Denmark	4.9	6.4	4.0	0.8
FB Bank Copenhagen	Denmark	11.7	14.3	10.7	1.3
Fokus Bank	Norway	8.0	9.1	7.3	0.6
Jyske Bank	Denmark	6.9	8.3	6.2	0.9
Nordea	Sweden	5.1	4.8	5.5	0.3
OKO Bank	Finland	7.0	7.4	6.5	0.4
Roskilde Bank	Denmark	13.6	14.6	12.9	0.6
Sampo Bank	Finland	6.2	6.5	6.1	0.2
Skandia Banken	Sweden	6.9	8.1	6.6	0.6
SEB	Sweden	4.7	6.6	4.1	0.9
Spar Nord Bank	Denmark	7.4	7.8	7.1	0.3
Sparbank Vest	Denmark	13.2	15.2	12.1	1.2
Svenska Handelsbanken	Sweden	5.1	5.3	4.8	0.2
Sydbank	Denmark	6.9	7.7	6.5	0.5
Swedbank	Sweden	6.1	6.4	5.6	0.3
Vestjysk Bank	Denmark	14.4	16.7	13.2	1.3

Source: BankScope

Table 4.7   Total risk in each bank, measured as the standard deviation in net profit before taxes to total asset ratio and the median capital to asset ratio

	Country	Total risk %	Median capital to asset %
SEB	Sweden	0.13	4.73
Danske Bank	Denmark	0.13	4.87
Swedbank	Sweden	0.13	6.11
Svenska Handelsbanken	Sweden	0.14	5.12
Bank of Aland	Finland	0.21	5.77
Sydbank	Denmark	0.22	6.86
FB Bank Copenhagen	Denmark	0.25	11.70
Nordea	Sweden	0.27	5.11
Skandia Banken	Sweden	0.28	6.88
OKO Bank	Finland	0.35	7.03
Spar Nord Bank	Denmark	0.41	7.42
Roskilde Bank	Denmark	0.42	13.58
Jyske Bank	Denmark	0.42	6.95
Sampo Bank	Finland	0.48	6.24

Continued

Table 4.7 Continued

	Country	Total risk %	Median capital to asset %
Arbejdernes Landsbank	Denmark	0.54	10.03
Sparbank Vest	Denmark	0.58	13.22
Fokus Bank	Norway	0.67	8.00
Vestjysk Bank	Denmark	0.75	14.39
Amagerbanken	Denmark	1.01	10.27

Source: BankScope

Table 4.8 Descriptive statistics regarding the capital adequacy ratio of Nordic banks

Capital Adequacy	Country	Median %	Max %	Min %	Standard deviation %
Bank of Aland	Finland	11.5	12.6	11.0	0.7
Amagerbanken	Denmark	12.3	14.9	10.4	1.8
Arbejdernes Landsbank	Denmark	12.8	13.6	11.8	0.8
Danske Bank	Denmark	10.4	11.0	9.6	0.5
FB Bank Copenhagen	Denmark	12.6	14.3	11.1	1.1
Fionia Bank	Denmark	11.0	11.4	10.1	0.5
Fokus Bank	Norway	11.0	11.9	9.5	0.9
Glitnir Bank	Iceland	12.2	12.7	9.7	1.2
Jyske Bank	Denmark	11.4	12.4	10.5	0.8
National Bank of Iceland	Iceland	10.2	10.6	8.7	0.7
Nordea	Sweden	9.5	11.1	9.1	0.7
OKO Bank	Finland	11.3	12.8	10.8	0.8
Roskilde Bank	Denmark	12.7	13.0	10.5	1.0
Sampo Bank	Finland	11.0	11.4	9.8	0.7
Skandia Banken	Sweden	10.1	11.9	9.7	0.8
SEB	Sweden	10.7	14.6	10.2	1.7
Spar Nord Bank	Denmark	10.5	11.2	9.4	0.6
Sparbank Vest	Denmark	14.1	15.3	11.7	1.3
Svenska Handelsbanken	Sweden	9.7	10.2	9.3	0.4
Sydbank	Denmark	10.8	11.5	10.0	0.6
Swedbank	Sweden	10.8	11.6	10.4	0.4
Vestjysk Bank	Denmark	12.7	15.3	11.7	1.2

Source: BankScope

authorities. Table 4.8 displays the capital adequacy ratios for each bank during the period.

Table 4.8 shows that the capital adequacy ratios for the banks varied from 8.7 per cent up to 15.3 per cent during the time period of this study. Even between median ratios, there seem to be significant differences. This fact

Table 4.9 Total risk in each bank, measured as the standard deviation in net profit before taxes to total asset ratio and the median capital adequacy ratio

	Country	Total risk %	Median capital adequacy %
SEB	Sweden	0.13	10.7
Danske Bank	Denmark	0.13	10.4
Swedbank	Sweden	0.13	10.8
Svenska Handelsbanken	Sweden	0.14	9.7
Fionia Bank	Denmark	0.18	11.0
Bank of Aland	Finland	0.21	11.5
Sydbank	Denmark	0.22	10.8
FB Bank Copenhagen	Denmark	0.25	12.6
Nordea	Sweden	0.27	9.5
Skandia Banken	Sweden	0.28	10.1
OKO Bank	Finland	0.35	11.3
Spar Nord Bank	Denmark	0.41	10.5
Roskilde Bank	Denmark	0.42	12.7
Jyske Bank	Denmark	0.42	11.4
Sampo Bank	Finland	0.48	11.0
National Bank of Iceland	Iceland	0.52	10.2
Arbejdernes Landsbank	Denmark	0.54	12.8
Glitnir Bank	Iceland	0.58	12.2
Sparbank Vest	Denmark	0.58	14.1
Fokus Bank	Norway	0.67	11.0
Vestjysk Bank	Denmark	0.75	12.7
Amagerbanken	Denmark	1.01	12.3

Source: BankScope

implies that factors other than the minimum regulatory requirement of qualified capital are being used by banks to determine the required capital structure. As to what extent the current Accord has influenced the decisions of the amount of capital to be held in the banks, this is yet to be determined.

Table 4.9 shows the regulatory capital adequacy ratio and the total risk for the banks during the period studied.

As can clearly be seen from Table 4.9, the correlation between the total risk and the capital adequacy ratio is positive ($\rho=0.53$), implying that the total risk of the banks has influenced the amount of capital held by them to a greater extent than was required under the regulatory framework of Basle I. It seems riskier banks tend to increase the amount of capital held, which has a positive effect on the capital adequacy ratio.

4.6   The financial funding of loans under Basle I

As we have remarked, the total amount of capital meeting the requirements of the current Basle Accord can be one of two types. While Tier 1 capital consists of core capital, Tier 2 capital consists of supplementary capital, limited to certain caps (e.g., as to maturity). Beginning around the millennium, however, additional categories have been imposed. These are Hybrid Tier 1 and Tier 3 capital. While Hybrid Tier 1 capital has been subjected to some discussion (see, for example, Chorafas, 2004), the regulatory authorities have accepted it up to 15 per cent of Tier 1 capital. Hybrid Tier 1 capital is actually subordinated debt with a higher cap than that of Tier 2. Tier 3 capital comes to a substantial extent from trading activities, making it highly volatile. Chorafas (2004) argues that the use of this type of capital is highly limited. He estimates it to be 3 per cent of total capital. Although, this estimate is based only on one single European bank, we believe it is reasonable to exclude this type of capital in our empirical study.

A relevant question to be answered, is to what extent the capital held by banks is equity (here Tier 1 capital) or subordinated debt (here Tier 2 capital), since both are presumed to have different costs, which is an issue that will be addressed in the following section. Table 4.10 shows the percentage of subordinated debt as a percentage of total capital for each individual bank.

The overall median value is 30 per cent subordinated debt to total capital. On average, the banks could be expected to have at least the following

Table 4.10 Subordinated debt to total capital for each bank (median values)

Subordinated debt	Country	Median %
Bank of Aland	Finland	28
Amagerbanken	Denmark	29
Danske Bank	Denmark	30
FB Bank Copenhagen	Denmark	42
Fokus Bank	Norway	34
Jyske Bank	Denmark	25
Nordea	Sweden	38
OKO Bank	Finland	37
Roskilde Bank	Denmark	35
Sampo Bank	Finland	28
Skandia Banken	Sweden	39
SEB	Sweden	25
Spar Nord Bank	Denmark	19
Sparbank Vest	Denmark	19
Svenska Handelsbanken	Sweden	31
Sydbank	Denmark	24
Swedbank	Sweden	48
Vestjysk Bank	Denmark	0

Source: BankScope

financial funding of an individual loan when the minimum required capital to the risk-weighted asset base is 8 per cent:

$$F_n = RWA_n*0.08*0.70*E + RWA_n*0.08*0.30*SD + (1 - RWA_n*0.08)*L$$

Where

F_n	= Financial funding of loan/asset n
RWA_n	= Risk-Weight of Asset n
E	= Equity
SD	= Subordinated Debt
L	= Liability

However, as we have seen, banks tend to have a higher amount of total capital than the regulatory minimum requirement of 8 per cent qualified capital in relation to risk-weighted assets. In reality, banks currently hold a capital adequacy ratio of approximately 11 per cent (median of all banks during the period). Under the assumption that the banks wish to maintain the current capital adequacy ratio, this should give the following financial funding or capital structure for each individual loan:

$$F_n = RWA_n*0.11*0.70*E + RWA_n*0.11*0.30*SD + (1 - RWA_n*0.11)*L$$

4.7   Estimating the impact of Basle II on banks' lending rates

In investment appraisal, the concept of the Weighted Average Cost of Capital (WACC) is often used to determine the appropriate hurdle rate for discounting expected cash-flows of an investment opportunity. Given that WACC could be calculated for each individual loan or group of loans, there should be a benefit for a bank to be facing a low minimum amount of regulatory capital required, since qualified capital is generally more expensive for the bank than liabilities like ordinary deposits.

Given that WACC could be presumed to show a positive correlation with the risk-weighted asset base, Basle II will have a direct effect on interest rates as it will change the capital requirements. Several banks confirm in their investor relationship documents that the return on economic capital is indeed an important parameter of the profitability analysis of their business segments (see, for example, Glitnir, 2006a; Svenska Handelsbanken, 2006).

In the following analysis we have assumed that banks could borrow at a risk-free rate. This proxy should hold, as banks have the possibility to assess the capital market at or very close to the official rate of the Central bank. The question is, then, how high an interest rate margin is required over the risk-free rate for subordinated debt and equity, respectively. If the interest rate margins increase with higher capital adequacy requirements, this should affect the cost of capital or the 'eigenkapitalkostensatz' displayed in Figure 4.1. We denote such an effect as an Interest Added for Capital (IAC). Hence, the impact of Basle II on bank lending rates, at a minimum requirement level, may be estimated using the following equation:

$$IAC_{RW} = RWA_n{*}0.08{*}0.70{*}\ (r_E = r_f) + RWA_n{*}0.08{*}0.30{*}\ (r_{SD} - r_f)$$

Where

IAC_{RW} = Interest Added for Capital at Risk Weight
r_E = Required return on Equity
r_{SD} = Required return on Subordinated Debt
r_f = Risk free rate

According to our findings, interest added for capital in Nordic banks could be derived at the 11 per cent capital to total risk-weighted asset base (i.e., the median of all banks) using the following equation:

$$IAC_{RW} = RWA_n{*}0.11{*}0.70{*}(r_E - r_f) + RWA_n{*}0.11{*}0.30{*}(r_{SD} - r_f)$$

4.7.1   Required return on equity

There are several methods available to determine the accurate cost of equity for a business firm, where the Capital Asset Pricing Model (CAPM) belongs to the most well known ones. Assuming efficient capital markets, CAPM shows the expected return on equity for a well-diversified investor implying that owners will only be compensated for the so-called systematic risk. This risk is inescapable since the investor cannot diversify away from the risk of the economy as a whole (cf. Copeland, Weston and Shastri, 2005). In practice it is difficult, if not impossible, to estimate an exact risk premium in accordance with CAPM. We do not have this ambitious aim in this analysis, but we will bear in mind that the risk premium $(r_E - r_f)$ should compensate for the non-diversifiable risk only. In Glitnir Bank, the target return on equity is said to be 6 per cent above the risk-free rate (Glitnir 2006a). Even though no other bank, to our knowledge, has made such an explicit statement regarding the target cost of core capital, several banks pinpoint the importance of financial performance measurements like Economic Value Added (EVA) and Annual Value Added (AVA). Svenska Handelsbanken (2006) also states that a main financial goal is to generate a higher return on equity than other comparable banks.

We will in this analysis use the target return of Glitner Bank, that is, we assume that the true (opportunity) cost of capital for the banks in this region should be close to what is stated by Glitnir. The assumption is, thus, that the risk premium to a diversified investor is 6 per cent, that is, the return on the bank's core capital is 6 per cent over the risk-free rate.

4.7.2   Required return on subordinated debt

In June 2006, Glitnir Bank issued USD 500m in subordinated bonds. The issue is classified as Tier 2 capital according to a recent press release (Glitnir, 2006b). It is for a term of 10 years that may be called in by Glitnir after 5 years. The terms of the transaction were 175 basis points over a 5-year US treasury bond or equivalent to 123 basis points over LIBOR. As a proxy for estimating the interest added for cost of subordinated debt, we will in this analysis use 120 basis points (i.e., 1.20 per cent).

According to our rough estimations, the following interest added for capital (IAC) should be applicable within this group at an risk weight (RW) of 100 per cent using the minimum capital adequacy requirement level:

$$IAC_{100\%} = 1 * 0.08 * 0.70 * 0.06 + 1 * 0.08 * 0.30 * 0.012$$
$$IAC_{100\%} = 0.36\%$$

At the average (median) level of capital currently held in the banks, this gives the following expected IAC:

$$IAC_{100\%} = 1 * 0.11 * 0.70 * 0.06 + 1 * 0.11 * 0.30 * 0.012$$
$$IAC_{100\%} = 0.50\%$$

The expected *IAC* should be linear through the origin of coordinates, since when using neither any Tier 1 nor any Tier 2 capital, the cost of that capital should be equal to zero. Moreover, any combination of 0 per cent and 100 per cent risk-weighted assets should prevent arbitrary opportunities of non-linearity. This presumption is also consistent with the theory, since when taking no risk at all, an investor should be rewarded with the risk-free interest rate only.

Certainly, both estimations of IAC may be regarded as rather rough. However, our main concern has not been to exactly estimate the level of IAC, but rather to demonstrate the main principles behind a bank's pricing of loans in practice with respect to capital adequacy requirements.

4.8   Empirical findings concerning expected effects of Basle II on Swedish ISBs

The managerial view of the management within ISBs on Basle II and its implications for the cost of capital and lending rates offered to different borrowers is interesting to study in more depth as ISBs are almost entirely concerned with retail banking. Moreover, despite the fact that these banks are mostly relatively small in size, they often play a very important role for local firms in their local geographical area.

Sparbanken Finn, with a business volume of about SEK 25,491m and 293 employees, is the biggest ISB in Sweden, whereas Kräklingbo Savings Bank on Gotland, with a business volume of about SEK 21m and 0.7 employees, is the smallest one (the Annual Report 2002). At present there are 69 traditional ISBs left in Sweden, which means a decline of about 10 per cent over the past decade. This reduction in the number of traditional savings banks does not depend only on mergers and acquisitions, but also on the fact that a number of independent savings banks converted into a limited liability company in the 1990s. This conversion era was initiated in 1995, when the ISB in Borås formed a limited company, Borås Savings Bank Ltd. In that respect this savings bank formed a foundation that took over ownership of the bank's shares. Thereafter Rekarne Savings Bank in Eskilstuna converted, when it formed Eskilstuna Rekarne Savings Bank Ltd in association with Swedbank. The novelty of this constellation was that the ownership was distributed evenly between the two parties, that is, 50 per cent of the shares were awarded the foundation and 50 per cent was awarded Swedbank.

The merger between Swedbank and Föreningsbanken in 1997 meant problems for a number of ISBs. Since Swedbank was a former savings bank, it had, and still has, many joint projects (such as real-estate mortgage loans, capital market activities and IT-systems) with ISBs. The remaining ISBs as well as Swedbank preferred not to start competing with each other by using branches formerly belonging to Föreningsbanken. Instead, the ISBs were offered the option of buying the branches within each individual bank's geographical area. In some cases, the capital held by the individual ISB was not large enough to buy the branches, which called for a joint ownership in order to avoid competition. Purchases of competing branches by an ISB were carried out almost everywhere in Sweden where a competitive situation had arisen. On Öland, for instance, where Föreningsbanken was a relatively large actor, the solution consisted in forming a limited company with a newly created foundation and Swedbank as common owners. The latter bank became the owner of 60 per cent of the shares, leaving the foundation with the remaining 40 per cent.

Of the total of 12 ISBs that up to 2002 have been reorganized into limited liability companies, there are also a number of banks that have chosen not to be intermixed with Swedbank in terms of ownership. Varberg's Savings Bank Ltd constitutes an example of this. It was reorganized with an owner foundation as a single-handed owner of the created bank limited company. It is worth noting that this bank was not pressed to change its association form by any economic problems or objectives.

Table 4.11 The capital to asset ratio in different types of ISBs in Sweden

	Number of banks	Number of observations	Minimum %	Maximum %	Mean %	Std. deviation	Median %
ISBs unconverted	69	207	10.2	45.0	20.8	6.1	19.4
Former ISBs entirely owned by a trust fund	5	15	12.4	29.8	20.7	5.6	19.0
Former ISBs partially owned by a trust fund	7	21	11.3	17.7	15.2	1.6	15.3

Source: The Swedish Savings Banks Association (2006).

Summing up, today four different types of ISBs exist in the form of a limited liability company. Such a bank or company may be:

1. entirely owned by a foundation,
2. majority owned by a foundation with Swedbank Ltd as a joint owner,
3. 50 per cent owned by a foundation with Swedbank Ltd as a joint owner,
4. majority owned by Swedbank Ltd.

The ISBs have a unique solvency situation in the Swedish banking industry. Table 4.11 provides detailed information about the capital situation in the ISBs between the years 2002 and 2004.

Obviously only a few, if any, of the ISBs seem to work under capital restraints. However, the Swedish savings banks are seldom market leaders and have been working close to the large commercial banks. This is especially true for Swedbank. The ownership structure is likely to feel a large impact from the method chosen under the first pillar of the new Basle Capital Accord. Since those banks, partially owned by Swedbank, have to use the same method as their owner, all of them are expected to use the IRB Foundation approach. Among the other ISBs, no bank is likely to consider any other approach than the Standardized approach. In this analysis it would have been suitable to divide the ISBs into two buckets separated by whether they are partially owned by Swedbank or not. However, as can clearly be seen in Table 4.11, this would have effects on the possibility of keeping to our promise of anonymity since one bucket would then have consisted of only five ISBs. Therefore, both the second and the third category in Table 4.11, that is, all converted ISBs, have been grouped together into one bucket.

4.9   The questionnaire study

Among the ISBs that have not changed the association form into a limited liability company, the answer of the respondents was generally negative to the question of whether they calculate a cost of capital that is adjusted for different types of borrowers (see Table 4.12). The respondents of ISBs that had converted into limited liability companies were, on the other hand, giving an affirmative answer. In most of the banks it was stated that they were already paying attention to IAC and that they intended to keep on doing so after the implementation of Basle II. Table 4.12 provides detailed knowledge about the *IAC* as perceived by the respondents of the different ISBs.

An interesting question is whether our rough estimation of the financial funding of loans is deviating from the estimations made by the ISBs. Table 4.13 provides evidence of the estimations made within these banks.

Table 4.13 implies that the rough estimation that we made gives a rather fair indication of the level of IAC. However, it seems that the assumption made that banks would want to maintain the current financial funding, that is, setting the level at the current capital to loan ratio, should provide a more accurate estimation than the one of setting the level in accordance with the minimum required capital to loan ratio.

The differences experienced in this preliminary enquiry lead to a few additional questions. If the market could be expected to price IAC at approximately 50 to 70 basis points when RW = 100 per cent, how would the true cost of capital then be estimated by the banks that answered that they do not intend to use IAC? In order to find out more about the increased ability of the ISBs to assess and price risk, personal interviews have been carried out with representatives of two ISBs. We have chosen to interview a representative

Table 4.12   Descriptive data over the ISBs perception of IAC

	Number of banks	Number of answers	Uses IAC to calculate interest rate under Basle I %	Will use IAC under Basle II %	Uncertain about usage of IAC under Basle II %
Savings Banks	60	28	14	50	7
Former Savings Banks	12	5	60	60	20

Table 4.13   Details of the level of IAC at RW = 100% as perceived by the ISBs

	Number of answers	IAC rate below 0.3% at RW = 100%	IAC rate between 0.3%–0.5% at RW = 100%	IAC rate between 0.5%–0.7% at RW = 100%	Will use IAC rate but uncertain about the level
Savings Banks	28	4%	4%	25%	18%
Former Savings Banks	5	0%	0%	40%	20%

for one of those ISBs that still remains unconverted and had answered that it does not, and will not, use IAC under the new regulatory framework. We have also chosen an ISB from the converted group that is currently using the IAC and responded that it will continue to use IAC under Basle II. Both these ISBs should be classified as major ISBs.

4.10   Case 1 (non-converted ISB)

The savings bank chosen is one of the larger Swedish ISBs. The respondent, called Bank A hereinafter, is CFO and a member of the Bank Board of Executives.

Bank A states that the efforts made under the new capital adequacy framework have indeed lead to better possibilities for the bank in foreseeing credit losses. The development of the IT-system, Bank A argues, has largely improved the possibility of bank loan clerks to predict future problems.

Bank A argues that it is mainly the quantification of risk that has made a contribution to the bank's pricing ability. In this case the savings bank has worked very closely to Swedbank. However, Bank A believes that it will take a considerable period of time to implement new skills usage within the bank. The employees of this ISB, A argues, are not relying to a full extent on the new and improved instrument, resulting in very low usage, if any at all, of the new system.

According to Bank A, the bank has evaluated the ability of the systems to predict future losses in comparison to the pricing methods the bank used previously. The result showed a largely improved prediction ability for the bank, which to some extent helped to convince the employees. Thus, Basle II seems to have served as an impetus among bank management and employees to work towards a better pricing of risk, at least to some extent, and better identification of customers with the highest probability of default. However, Bank A is careful to declare that there is still a long road ahead before risk-based pricing can be fully implemented in this bank.

The management report facility embedded in the system is one benefit of the improved system that Bank A brings up explicitly. Through the more detailed information, sorted in relevant order, the management achieves much better information about details, which according to Bank A, is expected to improve the bank's management of the loan portfolio.

This savings bank does not calculate interest added for capital to each loan. Instead, Bank A lets the competitive environment set interest rates. Therefore Bank A argues that to calculate the cost of capital for each individual borrower brings no benefit to the bank. As a consequence, Bank A believes that the bank will improve its ability of both predict and (at least in the long term) price risk through the implementation of Basle II. However, Bank A has no opinion about the relevancy of calculating IAC.

4.11   Case 2 (converted ISB)

This former savings bank is now a Savings Bank Ltd. It is also one of the larger ISBs in Sweden. The respondent at this bank is Head of the bank's lending activities, and also a member of the Bank Board of Executives. We will call this respondent 'Bank B'.

Bank B expresses that the capital market has been subjected to mispricing of risk over some years. The opinion is that the risk premium concerning lending activity to corporate customers has been far too little differentiated with respect to credit risk. This has resulted in a pricing of capital that is favourable to financially weak companies, and unfavourable to financially strong ones. In that respect Bank B argues that Basle II has and will lead to improved systems in the bank for pricing risks.

One of the benefits, as far as B is concerned, is that the quantification of the counter-party risk is built into the IT-system. Based on known information about the customer, the loan clerks will now be provided directly by the system with accurate risk premiums for expected credit losses. In this way, the effective pricing of risk based on the latest knowledge about customer behaviour and credit losses will be secured. According to the experiences of Bank B, there is yet another benefit. The risk premium will now be known and made explicit. This will provide better insight in the bank concerning the actual costs of different banking activities.

Bank B argues that Basle II is something that has also led to similar improvements of the pricing and IT-systems of competitors. By recruiting staff from competitors, Bank B has gained insight into the efforts being made in other large commercial banks. Bank B argues that personnel with skills in this field are highly mobile, which has indeed increased knowledge about the Basle II projects conducted in different banks.

Concerning the issue of charging individual customers an additional interest rate as a result of changes in the regulatory capital required due to Basle II, there was no confusion. Bank B replied, in a straightforward manner, that the current pricing of regulatory capital (i.e., IAC) is 0.56 per cent when the risk-weight is equal to 100 per cent. Moreover, on an explicit question, Bank B states that the interest added for capital as a function of regulatory capital is linear and starts at the origin of coordinates, that is, the added interest is 0 per cent for lending to the government and 0.28 per cent for real-estate mortgages (which has RW = 50 per cent under Basle I).

Bank B argues that the current interest added for capital (0.56 per cent at a 100 per cent risk-weight) is the result of the amount of capital currently being held within Swedish banks in general. The bank has reached its conclusion about this level by also taking into consideration the perceived or explicit IACs of other banks, particularly commercial banks. Bank B pinpoints that the current level is by no means any long-term defined solution, but rather it will be subjected to revisions in the future. Since the capital held by Swedish banks in total will decline due to Basle II, Bank B predicts that IAC will also decline over subsequent years. However, Bank B cannot predict how much lower IAC will be. (It is worth mentioning that one of the respondents of the questionnaire with a situation similar to Bank B, but with its banking activities in a totally different region of Sweden, estimated that IAC will drop from today's 0.56 per cent to 0.50 per cent at a risk-weight of 100 per cent when the new capital adequacy framework is implemented.)

4.12   Conclusion

According to our findings, many banks are already allocating capital with regard to their risk exposure. Moreover, we provide evidence that the current capital adequacy ratio is positively correlated with the total risk of the banks, leading to the conclusion that riskier banks allocate more capital to the banking business than is required by the current Basle Capital Accord. These banks could therefore be presumed to already work in line with the second pillar of the new Accord, that is, they make their own estimations of the economic capital required for each business activity.

With only one exception, the banks are using Tier 2 capital as a complement to the core capital. However, the usage varies a lot, and should reflect the decisions made by each bank. The benefit from Tier 2 capital, as we can see, should be to lower the WACC of the individual banks. It should be kept in mind, though, that we have not taken into consideration that the financial risk of the shareholders decreases with higher solvency. This of course has implications for the size of the risk premium.

The concept of WACC seems to roughly hold as an estimation of the true cost of capital as it is being perceived by the ISBs. Through the questionnaire study and the interview studies, we provide evidence of the estimations made that IAC should be expected to be somewhere close to 50 basis points when RW = 100 per cent. The personal interviews indicate that these estimations are strengthened through the ISBs' perception of the Swedish loan market.

There seems to be no doubt that the increased focus on accurately measuring the capital adequacy ratio has provided a deeper insight into risk estimations. Both the respondents estimate increased differences in the pricing of risk, and/or a better accuracy in credit evaluations. This improved skilfulness of banks should be expected to further increase differentiation in the interest rates on bank loans.

One troublesome effect with the new regulatory framework is that it might penalize financially weaker companies twice. When the improved system of pricing risk is in place, the weaker firms should be expected to pay a higher interest rate on lending just to 'cover' the expected risk of losses. Since this is due to the fact that their business is riskier, this should provide a more efficient pricing, leading to a better allocation of capital within the region.

However, when the probability of default (PD) is also used to allocate capital at the same time as the existence of IAC is recognized, the weaker firms will also be charged with an additional interest cost levied by the banks in order to cover unexpected losses, that is, to avoid the cost of bankruptcy or financial distress. That implication of the new Basle Accord is arguable. The negative effect on the weak firms could, as Repullo and Suarez (2004) conclude, be diluted if one presumes perfect competition and that the weak firms will borrow from banks using the Standardized approach to Basel II. However, as we have demonstrated, in a bank market such as Sweden, with a few (4) banks with a very large share of total banking activities, all of them assumed use of one of the IRB approaches. The small banks that use the Standardized approach could be expected to follow the same principles for pricing loan as made by the banks using an IRB approach to Basel II, leading to the double punishment of weak companies.

Notes

1. Basle I was complemented at the end of 1990s with an amendment concerning market risk.
2. There are several other countries that will implement the new Basle Capital Accord. This chapter, however, is mainly concerned with the situation in the Nordic Countries.
3. There are also additional data available for other types of exposures, such as lending to government or regional authorities. In this chapter we will focus only on retail and corporate lending.
4. In BIS (2003) the change in capital for banks that adopt the more sophisticated IRB Advanced approach is also studied. This approach is based on the internal calculations of LGD, EAD and M of each individual bank. Due to the delicate nature of such information, it is very difficult for academic researchers to get access to it. We will in this study therefore focus on the Standardized approach and the IRB Foundation approach.
5. In this chapter we will focus mainly on the relationship between the regulatory capital requirement and credit risks, even though we of course acknowledge the likely significant effect of operational risks on such requirements.
6. The regulatory capital needed to be held by a bank is currently based on externally based capital adequacy requirements stipulated by Basle I, whereas economic capital should be based on the bank's internal calculations of capital at risk using, for example, a Value at Risk method. In that respect regulatory capital and economic capital should be expected to converge when implementing Basle II.

References

Avery R. B. and A. Berger (1991). 'Risk-based capital and deposit insurance reform', *Journal of Banking and Finance* 15(4/5), 847–74.

Bank for International Settlement, BIS (2003). *Quantitative Impact Study 3 – Overview of Global Results*, Basel Committee on Banking Supervision, Basel, Switzerland, May.

Bank for International Settlement, BIS (2005). *Basel II: International Convergence of Capital Measurement and Capital Standards: A Revised Framework*, Basel, Switzerland, November 2005.

Barfield, R. (2004). 'The nature of risk: Deep impact – Basel in the European Union', *Balance Sheet* 12(5), 32–7.

Bergendahl, G. and T. Lindblom (2007). 'Risk management in banking – A review of principles and strategies', in H. R. Rao, M. Gupta and S. Upadhyaya (eds), *Managing Information Assurance in Financial Services*, Hershey: IGI Publishing.

Calem, P. S. and M. Lacour-Little (2004). 'Risk-based capital requirements for mortgage loans', *Journal of Banking and Finance*, 28(3), 647–72.

Carey, D. and A. Flynn (2005). 'Is bank finance the Achilles' heel of Irish SMEs?', *Journal of European Industrial Training*, 29(9), 712–29.

Cartwright, P. and H. Sarraf (2005). 'Leveraging regulatory investments with portfolio risk-based pricing', *Journal of Financial Regulation and Compliance*, 13(3), 215–23.

Chorafas, D. N. (2004). *Economic Capital Allocation with Basle II, Cost Benefit and Implementation Procedures*, Norfolk: Elsevier.

Copeland, T. E., J. F. Weston and K. Shastri (2005). *Financial Theory and Corporate Policy*, 4th edn, Boston: Pearson Addison Wesley.

Garside, T. and J. Bech (2003). Dealing with Basel II: The impact of the New Basel Capital Accord', *Balance Sheet*, 11(4), 26–31.

Glitnir (2006a). Annual Report 2005.

Glitnir (2006b). 'Glitnir Bank issues US$ 500 million subordinated bonds'. Press Release available at: www.glitnir.is of 2006- 06-13.

Grüner, J., V. Kleff, L. Norden and M. Weber (2002). 'Mittelstand und Basel II: Der Einfluss der neuen Eigenkapitalvereinbarung für Banken auf die Kalkulation von Kreditzinsen', *Zeitschrift für Betriebswirtschaft*, 72, 1045–64.

Hendricks, D. and B. Hirtle (1997). 'Bank capital requirements for market risk: The Internal Models approach', *Economic Policy Review (Federal Reserve Bank of New York)*, 3(4), 1–12.

Jones, D. (2000). 'Emerging problems with the Basel Capital Accord: Regulatory capital arbitrage and related issues', *Journal of Banking and Finance*, 24(1/1), 35–58.

Pitschke, C. and S. Bone-Winkel (2006). 'The impact of the New Basel Capital Accord on real estate developers', *Journal of Property Investment & Finance*, 24(1), 7–26.

Repullo, R. and J. Suarez (2004). 'Loan pricing under Basel capital requirements', CEMFI/CEPR working paper, Madrid.

Saunders, A. and M. M. Cornett (2004). *Financial Markets and Institutions – A Modern Perspective*, New York: McGraw-Hill/Irwin.

Svenska Handelsbanken (2006). Annual Report 2005.

5
Capital Market Frictions and Bank Lending in the EU

Yener Altunbaş[*], *David Marques*[**] *and Balzhan Zhussupova*[***]

5.1 Introduction

Modigliani and Miller (1958, 1963) suggest that in perfectly efficient markets a firm's capital structure does not affect market value, and the type of source of finance is irrelevant for investment decisions. The firm can raise enough capital to finance all its projects offering positive net present values. However, the violation of the perfect market assumption ascribes a role for financial factors in the company's value and investment decisions. Asymmetric information and costly enforcement of contracts can disrupt the functioning of capital markets, leading to a wedge between the cost of external finance and the opportunity cost of internal funds for the firm. This wedge, called the external premium, represents the deadweight costs associated with the agency problem that normally exists between lenders and borrowers. The costs include the lenders' costs of information acquisition, evaluation, and monitoring of the borrowers' projects. The wedge reflects the 'lemon' premium that is charged because the borrowers have more information about the investment projects than the lenders do. There are also costs associated with the risk that the borrowers can change behaviour due to moral hazard problems or the contracts' restrictions to contain moral hazard. Thus, the external finance premium is the difference in cost between the funds raised externally by issuing equity or debt and the funds generated internally by retaining earnings (Bernanke and Gertler, 1995).

The presence of information asymmetry implies that external funds will be more costly than internally generated funds and firm's investment decisions will depend on its financial decisions and profitability. In general,

[*] Bangor Business School, Bangor University
[**] European Central Bank
[***] A correspondent author, Bangor Business School, Bangor University

increases in profit lower the wedge between internal and external funds and investment increases with available internal funds. Those firms that are more financially constrained will exhibit greater sensitivity of investments to the internal funds proxy for the change in net worth than less constrained companies (Chirinko and Schaller, 1995; Fazzari, Hubbard and Peterson, 1988; Hubbard, Kashyap and Whited 1995). The positive relationship between the internal funds and firms' investments indicates that the firms are financially constrained. They are unable to fund all their investment projects because information inefficiencies and costly contracting increase the costs of external finance relative to the costs of internal finance (Hubbard, 1998; Fazzari, Hubbard and Peterson, 1988).[1] Accordingly, the relationship between investment and the internal funds is an indication of underinvestment, that is, the firms curb some projects with positive net present value because of the high cost of external finance.

The consequent constraints of informational asymmetry can be as much important for banks as they are for non-financial companies. Commercial banks mitigate information asymmetry problems of the capital markets that make firms' external financing costly (Diamond, 1984). Banks specializse in lending to firms with special needs that are costly to communicate to the market. Banks collect information in the process of loan screening and contracting, and then adjust this information over time by monitoring the firms' repayments on loan and other activities with banks. The private information produced by banks can itself create an asymmetric information problem for banks vis-à-vis financial markets. Outside investors may find it difficult to value a large portion of bank assets due to their high 'informativeness'. Bank management also has better information regarding the financial conditions and future profitability of the banks than outside investors do. The large store of private information possessed by bank management about the true value of their banks can create adverse selection and moral hazard problems (Diamond, 1984; Ross, 1977). Therefore, difficulty in valuing bank assets and the presence of incentive problems imply that banks can face similar information frictions in raising external funds as non-financial firms do.

A certain proportion of banks' external finance may be protected from asymmetric information related problems. Deposit insurance can explicitly shield bank creditors from the full effects of banks risk-taking and even lower their borrowing costs at a high level of leverage (Berger, Herring and Szego, 1995)[2]. However, in general, in deposit insurance schemes there is a limit to the amount in each account that is insured.[3] Therefore, when insured deposits are limited in supply those banks that want to expand their lending have to issue alternative financial instruments.

According to Stein (1998) information problems make it difficult for banks to raise funds with instruments other than insured deposits. Asymmetric information is relevant because uninsured external funds carry some level of risk exposure to a bank. Additionally, any attempt to substitute away from insured deposits can bring the potential for adverse-selection problems. Any incompleteness in debt insurance raises issues of evaluation and monitoring by lenders. The higher leverage can make bank creditors more sensitive to changes in bank asset value or risk. The tax advantages of debt can gradually offset the increased expected costs of financial distress associated with the increased financial leverage, which in turn can increase banks' borrowing costs.

Similar asymmetric information problems between the banks and the markets can limit banks' ability to raise equity in the primary capital markets (Froot and Stein, 1998; Stein, 1998; Van den Heuvel, 2004). New equity issues may signal to the market that managers possess some private information that justifies the equity issue. When investors believe that bank's shares are overvalued any equity issue will be priced at a discount, which implies higher financing costs. Therefore, the 'lemon premium' can cause a positive association between net worth and lending. The premium is, however, not significant for constrained banks since investors observe that constrained banks issue equity to meet capital requirements rather than take advantage of share overvaluation (Cornett, Mehran and Tehranian 1998; Park, 2006).

Unlike manufacturing firms, banks are required to maintain specified ratios of capital to their assets by the regulatory authorities. Hence, apart from asymmetric information, the presence of regulatory capital requirements can create a link between bank's net worth and lending. Loan growth can potentially be constrained by the growth of equity capital and debt. The research shows that an increase in capital requirements can lead to contraction in bank credits since banks may find it expensive to issue new equity from external sources in relation to internally generated funds (Furlong, 1992; Hall, 1993; Haubrich and Wachtel, 1993; Shrieves and Dahl, 1995). According to Park (2006) an adequately capitalized bank should not exhibit any correlation between lending and internal funds unless it faces information-related problems. Asymmetric information is the main reason why shortage of equity capital may impact investment decisions. Park (2006) models the bank's lending decision as determined by three factors: the profitability of lending, capital adequacy, and the cost of raising equity. While the optimal amount of lending can be considerably influenced by share valuation for banks with low capital ratios (constrained banks), it should be determined by the lending profitability for banks with relatively high capital ratios (unconstrained banks). The costs of raising equity should not influence well-capitalized banks which can expand their lending without raising equity.

In addition, the transaction costs of new securities issue can also lead to a wedge between the cost of internal and external finance. Banks can issue deposits debt at relatively low transaction costs. The transaction costs of securities issue can be substantially higher. The direct costs normally include the legal, auditing and underwriting fees for debt and equity issues. The indirect costs consist of the costs of the time and effort management spent on conducting the offer. There may also be ongoing costs associated with the requirement to supply information on a regular basis to investors and regulators (Ritter, 1998).

Furthermore, large information asymmetry between bank managers and outside investors can increase the transaction costs of banks' securities trading thereby inflating banks' costs of capital. The theoretical model by Diamond and Verrechia (1991) demonstrates that the greater public disclosure/ reducing information asymmetry in the market for firm's security can increase the demand from large investors due to increased liquidity of securities and, consequently, this can reduce its required expected rate of return – firm's cost of capital. Glosten and Milgrom (1985) also show a positive relationship between the presence of informed traders, the adverse selection component of the bid-ask spread and the firm's cost of capital.[4] Chilpakatti (2001) finds that increased banks' transparency as measured by the quality of banks' annual reports disclosure is negatively associated with the relative spread and price volatility of banks' shares. Laeven and Levine (2005) examine whether the diversification of activities of financial conglomerates influence their market valuations. The study finds that the 'Q' of a financial conglomerate is less than the Q it would have if the conglomerate were broken into a portfolio of firms each of which specializes in the individual activities of the conglomerate.[5]

Thus, asymmetric information and transaction costs of securities trading can impact the relative costs of internal versus external finance (and the relative costs of debt versus equity financing) (Berger, Herring and Szego 1995). If the private information that banks have about their portfolios can create adverse selection and moral hazard problems, it will be costly for the banks to issue uninsured debt or equity. Asymmetric information can considerably constrain bank lending by forcing banks with low capital ratios (low internal capital generation) to reduce lending instead of issuing new equity (Park, 2006). Consequently, given capital requirement constraints, 'informationally disadvantaged' banks with limited internal funds and liquidity holdings may be forced to reduce lending.[6] The decline in bank lending is an important policy concern if banks decrease lending because of their inability to raise external finance due to constraints stemming from capital market inefficiencies. Bank loans are the main source of intermediated credit for households and especially small firms who have limited access to other sources of financing. Reduction in bank lending can impair the financial ability of the borrowers and lead to reduction in investments and consumption and liquidation of even fundamentally solvent companies (Bernanke and Gertler, 1995; Gertler and Gilchrist, 1994). When the banks themselves experience financial difficulties, the funding problems of firms may become even more pronounced.

The purpose of this chapter is to examine whether finance constraints exist for European credit institutions. This research question has not been explicitly addressed by previous studies. Following Houston and James (1998) and Houston, James and Marcus (1997), the study assumes that capital market frictions generate a wedge between the cost of internal and external financing reflected in the sensitivity of bank lending to internal capital generation. The chapter investigates whether over the period 1999 to 2004 the sensitivity of banks' loan growth to internally generated funds varies among banks with different magnitudes of affiliation with bank and non-bank financial institutions.

Our study uses the degree of banks' affiliation with other financial firms as an indicator of the information positions of the banks. According to the literature, the information position of the firm reflects the extent to which the institution faces information related problems in raising external capital (Chirinko and Schaller, 1995). The criteria for identifying informationally disadvantaged firms ('constrained') that are likely to face a significant spread between the cost of external finance and internal finance and informationally advantaged firms ('unconstrained') include the firm's age, its size, the presence of credit rating, the firm's dividend policy, and membership in industrial or financial group. For institutions facing negligible information costs, an increase in net worth independent of changes in investment opportunities has no impact on investment. For companies that face high information costs an increase in net worth leads to greater investments, while a decrease in net worth leads to lower investments (Hubbard, 1998).

The literature shows that the correlation between the internally generated funds and investment should be stronger for the stand-alone institutions than for the companies that are affiliated with other firms. The internal markets for funds created among the affiliated companies can internalize the capital transactions and helps to mitigate the market frictions thereby alleviating financing constraints of the participating institutions (Alchian, 1969; Chirinko and Schaller, 1995; Gertner, Scharfstein and Stein, 1994; Stein, 1997; Williamson, 1975). The basic mechanism of capital allocation involves the direct transfer of funds between institutions in exchange for debt or equity rights.[7] In the internal equity market the bank can receive funds from either a parent bank or other affiliated firms in exchange for ownership rights. The transfer of dividends to the shareholders constitutes an important part of the internal equity market. In the internal debt markets the funds are allocated in exchange for debt titles in the form of interbank loans, subordinated notes and debentures, and so forth (De Haas and Naaborg, 2005). The loan sales market can be considered as an additional mechanism through which internal capital operate among financial institutions. Banks can originate the loans and consequently transfer them in part or completely from their own books to those of another institution (Holod and Peek, 2005).

The important consequence of internalization of capital transactions is the mitigation of information asymmetry between the borrower and the lender that increases the costs of firms' external financing (Liebeskind, 2000; Stein, 1997). The asymmetric information problems are less severe between the firm members of an interrelated group than those between firms and the external market. Firms enter into long-term relationships within a group which allow them to share private information about the individual projects' quality from a postion of trust (Chirinko and Schaller, 1995). Thus, internal capital markets can improve the information between lenders and borrowers and shield investment projects from the information and incentive problems that external finance normally suffers from (Alchian, 1969; Gertner, Scharfstein and Stein, 1994; Stein, 1997; Williamson, 1975). Overall, internal capital markets can reduce the costs and improve the reliability of capital supply and decrease the possibility of under-investment resulting from the fluctuations in capital supply and/or interest rates in the external capital markets.[8]

In the EU, merger and acquisition activities of banks during the last decade have resulted in complex banking groups or financial conglomerates (ECB, 2000, 2005). The financial firms within such groups are typically connected by both direct and indirect ownership links. In this study, we use the extent of ownership links between banks and other financial companies as proxies for the information positions of the banks. The use of information on bank shareholdings makes it possible to distinguish the behaviour of banks with the different magnitudes of affiliation with bank and non-bank financial firms. The study contrasts the banks in different information positions to test whether finance constraints exist and to identify whether they are due to asymmetric information. The main testing hypothesis is that lower sensitivity of loan growth to banks' internal funds will be observed among the 'low information cost' institutions (banks with a greater number and larger affiliations) than among 'high information cost' institutions (banks with fewer and smaller affiliations with other financial firms).

5.2   Bank lending, internal funds, and constraints: a review of the empirical literature

Empirical evidence confirms that US banks face market frictions and establish internal capital markets to allocate limited capital within the organizations. Houston and James (1998) compare the lending behaviour of banks affiliated with a multi-bank holding company (MBHC) with that of unaffiliated banks. The research finds that stand-alone unaffiliated banks are more cash constrained – that is, their loan growth is more highly correlated with internally generated funds and is influenced more by the bank's capital position and liquidity. The study further shows that those bank holding companies that face the highest underwriting fees for common stocks, preferred stocks, and subordinated debt, and therefore face the greatest wedge between internal and external financing costs, demonstrate the strongest sensitivity of lending on internal capital generation. Since in internal capital markets funds are obtained easier and at lower cost than from external financial markets, affiliated banks can do more lending than similar stand-alone banks. Houston and James (1998) shows that the rate of loan growth is higher among banks affiliated with bank holding companies than among unaffiliated institutions.

Klein and Saindenberg (1997) construct matching pro forma benchmarks from single banks for a sample of MBHC. The comparison analysis finds that MBHCs, on average, hold significantly less capital, and do significantly more lending, than their pro forma benchmarks.

Jayaratne and Morgan (2000) equate insured deposits to cash flows as a form of 'internal funds'. The study builds on the proposition that informational frictions exist in the market for uninsured liabilities and tests whether bank lending is constrained by the availability of insured deposits. The finding indicates that shifts in deposit supply have a stronger impact on small, unaffiliated banks that have no access to a large internal capital market.

De Haas and Naaborg (2005) confirm that bank debt from the parent or affiliated firms can be cheaper than that from third parties.[9] They also document that if banks are constrained by large exposure limits regarding intra-group transactions, the parent company can arrange a long-term syndicated lending for the banks and act as the syndication leader in it. In this situation, the terms of the lending may be more favourable since the parent organization has more and better information regarding the borrowing bank.

Furthermore, Berger and Udell (1993) suggest that membership in bank holding companies may reduce information asymmetry between the institutions thereby assisting banks' participation in a secondary loan market. Stand-alone banks may face difficulty in selling and buying loans in external capital markets while affiliated banks can be more active as a seller and buyer in the secondary loan markets. For example, Demsetz (2000) finds that membership in a multi-bank holding company significantly increases the likelihood of a bank participating in a secondary loan market, either as a buyer or seller. Membership helps banks to overcome reputational barriers to participation, therefore holding company acquisitions may enhance secondary market activity by increasing the proportion of affiliated banks and vice versa.

If, because of large loan losses or other factors, a bank's capital ratios approach supervisory minimum levels, the parent companies can inject capital into the bank to ensure that capital requirements are met. The transfer of equity capital can strengthen banks' capital positions and can soften the regulatory rules regarding large exposure limits on lending[10]

(De Haas and Naaborg, 2005). Overall, parent equity support can strengthen the stability of the banks. Gilbert (1991) documents that unaffiliated problem banks are less likely to receive a capital injection than affiliated distressed banks. Ashcraft (2004) also finds that over the period 1986 to 1999, an average US bank affiliated with a multi-bank holding company was significantly safer than either a stand-alone bank or a bank affiliated with a one-bank holding company.[11] The affiliation reduces the probability of future financial distress and the distressed affiliated banks are more likely to receive capital injections and recover faster than other non-affiliated banks. The effects of affiliation are weaker when the parent has less than full ownership of the subsidiary. Thus, a parent holding company may support a distressed subsidiary and an affiliated company is more likely to receive financial support than stand-alone bank.[12] Furthermore, instead of directly moving capital from well-capitalized subsidiaries to less capitalized subsidiaries, the parent bank can transfer loans from low-capital subsidiaries to highly capitalized subsidiaries through the loan sales market. Holod and Peek (2005) empirically shows that MBHCs shift resources internally not only by shifting capital from better capitalized to more poorly capitalized subsidiaries, but by moving loans from less capitalized to well-capitalized subsidiaries.

Finally, recent studies find an important implication of the relationship between lending and internal capital markets for transmission of monetary policy. The 'lending view' of monetary policy suggests that monetary policy operates primarily by changing the amount of bank lending: banks reduce their lending when monetary policy tightens, which negatively affects the real sector (Bernanke and Blinder, 1992; Bernanke, and Gertler, 1995; Kashyap and Stein, 1995). Recent US research finds that internal capital markets can shield bank lending from a monetary contraction. It suggests that in case of monetary tightening, the parent company of credit institutions can channel funds to their affiliated banks thereby counteracting the funding problems that affiliate banks might otherwise face (Ashcraft, 2001; Campello, 2002). The studies also suggest that the structure of financial conglomerates in the EU offers the potential to counteract the distributional effects of the bank lending channel (Ehrmann and Worms, 2001; Gambacorta, 2005). For example, Ehrmann and Worms (2001) show that after a monetary contraction, the necessary funds are received by the head institutions of German saving and cooperative institutions from the international interbank market, and then redistributed among their affiliated institutions via the internal interbank lending market. The available funds help these banks to keep their loan portfolio relatively unchanged under the monetary contraction. Thus, the affiliation of credit institutions with other banking firms may explain why the effect of monetary policy may differ among banks.

5.3   Bank lending and internal capital funds: data and methodology

The literature, thus, suggests that imperfections in external capital markets create a link between bank lending and internal capital funds, proxied by the change in bank capital. Frictions in capital markets can be evidenced if, given investment opportunities, the increase in internal funds leads to an increase in bank lending (Houston, James and Marcus, 1997; Houston and James, 1998). The studies on US banks investigate bank lending across two groups of institutions: affiliated and unaffiliated with bank holding companies, implying that asymmetric information problems are less severe between firm members of an interrelated group than they are between firms and the external capital market. To be part of a bank holding company means that the bank is involved in the operation of internal capital markets established by its parent organization. It is suggested that financial conglomerates take advantage of the created internal capital market to generate and reallocate resources within the firm. It is easier and less expensive for the banks' managers to obtain the funds within the integrated structure than from the external capital market (Houston and James, 1998; Houston, James and Marcus, 1997; Campello, 2002).

In this study we take a different approach to defining the degree of informational disadvantage of banks since the corporate structures of European credit institutions and US banks differ (Saunders and Walter, 1994). The regulation in the EU permits banks to participate in equities of banking, non-banking financial, and partially industrial companies.[13] Over the last few decades banks' merger and acquisition activities have led to the creation of complex banking groups and financial conglomerates within which financial firms are interrelated through direct and indirect ownership links (ECB, 2000, 2005). The study uses the extent of banks' shareholding of other financial firms to proxy for the information positions of banks.

This chapter is interested in equity shareholdings established by banks in three types of institutions (undertakings): (1) banks; (2) insurance companies; and (3) financial companies (other than bank and insurance firms). This information together with financial data for banks is available from Fitch-IBCA Bankscope.[14] The research samples European credit institutions[15] reported as active at the end of 2005. The credit institutions include commercial banks, cooperative banks, savings banks, real estate and mortgage banks, and medium- to long-term credit banks.[16]

Regarding the shareholding information, we collect data on the value of the total assets of undertakings and the percentage of shares directly held by the sample banks. It is important to note that BankScope continuously renews its shareholding dataset. Therefore, it is not possible to accurately compare the banks' shareholding structures over regular intervals of time.

There are also data limitations on defining the exact date when the banks acquired particular ownership. However, the study assumes that the ownership pattern is relatively stable over the medium time span (La Porta, Lopez-de-Silanes and Shleifer, 1999) which can allow us to credibly create a link between the shareholding pattern and financial performance of the banks for the medium-term period and eliminate the necessity to examine changes in the patterns of bank equity undertakings. Since we have only a single-year cross-section of ownership data (at the end of 2005), loan regressions estimated over a long period may use unreliable ownership information. The estimates calculated over a short period are also likely to be imprecise. Therefore, we compromise by using a six-year period from 1999 to 2004 in the results reported below.

The final sample of banks comprises 1270 credit institutions for which Fitch-IBCA BankScope supplies data on at least one equity undertaking and the required financial information for the period 1999 to 2004. In order to be included in the sample the credit institutions should meet the criteria for financial data: (1) positive values of total assets; (2) positive values of equity; and (3) non-missing values of net income for at least two years of the observed period. To prevent the influence of outliers we also eliminate bank-year observations with asset growth in excess of 50 per cent, those with total loan growth exceeding 100 per cent and those with total loans-to-assets ratios below 20 per cent. The former is to ensure that the research deals with credit institutions that are primarily engaged in traditional lending activities.

In order to differentiate among banks with different sizes of ownership affiliation, we constructed the affiliation index. The affiliation index indicates the size of a bank's affiliation relative to the average size within similar types of banks and the sample bank's country of origin. In particular, we compare the actual size of a bank's interest in the undertaking's total assets with its predicted asset size – that is, the asset size the bank would hold if the undertaking's total asset were equal to the national average within the same type of bank. Then, we compute an index for each bank's undertaking by dividing the actual asset stake by the predicted asset stake of the banks. An index score above 1 will indicate that the asset stake of the sample bank is larger than that of the average bank within the same bank category and the country of domicile. Since, banks have more than equity establishments across the three types of financial firms, we construct an aggregate index for each banks by averaging their individual index scores. An aggregate affiliation index score equal to or above 1 indicates that the banks have a higher degree of affiliation than that observed on average within the same type of bank in the country of domicile. We refer to these banks as 'low information costs' banks, experiencing less information asymmetry related problems due to the higher extent of their integration with other financial firms. Accordingly, we allocate banks to 'high information costs' banks if their average affiliation index scores are below 1.

The formula for calculating an affiliation index for an individual equity undertaking is as follows:

$$Index_{ic} = \frac{d_{ijc}{}^* a_{jc}}{d_{ijc} * \bar{a}_{sjk}}$$

where, d_{ijc} is the percentage of shares directly owned by i bank in c firm of the type j; j is either: (1) a bank, (2) an insurance company; and (3) a financial firm other than bank and insurance company; $\bar{a}_{jc}$ is the total assets of the c undertaking of the type j in which the sample bank holds equity interest; $\bar{a}_{sjk}$ is the total assets of the average undertaking of the type j observed within particular type of credit institutions s from the country k; s can be of five types: (1) commercial banks; (2) cooperative banks; (3) savings banks; (4) real estate and mortgage banks; and (5) medium- to long-term credit banks; k corresponds to the EU15 countries.

The study estimates the loan growth equation estimated over the sample period as follows:

$$\Delta Loan_{it} = \beta_1 + \beta_2 \left(\frac{\text{Internal funds}_{it}}{Loan_{it-1}} \right) + \beta_3 \left(\frac{\text{Equity}_{it-1}}{\text{Total Assets}_{it-1}} \right)$$

$$+ \beta_4 \left(\frac{\text{Liquid Assets}_{it-1}}{\text{Total Assets}_{it-1}} \right) + \beta_5 (Ln\text{Total Assets}_{it-1}) + \beta_6 \Delta \left(\frac{Credit_{kt}}{GDP_{kt}} \right) + \varepsilon_{it}$$

where, i is a subscript for a bank, t is a subscript for the year; k is the country of a bank origin.

The literature suggests that the investment spending of non-financial firms is a function of internally generated funds after firm-growth opportunities are controlled. In general, investment is changes in capital stock deflated by the value of firms' capital at the end of the previous year. Capital stock for non-financial firms typically includes various inventories, fixed assets, and equipment (Fazzari, Hubbard and Peterson, 1988). We follow several banking studies (i.e., Houston, James and Marcus, 1997; Houston and James, 1998) and consider $\Delta Loan_{it}$, bank investments, to be changes in the amount of loans outstanding and capital stock to be the value of loans outstanding at the end of the previous year. We examine the sensitivity of banks' loan growth to the internal additions to capital scaled by the value of loans at the beginning of the year, $Internalfunds_{it}/Loans_{it-1}$. Consistent with previous research, we measure internally generated funds as net income plus the changes in the provisions for general banking risks. To control for the initial liquidity and capital positions of banks we introduce ($Equity/Total Assets)_{it-1}$, the ratio of equity to total assets at the beginning of the year where the equity consists of share capital and equity reserves relative to the total assets of the banks; and ($LiquidAssets/Total Assets)_{it-1}$, the ratio of liquid assets to total assets at the beginning of the year, where liquidity assets are equal to the sum of assets due from banks, deposits with central bank and other banks, and government securities. $LnTotalAssets_{it-1}$, the first lag of the natural logarithm of the total assets, is added to control for the size of the banks.

Bank lending and deposit growth can change simultaneously because faster growth in capital and deposits may signal that the demand for loans is growing (Houston and James, 1998; Jayarante and Morgan, 2000). Therefore, the introduction of the variable controlling for loan demand is necessary to remove that part of correlation between the source of funds and lending due to the loan demand, rather than from the correlation caused by the presence of market frictions. A typical measure of firm's investment opportunity is Tobin's Q calculated as the market to book value of the firm's assets. Because the majority of our sample banks do not trade publicly, we control for differences in investment opportunities by using the ratio of loans extended by the monetary financial institutions to the country's GDP, and apply the first difference in this ratio in the analysis $\Delta(Credit_{kt}/GDP_{kt})$. The data for this variable were sources from the statistical database found in the European Central Bank's website.

Thus, we compare the banks in different information positions to test whether finance constraints exist and to define whether they are due to asymmetric information. The main testing hypothesis is that lower dependency of loan growth on banks' internal funds will be observed among the low information costs institutions (with higher levels of ownership affiliations with other financial firms) than among the high information costs institutions (with lower degrees of affiliation). Results supporting the hypothesis will indicate that sample banks face financial constraints and that their internal capital markets, established through affiliations with other financial institutions, lessen these constraints, reflected in weaker dependency of bank lending on the changes in capital, given that investment opportunities are controlled.

5.4   Results

5.4.1   Descriptive statistics: overview of European banks' equity holdings

Table 5.1 provides information on the distribution of the credit institutions according to the number and type of their equity undertakings. In total, 1,270 banks report on 10,568 equity investments in financial firms; 955 institutions have at least one equity undertaking in banks; 267 banks reported on their direct investments in equity of insurance firms and 876 banks hold equities of financial companies (other than bank and insurance companies). Overall, for 6248 equity undertakings the data on the size of banks' direct ownership is available.

Table 5.1 indicates that, on average, European credit institutions establish 6.9 equity undertakings. For a typical bank in the EU, the average number of

Table 5.1 Descriptive summary of banks' equity shareholdings

The shareholdings are the equity shares directly owned by the sample banks in other financial institutions. The shareholdings data as at 2005 is obtained from Fitch-IBCA BankScope.

Type of equity shareholding [a]	Number of banks [b]	Total number of shareholdings	Total number of shareholdings with correspondent value of the percentage of shares directly owned	Average number of equity undertakings per bank	Average total assets equity undertaking (USD mln.)	Average assets size of equity undertaking owned by banks (USD mln.)
1	2	3	4	5	6	7
Bank	955	4,614	3,001	3.89	33,290.1	3,375.0
Financial company	876	5,122	2,842	4.85	432.2	179.8
Insurance company	267	832	405	2.56	39,754.4	3,710.8
Total	1,270	10,568	6,248	6.97	22,964.9	2,518.6

[a] The type of a financial firm in which the sample banks hold equity interests.
[b] The number of credit institutions that report in Fitch-IBCA Bankscope on at least one equity shareholding with correspondent value of the percentage of shares directly owned.

equity investments in banks is 3.9, while the mean number of equity share-holdings of financial companies (other than bank and insurance companies) and insurance firms are 4.85 and 2.6, respectively. Furthermore, the average size of banks' equity stakes is USD 2519 million, while the average total assets of the undertaking are equal to USD 22,965 million. The mean bank also holds around 42 per cent of the total assets of the financial company (other than bank and insurance company) and approximately 10 per cent of the assets of insurance and bank firms, respectively.

Table 5.2 shows the descriptive summary for the equity shareholdings across the two groups of banks: 'high information costs' banks (group 1) and 'low information costs' banks (group 2).

The results indicate that group 1 banks establish fewer equity undertakings than group 2 banks. Moreover, group 1 banks tend to hold smaller owner-ship of other banks and financial firms (other than bank and insurance com-panies). For example, Panel A shows that the average percentage of shares directly owned in other banks by group 2 banks is 36.03 per cent, whereas this figure for group 1 firms is 2.6 per cent. However, on average, the size of equity ownership of insurance companies is higher for group 1 banks (47.8 per cent) than for group 2 institutions (42.6 per cent). Furthermore, column 9 indicates that group 1 banks hold around 1 per cent of total assets of bank undertakings while the analogous figure for the firms from group 2 is 13.4 per cent. A similar picture is observed for banks' shareholdings of insurance companies. To compare, the average bank from group 2 holds around 46 per cent of the assets of financial companies (other than bank and insur-ance companies), whereas the mean bank from group 1 owns only 3.4 per cent of total assets. Overall, the results show that banks from group 1 hold a smaller number and less concentrated ownership of financial intermediaries than the banks from group 2.

Table 5.3 presents descriptive statistics of the bank variables in total and for the two groups of banks categorized according to the average values of their index scores. It also shows the additional variables that we calculate to examine the possible differences in financial characteristics of the two cate-gories of banks. These variables include net loans to total assets ratio, the growth rate of customer deposits, the ratio of equity to net loans, the ratios of loans and liquid assets to customer deposits and short-term funding, interbank ratio, bank deposits to total assets, and bank loans to total assets ratios. Here customer deposits include the amount of total deposits except those extended to the government, bank and commercials. Short-term fund-ing includes money market short-term borrowed funds. Interbank ratio is the ratio of bank deposits to the deposits place with other banks.

The summary shows that the average bank from group 1 has total assets of Euro 6539 million. The typical bank from group 2 is significantly larger, with mean total assets of Euro 26,190 million. The median asset size of group 1 banks is also smaller (659 million versus 1670 million). Furthermore, the

Table 5.2 The descriptive summary of equity undertakings by the type and the bank group

The descriptive statistics are for the sample of active European credit institutions that report on at least one equity undertaking with correspondent value of the percentage of shares directly owned. Banks are divided into two groups according to the average score of their affiliation index. Group 1 consists of the banks with an average index score less than 1. Group 2 includes banks with an average index score equal to or above 1. Panel A shows a descriptive summary for the equity shares directly owned by the sample banks in other banks. Panel B presents a descriptive summary for the equity shares directly owned by the sample banks in insurance companies. Panel C show a descriptive summary for the banks' equity shareholdings of financial companies (other than bank and insurance firms). Panel D shows a descriptive summary of banks' total equity shareholdings irrespective of the type of undertakings. The shareholdings data as at 2005 are obtained from Fitch-IBCA BankScope.

Group	Average ownership size[a]	Median ownership size[b]	Minimum ownership size[c]	Maximum ownership size[d]	Number of equity undertakings	Average total assets of equity undertaking (USD mln.)	Average assets size of equity undertaking owned by the sample banks (USD mln)	The ratio of average assets of equity undertakings owned by the sample banks to the average total assets of equity undertaking
1	2	3	4	5	6	7	8	9
Panel A: Bank equity undertaking								
Group 1	22.60	0.59	0.01	100	707	22,841.0	232.4	0.010
Group 2	36.03	11	0.01	100	2294	33,166.2	4,453.8	0.134

Continued

117

Table 5.2 Continued

Group	Average ownership size [a]	Median ownership size [b]	Minimum ownership size [c]	Maximum ownership size [d]	Number of equity undertakings	Average total assets of equity undertaking (USD mln.)	Average assets size of equity undertaking owned by the sample banks (USD mln)	The ratio of average assets of equity undertakings owned by the sample banks to the average total assets of equity undertaking
Panel B: Financial company equity undertaking								
Group 1	47.2	27.6	0.01	100	424	218.8	7.4	0.034
Group 2	53.6	50	0.01	100	2418	503.8	230.3	0.457
Panel C: Insurance company equity undertaking								
Group 1	47.8	37.6	0.38	100	76	38,431.1	193.4	0.005
Group 2	42.6	26	0.02	100	329	38,286.4	4,645.6	0.121
Panel D: Total equity undertaking								
Group 1	32.8	5.01	0.01	100	1207	17,193.1	175.7	0.010
Group 2	44.9	25	0.01	100	5041	22,885.7	3,277.2	0.143

[a] The average percentage of shares directly owned by the sample banks.
[b] The median percentage of shares directly owned by the sample banks.
[c] The minimum percentage of shares directly owned by the sample banks.
[d] The maximum percentage of shares directly owned by the sample banks.

Table 5.3 Summary statistics of banks' variables

The descriptive statistics are for the sample of active European credit institutions that report on at least one equity undertaking with correspondent value of the percentage of shares directly owned. Banks are divided into two groups according to the average score of their affiliation index. Group 1 consists of the banks with an average index score less than 1. Group 2 includes banks with an average index score equal to or above 1. The financial data for the period 1999 to 2004 and the shareholding data as at 2005 is obtained from Fitch-IBCA BankScope.

Variable	Total sample				Group 1				Group 2			
	Mean	Median	Standard deviation	N	Mean	Median	Standard deviation	N	Mean	Median	Standard deviation	N
Total assets (Euro million)	19163.1	1123.2	73677.4	5487	6539.3	659.2	26528.0	1962	26189.5	1669.8	88999.4	3525
Loans/total assets[a]	0.601	0.614	0.165	5473	0.613	0.627	0.169	1956	0.594	0.603	0.162	3517
Loan growth[b]	0.105	0.103	0.098	4300	0.106	0.106	0.107	1510	0.105	0.102	0.093	2790
Internal funds/loans$_{t-1}$[c]	0.017	0.012	0.222	4472	0.024	0.012	0.371	1598	0.014	0.012	0.017	2874
Customer deposits growth[d]	0.077	0.071	0.096	4143	0.075	0.069	0.101	1428	0.078	0.071	0.093	2715
Equity/total assets[e]	0.095	0.085	0.060	5486	0.097	0.089	0.059	1961	0.093	0.084	0.061	3525
Equity/loans[f]	0.174	0.137	0.151	5473	0.180	0.144	0.186	1956	0.171	0.132	0.128	3517
Liquid assets/total assets[g]	0.221	0.202	0.152	5126	0.214	0.202	0.145	1845	0.225	0.202	0.156	3281
Liquid assets/customer and short-term funding[h]	0.337	0.298	0.279	5110	0.343	0.302	0.342	1842	0.333	0.295	0.237	3268
Loans/customer and short-term funding[i]	0.930	0.858	0.542	5435	0.976	0.891	0.619	1943	0.905	0.840	0.491	3492

Continued

Table 5.3 Continued

Variable	Total sample				Group 1				Group 2			
	Mean	Median	Standard deviation	N	Mean	Median	Standard deviation	N	Mean	Median	Standard deviation	N
Interbank ratio[j]	1.720	0.833	2.099	4185	1.831	0.946	2.148	1499	1.658	0.788	2.070	2686
Bank deposits/total assets[k]	0.149	0.074	0.191	5179	0.157	0.071	0.209	1891	0.144	0.075	0.179	3288
Bank loans/total assets[l]	0.108	0.078	0.102	4258	0.114	0.080	0.108	1566	0.105	0.077	0.097	2692

[a] Loans/total assets is the end-year ratio of net loans (gross loans net of loan loss reserves) to total assets.

[b] Loan growth is equal to the change in net loans divided by net loans outstanding at time t−1.

[c] Internal funds/loans is equal to net income plus changes in provisions for general banking risks divided by net loans at time t−1.

[d] Customer deposits growth is equal to the change in total customer deposits divided by customer deposits outstanding at time t−1.

[e] Equity/total assets is the end-year ratio of the sum of share capital and equity reserves to total assets.

[f] Equity/loans is the end-year ratio of the sum of share capital and equity reserves to net loans.

[g] Liquid assets/total assets is the end-year ratio of liquid assets (the sum of cash and due from banks, deposits with central bank and other banks and government securities) to total assets. This ratio is calculated by Fitch-IBCA Bankscope.

[h] Liquid assets/customer and short-term funding is the year-end ratio of liquid assets (the sum of cash and due from banks, deposits with central bank and other banks and government securities) to customer and short-term funding (total deposits and money market funding).

[i] Loans/customer and short-term funding is the year-end ratio of net loans (gross loans net of loan loss reserves) to customer and short-term funding (total deposits and money market funding).

[j] Interbank ratio is the year-end ratio of deposits with banks to bank deposits. This ratio is calculated by Fitch-IBCA BankScope.

[k] Bank deposits/total assets is the year-end ratio of bank deposits (liabilities) to total assets.

[l] Bank loans/total assets is the year-end ratio of deposits with other banks (assets) to total assets.

banks from group 1 hold a slightly higher proportion of loans relative to total assets than group 2 banks (61.3 per cent against 59.4 per cent). Table 5.3 suggests that there is no comparable pattern in banks' investment rate, as the rate of loan growth is quite similar at around 10.5 per cent across two classes of banks. However, the rate of the internal funds to the stock of loans is higher for group 1 banks than for group 2 institutions (2.4 per cent and 1.4 per cent, respectively). In addition, the average customer deposit growth is slightly lower for group 1 banks (7.5 per cent) than for group 2 institutions (7.8 per cent).

The difference in equity positions across bank groups is also evident. The equity to total assets ratio is slightly higher among 'high information costs' banks with a lower degree of average affiliation (group 1). Table 5.3 shows that the average group 1 bank maintains a capital ratio of 9.7 per cent against 9.3 per cent of the typical bank from group 2. The group 1 banks also have more equity in relation to their net loans than group 2 banks (18 per cent versus 17.1 per cent, respectively).

Although, the ratio of liquid assets to total assets ratio is lower for 'high information costs' banks, the ratio of liquid assets to customer funds and short-term funding is higher for the banks from group 1 than for institutions from group 2 (34.3 per cent against 33.3 per cent, respectively). Furthermore, net loans of group 1 banks constitute 97.5 per cent of their customer funds and short-term funding, whereas, for the group 2 banks this figure equals to 90.5 per cent.

Furthermore, Table 5.3 shows that banks from group 1 tend to hold larger proportions of other banks' assets and liabilities than banks from group 2. For example, the average group 1 bank funds 15.7 per cent of assets by bank deposits compared to 14. 4 per cent of the average bank from group 2. The percentage of assets placed with other banks is equal to 11.4 for the group 1 banks, whereas this figure for the group 2 banks is 10.5. In addition, both types of banks tend to participate in interbank market more as lenders than as borrowers. Table 5.3 shows that the interbank ratio is 1.83 for the group 1 and 1.66 for the group 2 institutions.

5.4.2 Sensitivity of bank lending: regression results

Table 5.4 reports the results of estimating equations for all banks and for the two bank categories: 'high information costs' banks (group 1) and 'low information costs' banks (group 2). The regressions are estimated using a fixed-effects specification.[17] The control variables include firms' financial characteristics: the lag value of natural logarithm of total assets and the beginning-of-period values of bank capital and liquid assets scaled by the value of total assets. We also control for the possibility that internal funds may proxy for the differences in the loan demand rather then in supply constraints across banks by introducing the loan demand conditions in the country and the past level of bank loan growth (Houston and James, 1998).

Table 5.4   The sensitivity of bank lending to internal funds

Fixed effects regressions relate loan growth to the internal funds and firm financial characteristics. The total sample comprises the active European credit institutions that report on at least one equity undertaking with the correspondent value of the percentage of shares directly owned. The banks are divided into two groups according to the average score of their affiliation index. Group 1 consists of the banks with an average index score less than 1. Group 2 includes banks with the average index score equal to or above 1. The financial data for the period 1999 to 2004 and the shareholdings data as at 2005 is obtained from Fitch-IBCA BankScope.

Variables	Total sample	Group 1	Group 2
1	2	3	4
Internal funds/loans $_{t-1}$[a]	1.273	1.969	0.911
	(6.67)	(5.6)	(4.05)
(Equity/total assets) $_{t-1}$[b]	0.598	0.862	0.442
	(3.44)	(2.87)	(2.07)
(Liquid assets/total assets) $_{t-1}$[c]	0.166	0.236	0.122
	(5.09)	(4.15)	(3.07)
Log total assets $_{t-1}$	0.019	0.013	0.021
	(4.36)	(1.88)	(3.85)
Credit/GDP[d]	0.056	0.041	0.074
	(3.15)	(1.57)	(2.94)
Intercept	−0.279	−0.244	−0.288
	(−5.69)	(−3.24)	(−4.42)
N (categories)	921	331	590

[a] Internal funds/loans $_{t-1}$ is equal to net income plus changes in provisions for general banking risks divided by net loans at time $t-1$

[b] Equity/total assets is the end-year ratio of the sum of share capital and equity reserves to total assets.

[c] Liquid assets/total assets is the end-year ratio of liquid assets (the sum of cash and due from banks, deposits with central bank and other banks and government securities) to total assets. This ratio is calculated by Fitch-IBCA BankScope.

[d] Credit/GDP is the first difference in the ratio of domestic loans extended by the monetary financial institutions to the country's real GDP.

The former is also used to correct for the autoregressive error structures and it is not reported in the regression results below.

The results in column 1 of Table 5.4 show that changes in capital proxied by the internal funds variable do have a significant impact on lending for the total sample of banks. Moreover, a stronger relationship between the internal funds and loan growth is observed among 'high information costs' banks (group 1) than among 'low information costs banks' (group 2). The coefficient on the internal funds variable is 1.97 for the group 1 banks against 0.91 for the institutions from group 2. This finding suggests that both types of banks are financially constrained. However, the wedge between the external and internal capital costs is smaller for banks with a higher degree of ownership affiliation with other financial institutions.

Furthermore, lending of the group 1 banks is more strongly determined by the beginning of the year capital and liquidity than that of group 2 banks. The estimated coefficients on the equity to total assets and liquid assets to total assets ratios for group 1 banks are 0.86 and 0.24 against respective 0.44 and 0.12 of group 2 institutions. Columns 4 show that the size matters more for 'low information costs' banks (group 2) than for 'high information costs' banks (group 1). Furthermore, group 2 banks are more perceptive to the changes in loan demand than group 1 institutions. The estimated coefficient for the first difference in the ratio of loans extended by the country's monetary financial institutions to GDP is positive and significant for the group 2 banks while it is positive, but insignificant for the group 1 institutions.

Jayaratne and Morgan (2000) consider banks' insured deposits analogous to internal funds since they are subject to deposit insurance scheme. A positive association between loan growth and insured deposit growth suggests that the supply of uninsured deposits for banks is inelastic. Our data source does not specify which banks' external debt is insured. We, however, decided to consider banks' customer deposits as an approximate for the banks' insured deposits. This variable is not precise; therefore, the results should be read with caution. In Table 5.5 we include the growth rate of customer deposits in estimation to identify the impact of customer deposits on bank lending and whether the presence of customer deposits alters the sensitivity of bank lending on the internal funds.

Table 5.5 indicates that the lending of the both categories of banks is sensitive to the internal funds and the growth of customer deposits. Moreover, the estimated coefficient on the customer deposits growth is slightly higher for group 1 banks than for group 2 institutions (0.26 versus 0.23, respectively). Further, the introduction of the customer growth variable reduces the sensitivity of bank lending to internal funds. The estimated coefficients on internal funds are still, however, higher for group 1 institutions. The impact of capital position is also significantly reduced, especially for group 1 banks, after we added the growth of customer deposits into the estimation. Table 5.5 also indicates that liquidity becomes more important than capital in influencing bank lending. For example, the coefficient on the ratio of liquid assets to total assets is positive and significant while the coefficients on the ratio of equity to total assets are not significant for both types of banks. Finally, for the both groups of firms the size and the loan demand are the important determinants of bank lending.

Table 5.5   The sensitivity of bank lending to internal funds and customer deposits

Fixed effects regressions relate loan growth to the internal funds, customer deposits, and firm financial characteristics. The total sample comprises the active European credit institutions that report on at least one equity undertaking with the correspondent value of the percentage of shares directly owned. The banks are divided into two groups according to the average score of their affiliation index. Group 1 consists of the banks with an average index score less than 1. Group 2 includes banks with an average index score equal to or above 1. The financial data for the period 1999 to 2004 and the shareholdings data as at 2005 is obtained from Fitch-IBCA BankScope.

Variables	Total sample	Group 1	Group 2
1	2	3	4
Internal funds/loans $_{t-1}$[a]	0.758	1.588	0.405
	(3.99)	(4.26)	(1.85)
Customer deposits growth[b]	0.244	0.260	0.235
	(12.81)	(7.83)	(10.04)
(Equity/total assets) $_{t-1}$[c]	0.141	0.160	0.117
	(0.78)	(0.48)	(0.55)
(Liquid assets/total assets) $_{t-1}$[d]	0.207	0.283	0.153
	(6.65)	(5.38)	(3.98)
Log total assets $_{t-1}$	0.014	0.013	0.014
	(3.89)	(2.33)	(2.82)
Credit/GDP[e]	0.061	0.060	0.063
	(3.59)	(2.44)	(2.68)
Intercept	−0.195	−0.208	−0.173
	(−4.76)	(−3.72)	(−2.89)
N (categories)	886	311	575

[a] Internal funds/loans $_{t-1}$ is equal to net income plus changes in provisions for general banking risks divided by net loans at time t−1.
[b] Customer deposits growth is equal to the change in total customer deposits divided by customer deposits outstanding at time t−1.
[c] Equity/total assets is the end-year ratio of the sum of share capital and equity reserves to total assets.
[d] Liquid assets/total assets is the end-year ratio of liquid assets (the sum of cash and sums due from banks, deposits with central bank and other banks and government securities) to total assets. This ratio is calculated by Fitch-IBCA BankScope.
[e] Credit/GDP is the first difference in the ratio of domestic loans extended by the monetary financial institutions to the country's real GDP.

5.5   Conclusion and implications

This chapter has examined whether European banks are financially constrained and whether affiliation with other financial institutions can decrease those constraints. The results show that the lending of banks is sensitive to the changes in capital proxied by the changes in internal funds suggesting that banks face market frictions in raising external funds. The market frictions make banks' external capital more costly than their internally generated funds. The findings also indicate that affiliation with other financial intermediaries can lessen banks' financial constraints. The lending of banks with lower degrees of ownership affiliation is more dependent on internal funds than the lending of banks with higher levels of affiliation.

Overall, the results suggest a financial rationale for integration among banks and other financial institutions in the EU. The equity links allow the creation of internal capital markets among the financial intermediaries that help banks to mitigate financing and liquidity constraints by securing cheap and reliable sources of funds. The internal capital markets can permit banks to raise funds easily within internal capital markets and keep the level of lending unconstrained. This is particularly important since contraction of supply of bank loans may have a negative impact on the real sector. The presence of a reliable source of funds also suggests that banks will be less likely to maintain capital ratios in excess of the regulatory requirements. Group membership can also increase banks' participation in the loan sales market. Finally, the dependence of loan growth on internal funds indicates that there is a possibility of a bank lending channel in the EU. However, the role of internal capital markets in reducing market deficiencies predicts that banks with greater numbers and larger affiliations may neutralize monetary shocks.

Notes

1. Another explanation of the positive relationship between investment and internal funds is the influence of future demand conditions on investment. Because there is a positive correlation between the internal cash flow and current and future output, internal funds can considerably determine investments even in the absence of finance constraints (Chirinko and Schaller, 1995).
2. The bank's uninsured debt can also received implicit protection if the investors believe that their debt is insured *de facto* or the safety net provides a whole subsidy for the banks.
3. Total insurance coverage normally extends only to small deposit accounts. The limits on the insurance coverage is set to create incentives for the holders of large deposits to monitor their banks and demand higher interest rates from more riskier banks (Gilbert, 1990).
4. In the market microstructure literature the bid-ask spread on a security is taken as a measure of the information asymmetry between the seller and buyer of a stock, specifically, and between managers and outside investors, in general. In a stock exchange the specialist market-maker defines the quoted bid-ask spread taking into consideration all the variable and fixed costs of securities transaction. The costs normally include: (1) the cost of processing transaction; (2) the opportunity costs of holding a particular security; and (3) the adverse selection costs that reflect the costs of dealing with insider trading. Increased volume and liquidity of securities trading can decrease the first and second types of costs. The opportunity cost of stock-holding also has a negative correlation with price volatility. The presence of insider traders increases the adverse selection cost of securities trading. The market-maker widens the spread to compensate the possible losses from the different valuations of the stocks due to the insider information (Chilpakatti, 2001).

5. Alternative explanation of the relationship between the securities prices and bank behaviour is suggested by the market discipline literature. The spreads on banks' outstanding shares and bonds increase as the response to the increased level of banks' risks (BIS, 2003).

6. Because of illiquidity and high costs of trade of loans and the high costs of failure, banks have incentives to hold larger amount of capital (a buffer capital above the regulatory minimum) and liquid assets to avoid failure and engage in risk management (Froot and Stein, 1998). Banks may hold large proportion of capital in order to be able to borrow additional funds quickly and at less cost if new investment opportunities arise. At the same time, large capital stock can protect banks from unanticipated shocks, especially in situations where the financial distress costs of having a low capital position are relatively large and the asymmetric information and transaction costs of issuing new equity are high (Berger, Herring and Szego 1995).

7. We use the term capital in general form as accepted in the finance literature to indicate the sum of the equity and the debt.

8. The internal capital markets can reduce the information asymmetry among project managers and investors and provide better resource allocation across the projects. The internal capital markets can, however, itself generate agency problems and inefficient subsidizations across projects (Rajan, Servaes and Zingales 2000; Scharfstein and Stein, 2000).

9. De Haas and Naaborg (2005) provide an example of KBC Bank capital management in regards to the subsidiaries' capital needs. The managers of KBC explicitly stated that they do not wish their subsidiaries to raise expensive subordinated debt themselves. Instead, KBC provides its subsidiaries (Kredytbank in Poland, in particular) normal and perpetual subordinated debt to maintain Tier 2 capital.

10. The regulation sets the large exposure limits to prevent large concentration of portfolios. The regulation limits banks' exposure to a single counterparty or group of related parties. The limit is calculated as the proportion of the bank's equity capital. Such limits can vary among the countries. For example, in the EU the maximum limit is 25 per cent of the banks' Tier 1 and Tier 2 capital (see EU Directive 2000/12/CE). The parent company can soften the regulatory rules by injecting additional capital to the subsidiary (De Haas and Naaborg, 2005).

11. The study uses CAMEL rating to evaluate the financial condition of the banks.

12. In addition, regulation itself may prescribe the parent companies of the financial institutions to act as 'a source-of-strength' to a distressed banking subsidiary. For example, in the USA the Federal Reserve can direct a parent company to offer assistance to problem subsidiaries and can hold up a parent company's plans for expansion if the assistance was inadequate according to the Federal Reserve. The Bank Holding Company Act's (1956) Regulation Y [12 USC 225.4(a) (1)] states that a bank holding company is expected to act as source of managerial and financial strength to its subsidiaries (see Ashcraft, 2004, for discussion of the source-of-strength doctrine).

13. In the EU, conglomeration and universal banking are permitted by the Second Banking Directive which has been implemented by all member states. In this directive, banks, investment firms, and insurance companies may hold unlimited reciprocal equity participations. The holding of shares in non-financial firms is, however, subject to certain limits. Individual stakes in industrial and commercial firms should not exceed 15 per cent of the bank's capital, while the sum of these participations should remain below 60 per cent of the capital. See Directive 2000/12/EC and Directive 2002/87/EC.

14. Bankscope is a database maintained by Bureau Van Dijk. It provides business and financial information for bank and non-bank credit institutions around the world and contains significantly more data on financial institutions than alternative sources of information (Laeven and Levine, 2005).
15. Europe is defined as the EU-15 and includes Austria, Belgium, Denmark, Finland, France, Germany, Greece, Ireland, Italy, Luxembourg, the Netherlands, Portugal, Spain, Sweden, and the UK.
16. Bankscope classifies the credit institutions into 12 general categories: bank holding and holding company, commercial bank, cooperative bank, investment bank and securities house, medium- and long-term credit bank, non-banking credit institution, real estate and mortgage bank, savings bank, Islamic bank, specialized governmental credit institutions and multigovernmental specialized credit institutions. We eliminated the banks classified as Islamic banks and investment banks because of the different business model and incentives that underlie their operations. We also exclude the non-banking credit institution, the specialized and multigovernmental specialized credit institutions and bank and holding companies.
17. We estimate the fixed-effects specification that includes a dummy variable for each institution. All estimated equations included a set of dummy variables to control for differences in the constant term for each institution (not reported in the tables). The statistical tests indicate that the fixed-effects model is more appropriate for this application. The Hausman (1978) test rejects the random-effects specification relative to the fixed-effects specification.

References

Alchian, A. (1969). 'Corporate management and property rights', in H. Manne (ed.), *Economic Policy and the Regulation of Corporate Securities*, Washington, DC: American Enterprise Institute.

Akerlof, G. (1970). 'The market for lemons: Quality uncertainty and the market mechanism', *Quarterly Journal of Economics* 84(3), 488–500.

Ashcraft, A. (2001). 'New evidence on the lending channel', Federal Reserve Bank of New York Staff Report, no. 136.

Ashcraft, A. (2004). 'Are bank holding companies a source of strength to their banking subsidiaries?', Federal Reserve Bank of New York Staff Report, no. 189.

Basel Committee on Banking Supervisions (BIS) (2003). 'Markets for bank subordinated debt and equity in Basel Committee member countries', Bank for International Settlements Working Paper, no. 12.

Berger, A. N. and G. F. Udell (1993). 'Securitization, risk, and the liquidity problem in banking', in M. Klausner and L. White (ed.), *Structural Change in Banking*, Irwin, Homewood: IL.

Berger, A. N., R. J. Herring and G. P. Szego (1995). 'The role of capital in financial institutions', *Journal of Banking and Finance* 19, 393–430.

Bernanke, B. S. and A. Blinder (1992). 'The federal funds rate and the channels of monetary transmission', *American Economic Review* 82, 901–21.

Bernanke, B. S. and M. Gertler (1995). 'Inside the black box: The credit channel of monetary policy transmission', *Journal of Economic Perspectives* 9(4), 27–48.

Campello, M. (2002). 'Internal capital markets in financial conglomerates: Evidence from small bank responses to monetary policy', *Journal of Finance* 57(6), 2773–805.

Chilpakatti, N. (2001). 'Market microstructure effects of bank transparency: A preliminary examinatio', Ohio Northern University, College of Business Administration.

Chirinko, R. S. and H. Schaller (1995). 'Why does liquidity matter in investment equations', *Journal of Money, Credit and Banking* 27, 527–48.

Cornett, M., H. Mehran and H. Tehranian (1998). 'Are financial markets overly optimistic about the prospects of firms that issue equity? Evidence from voluntary versus involuntary equity issuances by banks', *Journal of Finance* 53(6), 2139–59.

Coase, R. H. (1937). 'The nature of the firm', *Economica* 4, 386–405.

Demsetz, H. and K. Lehn (1985). 'The structure of corporate ownership: Causes and consequences', *Journal of Political Economics* 93, 1155–77.

Demsetz, R. (2000). 'Bank loan sales: A new look at the motivations for secondary market activity', *Journal of Financial Research* 23, 197–222.

De Haas, R. and I. Naaborg (2005). 'Internal capital markets in multinational banks: Implications for European Transition Countries', De Nederlandsche Bank NV Working Paper, no. 051/2005.

Diamond, D. (1984). 'Financial intermediation and delegated monitoring', *Review of Economic Studies* 51, 393–414.

Diamond, D. and R. Verrecchia (1991). 'Disclosure, liquidity and the cost of capital', *Journal of Finance* 46(4), 1325–40.

Ehrmann, M. and A. Worms (2001). 'Interbank lending and monetary policy transmission: Evidence for Germany', European Central Bank Working Paper, series no. 73.

European Central Bank (2000). 'Mergers and acquisitions involving the EU banking industry – Facts and implications', December.

European Central Bank (2005). Monthly Bulletin, May.

Fazzari, S., G. Hubbard and B. Peterson (1988). 'Financing constraints and corporate investment', *Brookings Papers on Economic Activity* 1, 141–95.

Froot, K. and J. Stein (1998). 'Risk management, capital budgeting, and capital structure policy for financial institutions: an integrated approach', *Journal of Financial Economics* 47, 55–82.

Furlong, F. T. (1992). 'Capital regulation and bank lending', *Federal Reserve Bank of San Francisco Economic Review* 3, 23–33.

Gambacorta, L. (2005). 'Inside the bank lending channel', *European Economic Review* 49, 1737–59.

Gertner, R., D. Scharfstein and J. Stein (1994). 'Internal versus external capital markets', *Quarterly Journal of Economics* 109, 1211–30.

Gertler, M. and R. A. Gilbert (1991). 'Do bank holding companies act as a source of strength for their bank subsidiaries?', *Federal Reserve Bank of St. Louis Economic Review*, 3–18.

Gertler, M., and S. Gilchrist (1994). 'Monetary policy, business cycles, and the behaviour of small manufacturing firms', *Quarterly Journal of Economics* 109(2), 309–40.

Gilbert, R. A. (1990). 'Market discipline of bank risk: Theory and evidence', *Federal Reserve Bank of St. Louis Review*, January, 3–18.

Glosten, L. and P. Milgrom (1985). 'Bid, ask and transaction prices in a specialist market with heterogenously informed traders', *Journal of Financial Economics* 14, 72–100.

Grossman, S. J. and O. D. Hart (1986). 'The costs and benefits of ownership: A theory of vertical and lateral integration', *Journal of Political Economy* 94, 691–719.

Hall, B. J. (1993). 'How has the Basle Accord affected bank portfolios?', *Journal of Japanese and International Economics* 7, 408–40.

Haubrich, J. G., and P. Wachtel (1993). 'Capital requirements and shifts in commercial bank portfolios', *Federal Reserve Bank of Cleveland Economic Review* 29, 2–15.

Hausman, J. (1978). 'Specification tests in econometrics', *Econometrica* 46(6), 1251–71.

Holod, D. and J. Peek (2005). 'Capital constrains, asymmetric information, and internal capital markets in banking: new evidence', College of Business, SUNY – Stony Brook.

Houston, J. and C. James (1998). 'Do bank internal capital markets promote lending?', *Journal of Banking and Finance* 22, 899–918.

Houston, J., C. James and D. Marcus (1997). 'Capital market frictions and the role of internal capital markets in banking', *Journal of Financial Economics* 46, 135–64.

Hubbard, R. G. (1998). 'Capital-market imperfection and investment', *Journal of Economic Literature* 36, 193–225.

Hubbard, R. G., A. Kashyap and T. Whited (1995). 'Internal finance and firm investment', *Journal of Money, Credit and Banking* 27(3), 683–701.

Jayaratne, J. and D. P. Morgan (2000). 'Capital market frictions and deposit constrains at banks', *Journal of Money, Credit and Banking* 32(1), 74–92.

Jensen, M. (1986). 'Agency costs of free cash flow, corporate finance and takeovers', *American Economic Review* 76(2), 323–9.

Jensen, M. and W. Meckling (1976). 'Theory of the firm: Managerial behaviour, agency costs and ownership structure', *Journal of Financial Economics* 3(4), 305–60.

Joskow, P. (2003). 'Vertical integration', MIT Department of Economics.

Kashyap, A. and D. Stein (1995). 'The impact of monetary policy on bank balance sheet', *Carnegie-Rochester Series on Public Policy* 42, 151–95.

Klein, P. and M. R. Saindenberg (1997). 'Diversification, organization, and efficiency: Evidence from bank holding companies', University of Pennsylvania Wharton School Center for Financial Institutions Working Papers, no. 97–127.

La Porta, R., F. Lopez-de-Silanes and A. Shleifer (1999). 'Corporate ownership around the world', *Journal of Finance* 54, 471–517.

Laeven, L. and R. Levine (2005). 'Is there a diversification discount in financial conglomerates?', NBER Working Paper, no. 11499.

Liebeskind, J. P. (2000). 'Internal capital markets: Benefits, costs, and organizational arrangements', *Organization Science* 11(1), 58–76.

Modigliani, F. and M. H. Miller (1958). 'The cost of capital, corporation financing and the theory of investment', *American Economic Review* 48, 261–97.

Modigliani, F. and M. H. Miller (1963). 'Taxes and the cost of capital: A correction', *American Economic Review* 53, 433–43.

Myers, S. and N. Majluf (1984). 'Corporate financing and investment decisions when firms have information that investors do not have', *Journal of Financial Economics* 13(2), 187–221.

Park, S. (2006). 'Effects of stock mispricing and regulatory capital constraints on bank lending', *Journal of Economics and Business* 58, 137–52.

Rajan, R., H. Servaes and L. Zingales (2000). 'The cost of diversity: The diversification discount and inefficient investment', *Journal of Finance* 55, 35–80.

Ritter, Jay R. (1998). 'Initial public offerings', University of Florida Working Paper, Gainesville.

Ross, S. A. (1977). 'The determination of financial structure: The incentive-signalling approach', *Bell Journal of Economics* 8(1), 23–40.

Rothschild, M. and J. Stiglitz (1976). 'Equilibrium in competitive insurance markets: An essay on the economics of imperfect information', *Quarterly Journal of Economics* 90(4), 630–49.

Saunders, A. and I. Walter (1994). *Universal Banking in the United States*, New York: Oxford University Press.

Scharfstein, D. and J. Stein (2000). 'The dark side of internal capital markets: Divisional rent seeking and inefficient investment', *Journal of Finance* 55, 2537–64.

Shrieves, R. E. and D. Dahl (1995). 'Regulation, recession, and bank lending behaviour: The 1990 credit crunch', *Journal of Financial Services Research* 9, 5–30.

Stein, J. C. (1997). 'Internal capital markets and the competition for corporate resources', *Journal of Finance* 52, 111–33.

Stein, J. C. (1998). 'An adverse-selection model of bank asset and liability management with implications for the transmission of monetary policy', *RAND Journal of Economics* 29, 466–86.

Stiglitz, J. and A. Weiss (1981). 'Credit rationing in markets with imperfect information', *American Economic Review* 71(3), 393–410.

Van den Heuvel, S. (2004). 'The bank capital channel of monetary policy', Department of Finance, The Wharton School, University of Pennsylvania.

Williamson, O. (1975). *Markets and Hierarchies: Analysis and Antitrust Implications*, New York: Free Press.

Williamson, O. (1979). 'Transaction cost economics: The governance of contractual relations', *Journal of Law and Economics* 22, 233–61.

6
Banks in the Microfinance Market

*Mario La Torre and Gianfranco Vento** [*]

6.1 Introduction[1]

In recent years, microfinance has taken over from the concept of microcredit. The fight against extreme poverty has become part of a wider objective in the fight against financial exclusion. The supply of products includes other financial services and technical assistance, as well as microcredit. Together with international donors and traditional NGOs, other typologies of microfinance institutions (MFIs) and commercial banks are now present on the market.

The entry of banks and other specialized profit-oriented institutions into the microfinance market has stressed the trade-off between the objectives of economic and financial equilibrium on the one hand, and the social goals of microfinance projects on the other. From this point of view, the chapter offers a new taxonomy for modern microfinance and discusses the definitions of 'sustainability' and 'outreach', identifying the various meanings of these broad concepts. It also analyses the key variables and the operational and management choices that a commercial bank should consider in order to reconcile the aims of sustainability with those of outreach, so as to implement 'ethically profitable' microfinance programmes.

6.2 A new conception of microfinance: the role of commercial banks

The expression 'microfinance' most commonly denotes the supply of modest financial services to zero- or low-income clients. Thus, broadly speaking, any small-scale activity characterized by limited funds and low-income beneficiaries may fall into the field of microfinance. Traditionally, microfinance is associated with programmes which benefit clients with

* University of Rome 'La Sapienza'

serious subsistence problems, mostly located in developing countries. For many years microfinance overlapped with microcredit – small loans, often without traditional guarantees, aimed at improving the life of clients and their families or at sustaining small-scale economic activities. The resources, which came mainly from funds donated by states and supra-national organizations, were channelled to their recipients most often through non-governmental organizations (NGOs), as well as local partners (Figure 6.1).

It is, in fact, a shared procedure that NGOs and donor countries operate together with other locally based organizations, such as municipalities, governments, development agencies or others from the third sector, which also help to better identify the needs of local communities as well as to facilitate the screening and management of credit positions. In order to reduce the physical, and often cultural, gap between intermediaries who provide credit and the beneficiaries of the microcredit, many institutions have recourse to a network of local promoters, known as 'loan officers', who visit potential clients to gather information during the selection and monitoring phases and, later, to collect instalments for loans granted.

Sociodemographic changes over the last few decades have significantly altered the world economic scene. For microfinance, the new situation has meant potential new beneficiaries, new products, and a greater involvement of financial intermediaries. Exclusion from the traditional financial system, seen as the inability to access basic financial services, effects millions of people today, both in developing countries and industrialized ones. Traditional poverty thresholds have shifted and new categories of 'poor' people have appeared, even outside developing countries. New beneficiaries have brought new financial needs with them. Over the past decade, new microfinance services have developed alongside microcredit. This development has also gained momentum from the observation that a more structured financial assistance increases the efficacy of the programmes, while at the same time improving the level of sustainability. The widening of the supplied services has taken at least six directions: credit products that represent alternatives to traditional loans, savings, payment services, insurance

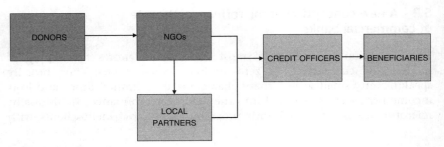

Figure 6.1   The standard microcredit structure

services, structured finance, and technical assistance. It is not surprising, therefore, that in the last few years financial intermediaries in industrialized countries have been taking greater notice of microfinance. It represents a way of reaching and gaining loyalty from new groups of clients and helps to improve corporate social responsibility.

6.2.1 The demand for microfinance

Thus, in the last few years microfinance has served different typologies of beneficiaries, largely distinct from the ones normally associated with micro-credit. Currently, potential microfinance beneficiaries could also include individuals who, although not living in poverty, experience a general difficulty in gaining access to the financial system. In this way, modern microfinance is broadening its target from 'the poorest of the poor' to all victims of financial exclusion. The phenomenon of financial exclusion has been defined in the literature as 'the inability to access financial services in an appropriate way' (Gardener, Molyneux and Carbo, 2004). Exclusion from the financial system may concern different products and services and can be due to a number of reasons. Firstly, there is *self-exclusion* which stems, in principle, from an individual's feeling of inadequacy with regard to the conditions required by financial intermediaries; 'the poorest of the poor' come under this category. Distance from the financial system may also be due to the failure of potential clients to meet creditworthiness requirements. In this case, we can refer to *access exclusion*, or exclusion following a risk assessment process carried out on clients by the financial intermediaries; in this category we find 'the poor'. 'The poorest of the poor' and 'the poor' are the two categories which represent the traditional target of microcredit programmes. However, as previously mentioned, sociodemographic as well as economic changes have heightened the significance of other forms of financial exclusion and have put forward potential new microfinance beneficiaries.

Exclusion from the financial system can be the consequence of exclusion from the sociopolitical system (*political and social exclusion*): the victims of this are, for example, immigrants or ex-convicts and those who are 'unregistered' and, consequently, 'not bankable'. Furthermore, there are individuals who cannot gain access to the financial system because they are unable to bear the costs and conditions of financial products offered. In this case, the 'disadvantaged' individuals are subject to a *condition exclusion*. Finally, another form of financial exclusion can be identified in those cases in which customers (mainly small-scale entrepreneurs) are considered 'marginal' by the intermediaries since they represent a low-value target when considered according to the traditional customer evaluation models (*marketing exclusion*). The 'unregistered', the 'disadvantaged' and the 'marginalized', despite their common distance from the traditional credit system, are characterized, ex ante, by increasing levels of professional skills and managerial ability, and, therefore, they demonstrate respective increasing levels of creditworthiness. The categories of beneficiaries thus identified are entitled to microfinance support as individuals or in groups. The assistance given to individuals recalls the traditional financing of sole proprietorship and micro-enterprises, whereas the support offered to groups resembles more closely the financing of associations and cooperatives.

The continuing involvement of 'unregistered', 'disadvantaged' and 'marginalized' people determines a greater complexity of the financial structure in microfinance programmes, as well as a greater involvement of financial intermediaries and, thus, a more decisive move away from the traditional patterns of microcredit.

6.2.2   The supply of microfinance

The institutions traditionally involved in microfinance are varied both from an institutional point of view and as far as their aims and objectives are concerned. Among the wide range of definitions adoptable for microfinance institutions, we here propose a taxonomy based on a regulatory approach. From a regulatory perspective, microfinance institutions can be classified into three main categories, depending on the regulatory thresholds of their organizational structures: informal, semi-formal and formal.

Informal institutions (self-help groups, credit associations, families, individual money lenders) properly do not have the status of institutions. They are providers of microfinance services on a voluntary basis and are not subject to any kind of control or regulation. *Semi-formal institutions* are usually registered entities, subject to all relevant general laws. They can be defined as microfinance financial intermediaries (MFFIs) and they represent the most traditional category of MFI: they are mostly credit-only institutions which provide various financial services but, generally, they do not collect deposits or, alternatively, they cannot grant credit, as is the case with postal saving banks. Therefore, MFFIs are subject to financial regulatory requirements, according to the wideness of their financial intermediation activities, but they are not under banking regulation. Within this category, it is possible to include different types of institutions with different structural and organizational complexity (financial NGOs, financial cooperatives, credit unions, postal saving banks). The most popular and widespread are, however, financial NGOs that operate principally by offering microcredit as part of development projects, often combined with the offer of technical assistance and other 'social intervention' for beneficiaries. To this aim the NGOs make use, in part or entirely, of funds donated by supranational institutions and agencies, as well as from donor states. Some of the most developed NGOs offer different types of financial services, raise private funds, and collect 'forced savings' from their clients. Finally, *formal institutions* can be further classified into three main categories:

- microfinance banks (MFBs)
- microfinance oriented banks (MFOBs)
- microfinance sensitive banks (MFSBs).

They can all offer credit and they are all deposit-taking institutions: for these reasons, they are all under banking regulation. Within MFBs, it is possible to list a limited number of pure microfinance banks (PMFBs), cooperative banks, and development banks.

PMFBs are banks specialized in offering only microfinance services. These may be the result of the upscaling of NGOs specialized in microcredit that have converted to banks in order to maximize the economic sustainability of their initiatives and widen their client base. Alternatively, such intermediaries may result from a process of privatization of public banks, with the aim of providing financial support to the local community. Lastly, they may be newly created banks which aim to enter into the microfinance market, attracted by the large profits and positive performances achieved by intermediaries specialized in micro-enterprises.

Microfinance services can also be offered by different types of cooperative institutions, which operate exclusively, or mainly, for the benefit of their own members. These include more organized credit unions – such as those based in the United Kingdom and Ireland – which offer credit and other services to their own members; the Rotating Savings and Credit Associations (ROSCAs), more common in developing countries, which provide rotating credit to their own members using resources from a centralized fund made available by the savings of the members themselves; and cooperative credit banks. Despite their differences, the common characteristics of these institutions lie in the legal status of cooperative companies and in the possibility to collect time deposits, mainly through partners. The chance to offer demand deposits, on the other hand, is largely prohibited by regulatory authorities, due to the higher complexity that would derive for those institutions in liquidity management, as well as for the higher contribution to the systemic risk. Development banks are large, centralized, and usually government-owned banks created to support specific sectors (small business development banks) or geographic areas (rural development banks); in some developing countries they can also take the form of private banks. Finally, in recent years, within formal microfinance institutions, it has been possible to include some commercial banks, banking groups and financial conglomerates. Here, two categories of intermediaries can be identified: microfinance-oriented banks and microfinance-sensitive banks.

In the area of microfinance-oriented banks it is possible to group together all the banks or financial institutions which are specialized in financing small to medium enterprises and micro-enterprises, and which are therefore professionally inclined to take an active part in microfinance programmes. These are mainly small, local banks, strongly rooted in the local territory, as well as financial institutions which come directly from local bodies. Finally, in the sphere of microfinance-sensitive banks it is possible to place all the banks and financial intermediaries that, for economic reasons or for the positive externalities deriving for their own image, view microfinance as an attractive opportunity. These consist, mainly, of banking groups, particularly large ones, or financial conglomerates which decide to enter into the micro-finance sector – downscaling their traditional activities – albeit to a limited extent compared to their own core business, creating specific companies or specialized divisions within their organizations.

6.2.3   Products and services in microfinance

Traditional microcredit programmes have based their success on simple structures. The progressive extension of target beneficiaries, from the category of the 'poorest of the poor' to that of 'disadvantaged people', has brought about the need to combine credit supply with the offer of other services. This requirement is based on two main factors: on the one hand, new target beneficiaries mean new financial needs to be met; on the other hand, some categories of entrepreneurs, especially disadvantaged and marginalized people, have a greater ability in organizing themselves in groups and bring about a greater complexity in the organization and running of the financed group. This, in turn, is combined with more sophisticated financial needs and calls for stricter controls by the microlenders.

For these reasons, it is necessary, in the context of modern microfinance programmes, to put in place a financial framework which provides other services, as well as supplying credit. These can be categorized as financial services in the strict sense or extended to non-financial services. In the first case, it is possible to identify the offer of deposits, as well as of insurance products. The need to channel the savings of beneficiaries appears stronger as the 'bankability' of the beneficiary himself increases, mainly because the percentage of the profits generated through their entrepreneurial activity, and not used for the self-subsistence of the customer, increases. Moreover, a higher rate of 'bankability' of the beneficiary generally coincides with a more structured organization that often outlives the project and that, to be sustainable, requires the setting up of a complete financial cycle. In this way, insurance products are also designed, on the one hand, to cover the specific technical and financial risks of the project and, on the other, can be extended to the whole economic activity of the financed companies.

Moreover, the organization of beneficiaries in cooperatives, or in other structured organizations, often goes with greater managerial autonomy. In such cases, the role of the investor is two-fold: to put controls in place to check respect of good managerial criteria, and to provide technical assistance to the project activities. Such assistance may concern the financial and administrative management, but can be extended to offering specific non-financial services. It is not uncommon, for example, for such well-organized beneficiaries need support in the commercialization and distribution of products, in particular when the sustainability of the project requires an opening into markets outside the local context.

6.2.4   A new taxonomy for microfinance

In light of the classifications made, it is possible to build a matrix of modern microfinance determined by the possible combinations of 'beneficiaries-services-institutions' (Figure 6.2). The new scenario identifies different business areas in the field of microfinance determined by the combination 'beneficiaries-services', each of which is relevant for specific categories of intermediaries. It is underlined that as the level of 'bankability' of beneficiaries increases the package of services which accompanies a microfinance programme is progressively more structured. In the same way, the involvement of microfinance financial intermediaries is increasingly supported by the intervention of other financial intermediaries.

In particular, MFFIs focus their activity on the 'poorest of the poor', the 'poor', and the 'unregistered', limiting the financial services offered to credit, insurance cover, and technical assistance, and only in a few cases to forced savings from beneficiaries. Conversely, formal MFBs find their most natural

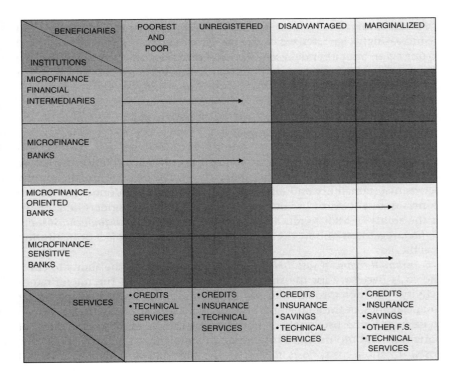

Figure 6.2   A taxonomy for a modern microfinance

targets, in 'disadvantaged' and 'marginalized' beneficiaries, and are involved in programmes with more structured products and more complex and consolidated financial structures.

It is useful to consider, however, that in recent microfinance experience it is possible to identify a trend which highlights operating models which are not easily classifiable. In particular, we are witnessing a crossover movement which is seeing a greater involvement of MFBs in programmes destined for 'the poorest of the poor', the 'poor', and the 'unregistered', and a parallel involvement of NGOs and other microfinance financial intermediaries in programmes aimed towards 'disadvantaged' or 'marginalized' beneficiaries. In fact, for microfinance-oriented banks and microfinance-sensitive banks in particular, the need to find new and more efficient ways of channelling and managing funds creates space for intervention even in programmes which are less structured, aimed at the poorest and the unregistered. At the same time, the efficacy of more structured programmes is increased by the contribution of microfinance financial intermediaries which contribute their local knowledge, important for improving relations between the intermediary and the beneficiary, as well as technical and operative expertise which is useful in the planning and monitoring of the project.

For the future, it is possible to foresee that microfinance programmes will be increasingly characterized by the presence of investors that are not linked to one actor, but rather represent a pool of mixed institutions which may see the presence of informal, semi-formal, and formal financial intermediaries at the same time.

6.3   Sustainability and outreach: can banks make ethical profit from microfinance?

The entry of banks and private investors into the microfinance market, as well as the increasing scarcity of public funds, has brought the dichotomy between sustainability and outreach to the attention of donors and practitioners in recent years. In microfinance, sustainability is understood, firstly, as the ability of MFIs to repeat loans over time (*substantial financial sustainability*), regardless of how the financial stability of the project or institution is achieved.

Substantial financial sustainability (Figure 6.3) describes the ability to cover the costs necessary for the start-up and management of the microfinance activity, whether through the profits from services offered, in particular financial ones, or through grants and soft loans. In a stricter sense, therefore, to be financially sustainable, a project or institution must receive a flow of donations and profits, from interest and commission, that cover operating costs, inflation costs, costs related to the portfolio devaluation, financial costs, a risk premium, and the return on capital brought by project investors or MFI shareholders.

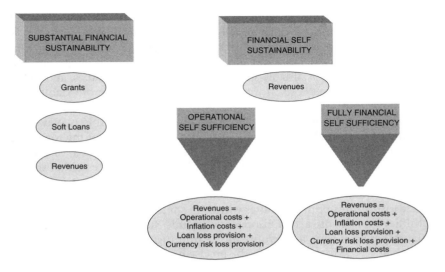

Figure 6.3   Different levels of microfinance sustainability

Financial self-sustainability should not be confused with substantial financial sustainability. When we refer to substantial financial sustainability, grants and subsidized funds are also included among the items which contribute to cover costs and to stabilize the income of a MFI; whereas, with financial self-sustainability, grants and soft loans are not considered in assessing the independent ability of the institution to cover costs. With regard to financial self-sustainability, it is necessary to further distinguish between *operational self-sufficiency* (where the operating income covers operating costs, the cost of inflation, loan loss provisions and currency risk loss provisions) and *fully financial self-sufficiency* (where the operating income is enough to cover not only operating costs, inflation costs and provisions, but also the financing costs which include debt costs and adjusted cost of capital).

Analysing sustainability is important for any type of business or economic activity undertaken. However, in microfinance and for MFIs especially, it represents a crucial element for two reasons. Firstly, MFIs work with marginalized clientele, who are not accepted in the formal financial system as they are considered too risky and not profitable enough. Therefore, it would be logical to assume that the institutions which decide to work with such clientele have greater problems in covering costs with an adequate profit flow in the medium to long term.

Secondly, the operating costs necessary for the screening of trustworthy individuals and small business and the monitoring of those borrowers are such that when compared to the profit made from a single client, they could show little advantage in working for such small amounts. However, a project or an institution may be substantially financially sustainable, in that it is able to attract a constant flow of subsidized funds over time which significantly reduce financial costs and allow the profits to cover residual costs, but not financially self-sustainable since, due to the lack of subsidies, and therefore funded at market costs, it would be unable to achieve profit stability.

It follows that, in analysing sustainability and in distinguishing between substantial sustainability and self-sustainability, a central role is played by subsidies, from which, in different ways, the vast majority of microfinance programmes and MFIs have benefited. In fact, although the goal of leaving aside the donors' funds has been considered by many as an essential step in order to make microfinance a stable instrument to sustain the poorest people, as well as those financially excluded, there are few cases of microfinance institutions or programmes which, in some form, have never received subsidies and are in a condition of economic stability. The search for a balance between costs and profits in the running of MFIs brings us back to the debate in the literature about the precise nature of microfinance. Thus, it is important to examine more closely the type of aims and benefits that should inspire microfinance programmes, and which are addressed towards *outreach*.

Although the literature offers various taxonomies of the values that express outreach, it is possible to define the concept in two partially opposing ways: *depth* and *breadth* (Figure 6.4). Depth represents the poverty level of the beneficiaries involved, whereas breadth concerns the number of clients reached. In the first case, in terms of overall benefit, outreach towards poorer beneficiaries is preferred in spite of the total number of potential customers. Assuming that in social welfare the community prioritizes the poorest individuals, the depth of a microfinance involvement is proportional to the net benefit that derives from the offer of financial services to those people. The basic idea is that, for the poorest individuals, the benefit of receiving a loan is greater than for people at a higher social level. On the

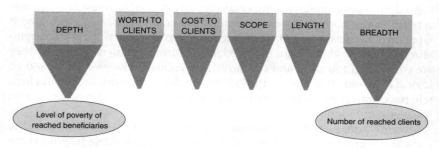

Figure 6.4   Dimensions of microfinance outreach

other hand, priority to breadth implies a preference towards a wider consideration of customers, although they are not all categorized as 'the poorest of the poor'. In a context in which the demand for financial services from the poorest and the financially excluded people is higher than the supply, the ability to reach a larger number of beneficiaries becomes a goal itself.

In the literature, other aspects of outreach are often mentioned, which, however, are referable to simple proxies of breadth and depth. An important initial indicator of the depth of the programme is the loan amount, since most financially excluded clients tend to ask for smaller loans. Furthermore, outreach can be considered as *worth to clients*, that is, an indication of the client's attitude towards paying for services, since these significantly meet their own financial needs. It indicates the maximum amount that the borrower would reach in order to obtain a loan. A poorer beneficiary obviously accepts to pay more. A greater *worth to clients* may correspond to greater depth.

The third variable of outreach consists in the *cost to clients* for the financial services achieved. This represents the cost of the loan for the debtor. It is the sum of direct cash payments for interest and fees, plus transaction costs. Generally, the cost to client is positively related to depth, because, in theory, greater depth implies riskier clients as well as fixed operating costs are shared by a smaller number of beneficiaries. The fourth proxy of outreach is *scope*, that is, the number of typologies of financial contracts supplied by MFIs.

The fifth profile of outreach regards the *length* of the microfinance programme. It represents the period of time during which microfinance services are offered. An indirect proxy of length is the obtainment of profits that guarantee the carrying out of the programmes, even without lasting donations. The underlying idea is that the offer of microfinance should not run out in a short space of time. Consequently, it is assumed that the offer is positively correlated to profits generated by MFIs. The greater the variety of the products and financial services that are offered, the greater is the length of operations and, presumably, the greater is the outreach. Scope and length, however, can be associated to programmes which prioritize depth as well as those that focus on breadth.

6.3.1 The microfinance dilemma: Sustainability versus outreach

As stated in the previous paragraphs, sustainability represents the essential prerequisite for MFIs – especially for microfinance banks which by definition are profit-oriented – to continue to provide their services in the medium and long term, as any other firm. On the other hand, in cases of financial exclusion – in which the demand for financial services from disadvantaged individuals greatly exceeds the supply – an analysis concerning outreach is necessary in order to address the resources, which are by definition scarce, towards financing productive micro-activities that are able to provide the highest return.

In the literature and among practitioners, sustainability and outreach have been deepened in order to verify the existence of a trade-off between the objectives of economic and financial equilibrium and the social goals. Considerations concerning a preference towards providing stronger support to depth goals rather than breadth goals are typical dilemmas in welfare economy, which are difficult to deal with without an exhaustive analysis of the context. Furthermore, it is common to find an orientation in the literature aiming to stress the need to carry out corner choices between sustainability objectives and outreach goals. Hence, this chapter avoids revisiting a historical debate regarding the priority to be assigned to different models of outreach and their compatibility with sustainability. Instead, it is more useful to examine the managerial aspects that allow one to find a better equilibrium between sustainability and outreach.

The dimensions of outreach must be taken into account by those who intend to put together a microfinance programme, but should be evaluated in the context of single programmes or the medium- and long-term strategies of MFIs. According to MFIs' codes of conduct, the different aspects of outreach can have different relevance, by increasing, falling, or even being cancelled.

Pricing policies adopted by MFIs, and in particular by microfinance banks, show the dichotomy between sustainability and outreach. When, for example, an institution decides to improve sustainability, by raising clients' commissions, there is the risk of not reaching all potential beneficiaries with the service; consequently, the value of breadth goes down, whereas the value of depth increases. In this case, the cost to the user increases because the increase in operational costs is transferred to the customers. When a MFI decides to keep the cost to user low, this means a decrease in operating margins and consequently in length – and ultimately in sustainability.

If an MFI, including microfinance banks, fixes high interest rates to cover operating and funding costs, both depth and breadth risk being affected. In this case, applying interest rates higher than the market ones can be justified by the fact that, for financed individuals, the financial costs are totally compensated by the benefits deriving from access to the credit. If, instead, a MFI, in trying to keep interest rates on credit low for outreach purposes, cannot achieve full sustainability, it is likely to create some distorting effects. In fact, firstly, the offer of financial services, especially microcredits, at lower interest rates than the market, distorts competition between those financed by MFIs who take this approach and the micro-enterprises which are financed in market conditions. Moreover, the fact of not achieving full sustainability leads some MFIs over time, and in particular microfinance oriented banks and microfinance sensitive banks, to leave the market, which can cause serious problems for clients who had deposited savings with them but also for the micro-enterprises that lose their prevalent source of funding.

However, it is useful to underline how for some categories of beneficiaries the dichotomy between sustainability and outreach is less important. In fact, non-bankable individuals who are able to create products and services that can be placed on the market, are able to obtain margins for which the difference between the cost of funding, available at market rates, and the higher one actually obtained from the MFIs, does not have a significant effect. In this way, supposing that the microcredit beneficiary – being a small producer by definition and therefore unable to shift the supply curve as a price-taker – has the productive capability to achieve significant margins, he will be able to pay higher interest rates during the period in which he will continue to be considered unbankable, and at the same time he will remain in economic equilibrium. If, however, the spread between the market rate and that applied by MFIs could jeopardize the profitability, and therefore the sustainability of the funded micro-enterprises, it is unadvisable to proceed with the funding both in the interest of the beneficiary and also of the MFI.

6.4   Policies for improving sustainability: a lesson for banks and traditional MFIs

In analysing sustainability in managerial terms, the balance between revenues and costs in offering microfinance services can be seen as a matter of analysis and improvement of the performance over time. From this perspective, it results in being a crucial issue, especially for profit-oriented banks entering the microfinance market. Thus, here we present three key variables that, among others, can determine the success of a microfinance programme run by traditional MFIs as well as banks.

6.4.1   Portfolio management

With regard to profits, the main source of income in microfinance, and in some cases the only one, is the interest from the loans portfolio and related commission. For this reason, it is vital for MFIs' stability that they maintain a high-quality credit portfolio and adequate credit risk management in order to minimize loan losses. It has often been verified that the average quality of MFIs' loan portfolios are, in many cases, higher than that of formal financial intermediaries working in the same operational context. These elements, besides shattering the myth that less wealthy borrowers are not good clients, highlights a more effective incentive system to repay, a better credit selection process and a subsequent improved monitoring by microfinance banks and institutions, compared to traditional intermediaries, which should be better recognized.

As far as the selection process is concerned, the elements that seem to affect the quality of the portfolio the most can be identified in the proximity and deep acquaintance between the MFIs' credit officers and the funded borrowers, in the use of specific technicalities conceived for microfinance – such as peer monitoring, dynamic incentives, and so on – and in the decision to lend to customers who have technical and operating skills but lack of funds. Instead, the quality of monitoring on the financed borrowers significantly depends on the ability and reliability of the credit officers, on the existence of at least two levels of control and, more generally, on the analysis and standardization of processes, which even smaller MFIs must somehow formalize. Furthermore, monitoring is made more efficient and timely by technological development, which allows MFIs to process a significant amount of data in less time and at a lower cost, like traditional intermediaries. The considerations made above do not rule out the possibility that MFIs should further improve credit management and operational procedures. Thus, the contribution that banks entering the microfinance market and other financial intermediaries can offer to traditional MFIs may have a great importance: the use of risk measurement and management models used by banks and the outsourcing of some phases of the production process may, in fact, be the key to a more efficient management. In this regard, there is a number of downscaling commercial banks that are starting to operate with financially excluded segments by using more simplified methodologies compared to those used with retail customers, but only with those clients previously selected by MFIs' partners.

6.4.2   Pricing policy

Interest rate policies are one of the most disputed topics in microfinance. In defining interest rates and commissions, banks and traditional MFIs cannot neglect the need to cover the costs of funding, the operational costs to be spread on each loan, the devaluation of purchasing power of currency due to inflation, loan losses and currency loss provisions, and a risk premium to remunerate for business risk.

In addition, the process of fixing interest rates must also consider a further four factors. First, microfinance banks and institutions must consider the pricing policies adopted by other intermediaries, formal and non-formal, operating in the same context, in order to avoid offering products too far from market conditions, and thus risking lack of demand. Second, like practices in use in traditional intermediaries, interest rate policies should reflect the higher or lower recovery rate implicit in the different technical lending products, considering the existence of collateral or other factors that may determine a pre-emption right for MFIs in case of default of the borrower. Furthermore, the fixing of interest rates cannot avoid considerations regarding triggering adverse selection and moral hazard processes, where interest rate levels are considered too high by the borrowers. Finally, the experience of many microfinance programmes carried out at particularly favourable interest rates have shown how such programmes attract different individuals from the original beneficiaries to apply for a loan; this leads to very modest performance levels for MFIs.

Therefore, in order to achieve pricing which meets sustainability objectives, MFIs must consider both internal management variables and external market variables. However, it is also true that a greater efficiency in the credit process and in the measuring of credit risk by MFIs could contribute to reduce, other conditions being constant, the cost to users without compromising sustainability. Also in this case, collaboration with banks and other financial intermediaries could help traditional MFIs in such strategic activities.

6.4.3 Efficiency

On the cost front, the situation seems equally critical, since it is affected by the contexts in which the different banks and traditional MFIs decide to work. As far as financial costs are concerned, the vast majority of traditional MFIs, as previously mentioned, are highly dependent on external funds, in the form of subsidies and soft loans. These funds have very low or no costs but are somehow unstable and uncertain over time, depending on donors' evaluations, on which MFIs have no influence. Therefore, obtaining subsidies is not necessarily a negative factor in itself; it is actually useful for sustainability. What is worrying is the unpredictability of these subsidies. Thus, the efficiency of a traditional MFI should not be measured so much on a lower dependence on grants and loans, as on the capability to keep these funding sources stable over time. This capability represents an intangible asset for MFIs that allows for a lower cost to the user and facilitates the goal of sustainability. Moreover, given that most of the MFIs that are not self-sustainable receive external subsidies, a deeper analysis of the optimization of subsidies is necessary. In this regard, it is believed that subsidies should mainly be finalized to finance the start-up phases of MFIs, bridging the gap between revenues, which at the start-up stage are usually not enough, and costs. Vice versa, if subsidies were used by banks and MFIs to keep the intermediation costs low, the effect of this policy would be to distort allocation processes, to alter market competition, and probably to worsen the portfolio quality in the long run.

In the same way, the capacity to differentiate sources of funding should be evaluated. Many MFIs, with the aim of reducing their dependence on external funds, have for a long time extended their activity in collecting savings from the public. From this perspective, microfinance banks have a greater advantage compared to traditional MFIs. In fact, experience has shown in practice how even the poorest individuals have a savings capability, often not held in monetary form. Such savings, if reintroduced in the financial system, could usefully contribute to funding investment projects. The collection of deposits, however, is not always permitted by prudential regulations to all typologies of MFIs, and, nevertheless, it exposes the depositor to the risks deriving from the misuse of funds by MFIs in excessively risky business, triggering agency problems. Finally, the reduction of funding costs can also be achieved through recourse to types of collection related to ethical finance, not as yet exploited much by MFIs, with particular reference to the collection of Ethical Investment Funds and Ethical Pension Funds.

The second variable that affects the efficiency of MFIs, including microfinance banks, and their capability to exist is their ability to keep operational costs low. Managing numerous microloans as well as the high-frequency repayment of loan instalments entails a significantly high level of operational costs, mainly due to personnel costs. The main effort of the most sustainable MFIs, therefore, is focused once again on the standardization of procedures, without transforming the universally acknowledged strong points of microfinance, such as close contact and deep mutual acquaintance between institutions and beneficiaries. Even in this sphere, interaction with banks and other financial intermediaries can be the key to success.

The factors discussed do not cover the full panorama of policies towards improving sustainability. The solutions offered by the market for sustainable outreach are many and varied. As such, the microfinance market must look more trustingly towards the traditional financial systems. The expansion of a network between the non-profit sector and the profit sector could help the search for other alternative solutions, which are able to exploit all the processes and products of financial innovation that are available in more developed financial markets.

On the other hand, so far the policies to expand sustainability described here are actually implemented by a very small number of formal MFIs. The creation of a structured network, and a greater collaboration between traditional MFIs and banks willing to enter the microfinance market would allow semi-formal and formal institutions to improve their own operations and to enhance their operating and management standards.

6.5   Conclusion

In recent years the microfinance market has experienced many important changes. The beneficiaries of support are no longer only poor people in developing countries. The offer of products includes other financial services and technical assistance, as well as microcredit. Together with donors and non-profit institutions, microfinance institutions, banks and other traditional financial intermediaries are present on the market. Therefore, modern microfinance offers more alternatives compared to the past experience of microcredit as it: targets a wider potential number of beneficiaries; tailors interventions to the effective needs and characteristics of clients and in selected intervention areas; allows for more structured financial and technical assistance.

In the face of growing financial sophistication, greater transparency and more efficient management system, microfinance risks losing its real nature of immediacy and ethicality which mark its origins. The search for a balance between the sustainability objectives of microfinance institutions and the pursuit of social aims represents a big trade-off in microfinance. This contrast is inspired by two different theoretical approaches, on the basis of which microfinance is seen either as a method of diversifying the offer of financial services to financially excluded individuals, or as an instrument to support the development of the poorest sectors of the population.

The discussion between supporters of sustainability and defenders of outreach seems best represented by a scheme in which some MFIs focus on the social mission, while others, mainly microfinance banks, put the economic mission first. This means that the first type of institutions must somehow be subsidized, whereas the second can progress towards self-sufficiency. The analysis of the determining factors of sustainability and outreach has shown that there are operating and managerial policies which can bring together these apparently conflicting objectives. Traditional policies can be aided by more innovative solutions when microfinance operators form profitable collaborations with banks and other financial intermediaries. An integrated network for microfinance, which is now experienced in several countries, represents the most advanced and tangible way towards sustainable outreach.

Encouraging the development of microfinance, today, means especially to find operational and managerial models able to yield balanced cooperation between the non-profit system and the traditional financial system. The practitioners and the institutions of microfinance have to benefit from the expertise of banks and financial intermediaries to achieve a higher level of efficiency in resource management. Financial intermediaries can regain, with microfinance experience, proximity to local territories and customer care. Together, the non-profit system and the traditional financial system must collaborate to achieve the highest level of ethicality of financial intermediation for microfinance, compatible with the objectives of sustainability and performance.

Note

1. Although the chapter has been jointly written by both authors, paragraph 2 is attributed to Mario La Torre, and paragraphs 3 and 4 to Gianfranco Vento.

References

Armendariz de Aghion, B. and J. Morduch (2005). *The Economics of Microfinance*, Cambridge, MA: The MIT Press.

Calderon, M. L. (2002). *Microcréditos. De pobres a microempresarios*, Barcelona: Editorial Ariel.

Carbo, S., T. Gardener and P. Molyneux (2005). *Financial Exclusion*, Basingstoke: Palgrave Macmillan.

Gardener, T., P. Molyneux and S. Carbo (2004). 'Financial exclusion: A comparative study', Paper presented to the 2004 Annual Conference of 'European Association of University Teachers of Banking and Finance' Krakow, Poland.

Harper, M. (ed.) (2003). *Microfinance: Evolution, Achievements and Challenges*, London: ITDG Publishing.

Hulme, D. and P. Mosley (1996). *Finance Against Poverty*, vols 1 and 2, London: Routledge.

Jenkins, H. (2000). 'Commercial bank behaviour in micro and small enterprise finance', Development Discussion Paper, no. 741, Harvard Institute for International Development, February.

La Torre, M. and G. A. Vento (2005). 'Per una nuova microfinanza: il ruolo delle banche', *Bancaria*, no. 2.

La Torre, M. and G. A. Vento (2006). *Microfinance*, Basingstoke: Palgrave Macmillan.

Ledgerwood, J. (1999). *Microfinance Handbook*, Geneva: The World Bank.

Rhyne, E. and M. Otero (1998). *El nuevo mundo de las finanzas microempresariales*, México: Plaza y Valdés Editores.

Vento, G. A. (2004). 'New challenges in microfinance: The importance of regulation', Documento de Trabajo, Centro de Estudios de la Estructura Económica (CENES), Universidad de Buenos Aires.

Vento, G. A. (2005). 'La via italiana alla microfinanza: il contributo del sistema paese per una microfinanza sostenibile', Dirigenza Bancaria, no. 112, marzo – aprile.

Vigano, L. (a cura di) (2004). *Microfinanza in Europa*, Milan: Giuffrè Editore.

7
Migrants and Financial Services: Which Opportunities for Financial Innovation?

*Luisa Anderloni and Daniela Vandone**

7.1 Introduction

Since the middle of the 1990s, international migration has been growing rapidly in most developed countries, with features indeed unique from several viewpoints: size, complexity, diversity, and social implications.[1] The implementation of effective policies to ensure immigrant integration, to attract the required skills to satisfy domestic needs, and to fight against irregular entry and employment has become primary in the policy agenda of many countries over the past decades. An interesting aspect is that of financial inclusion of migrants, that is, access to the mainstream financial sector by immigrants. However, this is still a largely unexplored area, although some countries have experienced benchmark initiatives in promoting financial inclusion and, more specifically, in migrants' financial inclusion, sometimes through financial innovations.

This chapter discusses the potential of migrants as banking customers and analyses areas of innovation in order to better serve this market segment. The first part of the chapter provides an overview of the dimension of this untapped market segment and follows on by introducing the issue of financial exclusion and the position of migrants as clusters at risk of

* Luisa Anderloni is Full Professor of Financial Intermediaries and Markets, DEAS (Department of Economics, Management and Statistics) – University of Milan (Italy): luisa.anderloni@unimi.it Daniela Vandone is Assistant Professor of Financial Intermediaries and Markets, DEAS (Department of Economics, Management and Statistics) – University of Milan (Italy): daniela.vandone@unimi.it. The chapter is the result of intense collaboration between the two authors. However, sections on migrants, financial exclusion, and migration phases are attributable to Luisa Anderloni, and the sections on areas of financial innovation and product innovation to Daniela Vandone. The introduction and conclusions sections have been written jointly.

149

financial exclusion. We then outline the migration phases and personal variables as key elements to evaluate customer relationship issues in the context of migrant life cycles. The following sections look at various product and financial innovations that can be used to target this market segment. The final section provides the conclusion.

7.2   Migrants: a new market segment for banks and financial institutions

The migratory phenomena registered in recent years in many European countries are the result of structural changes in the labour market and in our modern social organization. Together with complex concomitant demographic, political, and social causes they have become expressions of lasting tendencies that are likely to grow significantly over the next few years.

The size of the migrant population is already quite high in many European countries (such as Austria and Germany 13 per cent, Belgium and Ireland 11 per cent and 10.6 per cent, and France and the UK with 10 per cent and 9.3 per cent)[2] as shown in Figure 7.1. In other countries such as Italy, Spain, and Portugal, the size of the migrant population is significantly smaller. If, however, instead of considering the number already present we consider the flow of immigration, a trend of marked growth can be seen.

These figures suggest the idea that immigrants represent a new source of demand for banking and financial services. In banking, markets that show clear signs of maturity and growing competitiveness, identifying new market segments represent an opportunity for banks to expand their services and regenerate the industry through new initiatives based on the demand expressed by this new segment. Indeed, on the demand side, in retail banking, after initiatives aimed at promoting mass use of banking services in the 1950s and 1960s, demand seems to be almost totally saturated. Even the supply of new products in new and emerging areas of intermediation and services (such as pension funds and electronic payment systems) usually results in a shifting market share from one business area to another. In itself, however, it has limited scope for increasing overall demand in the market. Growth potential is also connected to the growth of the economy and to an intensifying of financial relations. Nevertheless, it should be noted that reduced rates of actual growth in mature economies offer limited scope for further enlargement of the retail banking market.

On the supply side, competition has also intensified in the retail markets. This is due, firstly, to the removal of institutional barriers that, generally in many countries, artificially segmented the market. Subsequently, it was also due to international openings and domestic and cross-countries mergers and acquisitions which redesigned the morphology of the banking system and the dynamics of competition.

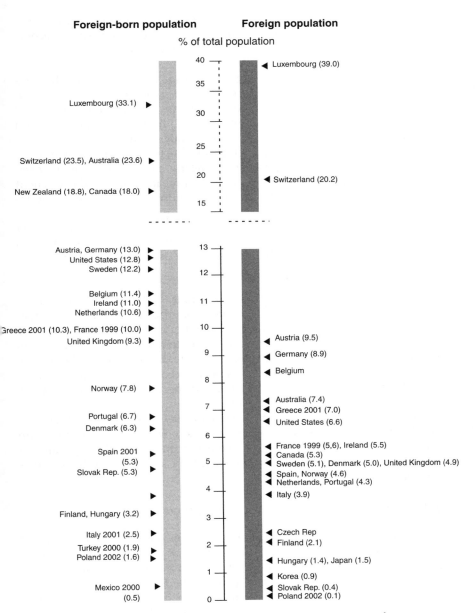

Figure 7.1 Stock of foreign-born populations in selected OECD countries[1]

[1] 2004 unless otherwise stated.

Sources: Foreign-born population: estimates by the Secretariat for Canada, the Czech Rep., Germany, Ireland, Luxembourg, New Zealand, Portugal and Switzerland; for the other countries, please refer to the metadata for Table A.1.4. of the Statistical Annex. Foreign population: please refer to the metadata for Table A.1.5. of the Statistical Annex. World Bank (2006), p. 44.

In addition to the statistics on the high number of immigrants, other qualitative factors emerge, such as how immigrants can more easily become a target market for banking services. The following should be noted:

- In general, the presence of immigrants tends to be evenly spread throughout countries and not concentrated only in some of the main towns or certain geographical areas. There is, therefore, demand for immigrants' banking services almost everywhere, and it is not a phenomenon restricted to a few regions with a heavy immigrant presence;
- families are increasing in number; this is due to the policy, which many countries have, of making it easier for relatives to join a family member, and to migration models which envisage more long-term and permanent stays in the country, as well as to the beginnings of a build-up of successive generations of immigrants;
- greater variety in the jobs carried out, including also the growing number of self-employed immigrants and small entrepreneurs in countries in which immigrants normally worked as care assistants, domestic staff or company employees.

Moreover, if we consider that migration causes a brain-drain effect from richer countries at the expense of emigrant countries and at times even brain waste, so that there is a net loss of skills and talents, we reinforce the idea that access to the banking system can play an important role in the promotion of an individual's economic and social life. In other words, because of inconsistent use of its full capabilities in the labour market, human potential, which is often not fully appreciated, is demeaned even further by a lack of suitable banking and financial services.

The information above about the scale of present and potential demand and the forecasts on further growth over the next few years, together with qualitative factors, should make us consider the economic opportunities carefully in order to strategically direct banking services towards these new segments.

7.3   Financial exclusion and inclusive policies

The issue of migrants' access to banking services is not a priority compared to other livelihood needs and to other aspects of their economic and social integration. However, in recent years this concern has become more important, due to various causes. Some of them are specifically related to migrants, and others are more generally related to all persons who find it difficult to access the banking system and to establish financial relationships and consequently risk being financially excluded.[3]

It is worth mentioning that financial inclusion is a recent issue debated in developed countries. Indeed, while on the one hand the link between finance and growth has been thoroughly studied by several analysts from a macroeconomic perspective, with theoretical approaches, methodological issues, and empirical analysis that are still 'pending',[4] less attention has been paid (until recently) to access to bank relations within developed countries. Since the 1980s, special attention has been devoted to the issue of financial exclusion, seen as part of the wider issue of social exclusion. This has been particularly true for the United States, as well as for some European countries – the United Kingdom and France in particular.

Several current trends in the bank systems and, more generally, within the organization of economic and relational activities, have often enhanced the risk that, on the supply side, the low-moderate income segment is excluded from banks' strategies. Interests to promote a financial inclusive society arise from several areas: from the social point of view, the importance for everybody of promoting the opportunity to participate in financial processes and to benefit from the basic mechanisms that represent major channels to economic independence opportunities[5]. As to society's economic interest, individuals that are excluded from financial transactions and from payment systems can cause some frictions within the financial system and, therefore also a social cost. Further more, individuals that are financially excluded and that are also at risk of being socially excluded, are not able to fully take part in the production of value and therefore are less likely to make a positive contribution to the system.

Financial exclusion has been identified as a multidimensional construct[6] and different definitions have been suggested.[7] Sometimes, the concept of financial exclusion also encompasses the distinction between 'unbanked' individuals (who are totally excluded from the banking offer) and 'under-banked' individuals who, while they do in fact have a bank account (they are not 'unbanked') make limited use of their account as they have a pattern of living in which they mostly use cash or prefer to use other channels outside the mainstream financial sector.[8]

In light of these features, it seems appropriate to adopt a wider definition of financial exclusion such as the following: 'The inability to access necessary financial services in an appropriate form. Exclusion can come about as a result of problems with access, conditions, prices, marketing or self-exclusion in response to negative experiences or perceptions'.[9] The advantage of such definition is that it effectively encompasses both objective circumstances, 'lack of access to financial services', as well as specific assessments: whether, as a matter of fact, the services offered are appropriate to needs. Furthermore, it also links the objective situation to various circumstances that, whether individually or jointly, lead to exclusion. These include both obstacles from the supply side as well as barriers from the demand side, such as lack of knowledge or awareness. In the case of migrants, the concept of 'under-banked' is often more appropriate, as services are often not adequate to their needs.

Another useful distinction focuses on the causes of financial exclusion and explores concepts such as affordability and access, with an emphasis on economic variables, on the one hand and, on the other, behavioural variables.[10] A further relevant distinction to be made is between: (i) access and possibility to use financial services; and (ii) the actual use of financial services.[11]

In many cases, 'alternative financial services providers' play an increasingly important role, especially in the context of payment services (exchange, cheques, and transfer of remittances to the original country for immigrants, and loans for immediate cash needs). Therefore, among the unbanked there are those that deal with other formal institutions like the above-mentioned cheque-cashing agencies, pawnshops, pay-day lenders, tax refund advances, and other finance companies operating outside the traditional financial system. As a consequence, they are 'formally included', but generally pay high charges and fees and 'usurious' interest rates; in addition, they do not have easy access to further services. Often people on low-incomes with social and economically precarious conditions can have access to – or prefer to deal with – financial services providers that operate informally without binding contracts, transparent conditions, and, often, fair prices. Concluding, among the 'financially served', that is, among people who are not financially excluded, there are groups that do not satisfy their financial needs dealing with the mainstream financial institutions. This happens not only in developing countries, but also in the developed world where the evolution of the banking system and the business strategies of high-street banks do not consider the segments of low incomes and poor people. In the past these marginal segments were often served by local community banks or by postal offices, but these special categories of banks are gradually disappearing.

Migrants are often subject to social and financial exclusion or, according to Figure 7.2, they are unbanked, but 'formally included' as they use other formal intermediaries.[12] Sometimes they are 'financially served' as they

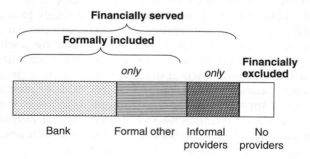

Figure 7.2   Different forms of financial inclusion/exclusion: from formal to informal providers

Source: Concept and graphic representation from World Bank (2005).

resort to informal providers. In many countries, most belong to the lowest income group, especially when they first arrive in a country, and in some cases for longer periods of time they do not have regular permits to stay or evidence of a regular, declared, job and therefore they prefer to operate in the informal market.

It's a vicious circle, where – amongst migrants – social exclusion increases the difficulties they have in accessing financial services. Unstable income and low savings mean that many banks see them as unexciting – if not undesirable – customers, associated with higher credit risks, higher operational costs and lower profit margins. At the same time, exclusion from financial services is also an obstacle to migrants' social and economic integration. Bank accounts can help build savings and make payments easier. Mortgages give immigrants opportunities to own property that not only can offer better living conditions, but that also can become useful collateral for future business loans. Loans to finance new businesses can help immigrants create new job and business opportunities, and thus provide them with more chances for economic and social integration. In many enterprises, wages are paid directly into employees' bank accounts, so that bank accounts are necessary.

In many developed countries initiatives have been taken to promote financial inclusion, adopting different models of dealing with the phenomenon: from the market model to sector self-regulation and to government intervention as mediator or regulator in addition to affirmative action.[13]

In our opinion, immigrants are a market segment where market responses can be provided quite easily. Several banks have started to consider the market segment of immigrants in terms of the potential for business development. An answer to the question of whether the migrant population is seen to have specific financial needs that require a targeted and dedicated response, or whether they are to be seen as low priority customers for whom the cost of providing services is inadequately covered by earnings and risk coverage margins, can be found by looking at the issue from a perspective that includes the changing dynamics of needs and how these will change over time.

An understanding of needs within this more dynamic context can help explain whether the limited financial inclusion of, possibly large, groups of immigrants may be due to the lack, or at least limited extend, of needs that can be met by the banking system or, on the other hand, whether difficulties in access are rooted in cultural, linguistic factors, procedural aspects, or assessments of cost, or even to other factors of individual psychology and the views individuals have of banking relationships. It could also help understand whether, as an alternative or in addition to these shortcomings on the demand side, there might also be something lacking as regards what they are offered, either because products and services are unsuitable to their needs, or because the procedures, communication methods, or pricing policies adopted have the effect, whether by design or by chance, of discouraging access to banking relations. Taking a dynamic approach and a longer term perspective opens the way to a modification of both views: on the one side immigrants might appreciate the convenience of access to the banking system, on the other side banks might see the benefits in targeting the immigrant market. As a result it might be easier for supply and demand to come together.

Adopting this approach might also make it easier to provide an accurate assessment of remittance services, which are specific and exclusive to the migrant population. In recent times they have been analysed on a number of occasions and from several viewpoints, taking into account the connection this issue has with other macro- and microeconomic questions.[14] Remittances are a primary need, generally used recurrently by immigrants, though remittance models vary depending on the reasons the person saves money to send back home, on how long they have been living in the host country, and on their plans for the future.

The following sections outline an approach that looks at financial needs taking into account the phases of migration that mark stages in the life cycle and of migrant's actual plans. This makes it possible both to provide a comprehensive assessment based on individual personal variables (social, cultural, and psychological characteristics) and to demonstrate that the range of products and services supplied is likely to become broader. This is especially the case as the initial need to access an account to make deposits and use payment instruments (and the need to make remittances) is supplemented with additional financial requirements for increasingly complex services that are likely to be profitable.

7.4   Migration phases and personal variables as key elements of financial needs[15]

As previously stated, immigrant groups often show characteristics and attitudes typical of other socially excluded groups, such as low income, low skills levels, a lack of language knowledge and of technical – that is, legal and financial – aspects, mistrust of suppliers, and also psychological barriers including lack of confidence. These characteristics are partially related to migration phases and levels of integration in the host country, as well as to economic, social, and educational levels, as well as to the type of banking system existing in the country of origin.

However immigrant groups may differ, under certain conditions, from other socially excluded groups. In particular, second-generation immigrants, those in the last phases of their migratory projects, or immigrants from certain ethnic groups, can gradually overcome initial economic exclusion, when they obtain a regular job and a house, and when they start saving and using bank services and products. Eventually they may become sought-after customers who will be supplied by bank service providers with a range of services. However, this is not the case for all immigrant groups. Thus, the migrant universe is a complex one, made up of various ethnic groups that differ widely. Consequently, theoretical considerations may apply to one situation, but not to another.

Migrant social and financial exclusion also differs according to geographical context, with considerable variation to be found in Europe. Some countries, such as the United Kingdom, France and Germany, have experienced migration flows for many decades, and their 'integration problems' are different from those experienced by countries with recent, more varied migration flows, such as Italy and Spain. Recent migration flows are much more mixed than those in the past: in countries where migration is more recent, there are many different nationalities of immigrants, from Asia, Africa, Eastern Europe, and Latin America.

7.4.1 Demand for financial services aimed at immigrants

In drawing up a theoretical framework based on variables that may influence migrant demand for financial services and products in the host country, we should remember that financial needs are generally considered to be 'secondary level' needs, rather than the 'primary level' basic needs required for survival in a foreign country.[16]

With this in mind, we need to consider the relationship between the following variables:

- migratory project (phase and goals of migration plan);
- priority of basic needs and resulting prioritization of intervention by social and governmental institutions;
- structure of banking markets, extent of development of a cashless society in the host country.

The implementation of plans to move from one country to another can be divided into a succession of phases,[17] each of which has differing priorities in terms of both basic and financial needs.

The first phase is 'initial settlement', when immigrants first enter the host country. Basic needs in this phase relate to labour (finding a job or obtaining money for basic living needs) housing (finding a place to live, often shared with many other immigrants) and language. In this phase financial needs relate mainly to the use of money for survival. The key variable in the initial phase is the issue of legal or illegal entry, as this heavily influences immigrants' way of life and the visibility of their activities. Whether immigrants have entered the country legally or not has implications for how easy it will be to find jobs and housing, both of which are very important basic needs in the initial phase. Generally illegal immigrants have no official access to the services provided by financial institutions.[18] It is practically impossible for immigrants to save money during this economically unstable first phase. Housing problems may lead to financial needs, such as the need to obtain a bank guarantee to rent a house, in cases where immigrants favour, or are able to choose, the legal approach and do not have to rely on the 'irregular' rental market. More often, immigrants share housing with friends, relatives, or simply other immigrants from the same country or ethnic group. Illegal entry is, furthermore, often associated with incurring large debts to finance the journey.

The second phase is characterized by the following basic needs for illegal immigrants: to obtain a regular residence permit; to have a regular job, and to work towards reuniting the family. This need shapes choices in different ways, depending on what their main goal in coming to a country has been. If the goal has been to stay permanently in the host country, immigrants often try to arrange for other family members to join them. If they only want to stay on a temporary basis, they prefer to help the family while staying in the host country and will send them money for food, housing, education, and emergency medical services. In this phase, financial needs consist mostly in saving and transferring money abroad through remittances. How often they send money depends on how important an individual's help is for the survival of their family in their country of origin and the amount will depend on how much they manage to save, given low salaries and high expenses.[19] Other financial needs may include personal loans or consumer credit to buy furniture or household appliances, or microcredit for the self-employed to purchase business equipment. Sometimes the demand remains latent due to failure to meet the requirements that banks generally stipulate in order to grant a loan in the first place.

The third phase of 'stable settlement' involves a greater degree of integration in the host country. Priorities may shift to setting up business or commercial activities (such as shops, restaurants, or small businesses in the services or industrial sector) to buying 'superfluous' goods or services (such as a car, or more furniture, or entering into a rental agreement) and in certain cases even to buying a house. In this phase, saving is characterized by more medium-term goals, and immigrants look for basic savings products. As far as credit is concerned, demand will focus on micro or consumer credit, mortgages for house purchase, and business loans. The amount and frequency of remittances generally decreases as many immigrants by now have a family living with them in the host country and prefer to invest most of their resources in improving their life in their adopted country.

The exact features of the fourth phase of 'consolidation' will depend on the original plan or model of migration.[20] If the plan follows the 'transit' model, where the aim is to work abroad for a certain period of time, to save money for the family in the country of origin, to be able to buy, build, or refurbish a house and then return home, needs are similar to those in the previous phase. An untapped area of offer for this segment of immigrants may be that of savings and transferable pension schemes and the formation of deferred annuities.[21] If the project follows the model of 'final settlement

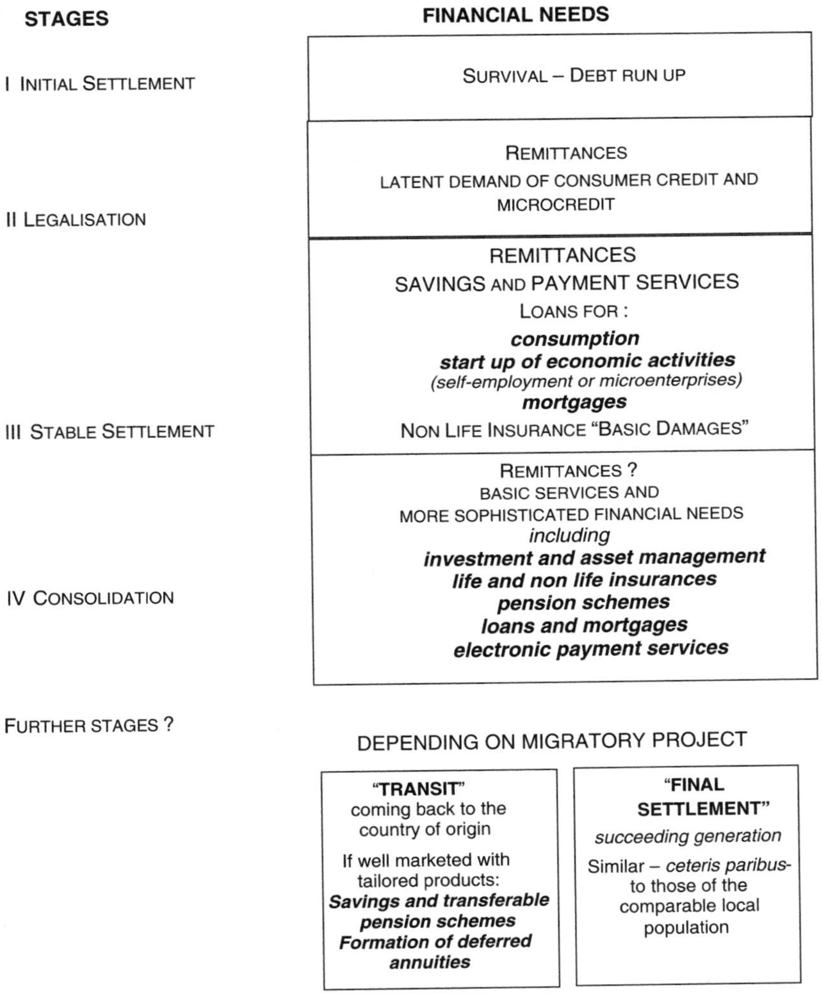

STAGES	FINANCIAL NEEDS
I INITIAL SETTLEMENT	SURVIVAL – DEBT RUN UP
II LEGALISATION	REMITTANCES LATENT DEMAND OF CONSUMER CREDIT AND MICROCREDIT
III STABLE SETTLEMENT	REMITTANCES SAVINGS AND PAYMENT SERVICES LOANS FOR : **consumption** **start up of economic activities** *(self-employment or microenterprises)* **mortgages** NON LIFE INSURANCE "BASIC DAMAGES"
IV CONSOLIDATION	REMITTANCES ? BASIC SERVICES AND MORE SOPHISTICATED FINANCIAL NEEDS *including* **investment and asset management** **life and non life insurances** **pension schemes** **loans and mortgages** **electronic payment services**

FURTHER STAGES ?

DEPENDING ON MIGRATORY PROJECT

"TRANSIT" coming back to the country of origin If well marketed with tailored products: **Savings and transferable pension schemes** **Formation of deferred annuities**	"FINAL SETTLEMENT" *succeeding generation* Similar – *ceteris paribus-*to those of the comparable local population

Figure 7.3   Financial needs and migrant life cycle

and succeeding generations', the financial needs will become more sophisticated, and resemble those of people in the host country with the same characteristics. Remittance services become less important than in previous phases.

Further stages are those of second and succeeding generations. Only countries with a long tradition of incoming migrations (the US, the UK, and

France) have already experienced these stages. However, in all these phases, remittance is an important service for migrant populations, even though its relative importance tends to decrease as other needs increase.

Therefore, considering that remittances are only one type of financial service a person may need, we should remember that migrant demand for financial services and migrant financial behaviours are also influenced by such factors as:

- country of origin
- personal attitudes
- ethnic group.

One factor relating to the country of origin is the level of economic development in that country. In very poor countries, even very small remittances may be of major significance in the survival of the families of immigrant workers. In these countries, too, relatively small savings in European terms may have much greater purchasing power locally. Medium-term saving may facilitate the creation of a business or house purchase on return to the home country. Furthermore, economic development in their home country also has an indirect effect on immigrants' knowledge of the products, services, and technologies normally available in the host country and may influence their lifestyle in the host country as soon as they start to work and earn income. This has an indirect effect on purchasing decisions, saving capacity, and also on access to financial services.

The level of development of the banking systems in countries of origin also has an indirect effect both on the financial awareness of immigrants, since they may already know about certain banking products and services, and on their use of banking channels for services and for remittances. If in their country of origin the banking system is not well developed, with very few branches, it is more likely that immigrants will access non-banking channels in the host country to send remittances. The distance between the country of origin and the host country also has an influence on the channels used for remittances. If the country of origin is not far away from the host country, informal channels are more likely to be used. The characteristics of different ethnic groups, in terms of level of network cohesion and of social control, also play an important role in this case. If cohesion and social control are low, immigrants from countries located near the host country prefer not to use informal channels.

Individual immigrants' own particular social, cultural, economic, and psychological characteristics have a strong impact on their access to financial services. Each person is an individual with his or her own ideas, behaviour, and plans for the future. Furthermore, their position in the labour market (employee or self-employed; open-ended or temporary contract) and social position in their home country can influence the economic activity undertaken in the host country. Level of education is an important factor: the ability to read and write, knowledge of a foreign language and knowledge of basic mathematical concepts enable better integration and facilitate access to banking services in the host country.

Psychological factors may include a perception of how immigrants are viewed in the host country, and consequently influence their behaviour in approaching host country institutions, particularly banks. If they sense that there is a hostile or discriminatory attitude towards foreigners (or immigrants, or non-Europeans) they may prefer to access non-banking institutions, especially if other immigrants run these. Another psychological factor is the extent of their attachment to their own ethnic community lifestyle and whether they are likely to develop a different lifestyle as time goes on: if they remain in areas with high concentrations of their compatriots and their working relationships are restricted to members of that particular community, they are unlikely to access institutions in the host country since they will first turn to their own community to find solutions to financial problems.

Ethnic group characteristics and initiatives play an important role in shaping migrants' access to financial services. The ability to act and communicate is a very important variable. One important factor that influences aggregation and communication mechanisms is the degree of geographical concentration of immigrants' homes and workplaces.[22] Ethnic associations and informal groups can help to facilitate access to financial services for their members.[23] Ethnic groups can also be channels of information, facilitating bank credit analysis: they may know their members well, understand the significance of the cultural factors in behaviour, and can then act as cultural mediators between banks and other immigrants.

Community associations can also make agreements with banks to facilitate migrants' access to financial services. Price agreements are the most popular initiatives, but agreements with cultural mediators or interpreters who can help immigrants when they enter bank branches are also common. Another important role played by ethnic associations is that of developing innovative approaches to the financial literacy of their members and in facilitating access to finance for them by, for instance, guaranteeing loans taken out by members.

The study of the life cycle of migrants, their migration project and other factors such as their country of origin, individual situations and differences among ethnic groups should help banks in developing strategies to address this untapped market segment. In the early stages migrant financial services demand will mainly be for elementary services; however, over time these are likely to evolve into more sophisticated products and services developing into a profitable business area.

7.4.2   The special role of remittances

Remittances represent a major area of financial intermediation for a variety of reasons. As the previous section pointed out, they are a service which represents an exclusive need for this market segment, even though their importance in the immigrants' portfolio of services and products generally changes throughout their life cycles. Remittance services can therefore be considered a way of starting off a relationship with a bank. The relationship gradually strengthens and, eventually, more complex services are used that incorporate greater added value.

It should also be pointed out that recently, considerable attention has been paid to this area of business from a number of perspectives which are not just restricted to the strategies of individual banks or financial operators, but which also involve international financial organizations (starting with the World Bank, the United Nations, and the IMF) policy-makers, and international and national regulatory and supervisory bodies.

The reasons for this interest can be summarized as follows. As far as the macroeconomic aspects are concerned:

- Flows of remittances represent highly significant qualitative and quantitative flows of capital, not only for individual families, but also for local communities and national economies.
- The direct impact is mainly on current family incomes, but families also use them to pay school fees for children in the home country, therefore investing in human capital for the next generation. Furthermore, some remittances are channelled into investment goods, such as machinery, tools, and as a source of operating capital for small businesses. There is, therefore, growing interest in using these flows to invest in human capital and in entrepreneurial and microbusiness capital.
- Remittances are also used to purchase land or homes, as well as to repair and refurbish homes, sometimes producing disorderly and erratic agricultural and urban 'development'. This means that the potential for development runs the risk of being demeaned and that environmental and social consequences are negative.

As far as the functioning of banking and financial markets are concerned:

- A large part of remittance flows are channelled outside the banking system both by specialized agencies that belong to the official system as well as through informal channels of various kinds. This has clear consequences for the following aspects;
- The cost of remittance services in its various forms has considerable impact on the amounts sent. The composition of cost elements can vary and can include commissions and administrative costs in the country from which the money is sent and even in the country it is sent to, as well

as a currency exchange commission, while the exchange rate applied can also contribute to overall costs. It is therefore difficult to calculate these costs in abstract terms (rough estimates frequently calculate a cost of 10 per cent for average amount remittances). In any case, these charges represent a drain on the resources of the poor population in the country where the money is received and of the workers who have to make a considerable effort to save the money. Therefore, it seems important to raise public awareness on the issue.

- The infrastructure of the payment system is very important in this field. Improvements could increase efficiency, reduce costs, and offer a higher level of welfare both from the point of view of the individual families involved as well as in terms of their countries;

In terms of regulation, the issue of remittances is particularly relevant to:

- how payment systems relate to deregulation of the markets and functioning of the single European market, both in terms of guaranteeing solvency conditions and efficiency of consumer protection as well as, more generally, of the individual customers. In terms of the latter, the importance of enforcing transparency regulations should be stressed, regarding conditions and user-friendly procedures that can be used in the event of breech of contract and disputes;
- the problems involved in using financial systems for money laundering and money dirtying transactions. The latter includes, in recent times, the problem of financing terrorist activities.

Indeed, discussion on global remittances is an area where debates and the process of regulation are ongoing.[24] These are complex regulatory procedures because often they must be coordinated with different concerns and various legal systems – from international law to private and banking law. Moreover, it is now a commonly shared opinion that every regulatory change must carry out an assessment of the regulatory implications, with a cost estimate and an evaluation of the benefits of the regulation. The point that should be emphasized is how these regulatory or re-regulatory processes can represent a kind of institutional innovation, which in turn can stimulate innovations in remittance products and processes.

As regards the innovation in the institutional context, the most important stimulus is the likely introduction of a new European Directive on Payment services in the internal market.[25] Among the three main building blocks of the proposal, with reference to the right to provide payment services to the public, a new category of service providers, named 'payment institutions', is created.[26] Payment institutions should be subject to a set of conditions and prudential requirements proportionate to the operational and financial risks faced in the course of their business.[27] It is worth mentioning that money remittance services are included in the list of 'payment services'[28] contained in the directive. As regards the area of activity and the way of rendering payment services, payments institutions should be prohibited from accepting deposits from users and permitted to use only funds accepted from users for supplying payment services. This provision limits the area of innovation for money transfer operators, while banks, as credit institutions, can offer services with higher added value. The approach of the European discipline is indeed – in principle – flexible in order to avoid the risk of some institutions being 'forced into the black economy': mechanisms are therefore suggested with the aim to allow that providers unable to meet all the conditions may nevertheless be treated as payment institutions.[29]

Another important improvement in the institutional context is that of transparency and of understanding of conditions. The underlying objective is to facilitate payment service users to make well-informed choices and to be able to shop around with different providers. Adequate information should be given to payment services users with regards to both the payment service contract as well as to the authorization and execution of a transaction. In this area a balance should be found between full details of information and the real needs of the users; a standard form of communication of the conditions is suggested to the Member States with the recommendations that they have to be set out in easily understandable words and in a clear and readable form. In this context there is also room for enhancing transparency regarding fees, charges, and exchanges rates for currency conversion applied to the payments.

The Payment Services Directive, in providing an institutional framework for the activity of payment institutions, also creates a prerequisite for rendering these operators subject to a more effective anti-money laundering and anti-terrorist financing requirements. This need has caused some countries to regulate the sector of money service businesses, which includes money transfers, bureaux de change, and cheque cashers.[30]

Another boost towards an improvement of remittance services and in facilitating access to financial services for migrants comes from the publication of general principles by the Bank for International Settlements and World Bank.[31] These principles are aimed at achieving safe and efficient services. The main idea is that remittance services are part of the broader retail payment system, both domestic and cross-border, and that an efficient infrastructure is key in reducing costs of remittances. This is particularly true of receiving countries, where these services are usually expensive, slow, inconvenient, and sometimes unreliable. Moreover new remittance products improve value to the user in the short term and gives access to other financial products in the long term, moving transactions to the formal sector. We should also consider that new technologies may significantly help to offer better quality at lower costs.

Synthesizing these principles, the general regulatory principles applied to remittances, these are related to: (1) transparency and consumer protection;[32] (2) payment system infrastructure;[33] (3) legal regulatory environment;[34] (4) market structure and competition;[35] and (5) governance and risk management.[36] In addition, there is also a call for taking action both from remittances service providers (which should participate actively in the application of the general principles) and public authorities (which should evaluate what actions to take to achieve the public policy objectives through implementation of the general principles).

This convergence of interest in the field of remittance services from different perspectives strengthens our conviction that in the near future this market will be the theatre of stronger competition and innovation. This idea is reinforced by the belief that, in terms of volume, remittances may represent a larger potential source of funding for the development of receiving countries. However, their development impact could be further enhanced by adding incentives for more virtuous plans of savings and investments that see banks or money transfer firms to cooperate with not-for-profit organizations in achieving these goals.

7.5 Areas of financial innovation

As previously stated, migrants constitute a market segment with a specific demand for financial services, varying according to migratory project. As with any other market segment (e.g., women, students, the elderly) banks may develop dedicated products in order to satisfy migrants' specific financial needs. However, unlike in other market segments, the business strategy of developing new products is not enough to serve immigrant customers because barriers exist that sometimes keep them away from the banking system or make the access more difficult.

In order to serve this market segment, and thus achieve advantages in terms of business volume, income and customer relations, banks need both to develop strategies to reduce these barriers and to create new products. Hence, the immigrant segment acts as a driver for two areas of innovation in financial services:

- innovation in customer relations; and
- product innovation.

We will first focus on strategies that banks can adopt in order to bring immigrants into the mainstream financial system[37] and establish long-term banking relationships. We then focus on the development of financial products which can reach this niche segment.

7.6 Re-inventing customer relations

Various barriers may keep immigrants away from the financial system. Some, such as language barriers, cultural differences, location inconvenience, and banking service hours, relate particularly to the migrant population. Others relate more to the unbanked population in general, such as low levels of financial literacy, lack of information about appropriate products and services, and a general distrust of banks.

Serving immigrant customers means developing strategies that can reduce the above-mentioned barriers, build trust in the banking system, and thus avoid immigrants remaining unbanked.[38] To this end, banks have to re-invent customer relations and develop strategies, such as tailored outreach and targeted marketing, that bring these products and services to immigrant consumers.[39] Re-inventing customer relations is important both in order to establish basic connections with new immigrant customers and to strengthen these relations by matching customers with higher-end financial products, such as housing loans and pensions.

Although the cost of these strategies is high, the business opportunity is clear: financial institutions looking to increase their customer base have become increasingly interested in reaching out to untapped immigrant markets, bringing them into the financial system and establishing long-term banking relationships.

The following four areas are drivers of innovation. The first three areas, which involve increasing levels of complexity, require adjustments in aspects of bank staffing and procedures. The fourth area requires the direct involvement of local communities in order to build trust:

- multilanguage material
- multilanguage staff
- dedicated branches
- community partnerships.

7.6.1   Multilanguage information and marketing material

Providing information, contracts and agreements in immigrant languages promotes transparency and clarity, and is the first step to reducing the barriers that block immigrants' access to the banking system.[40] Banks must provide informational material that is easy to read and can contribute to the financial education of immigrants; it should not be merely a translated version of information already available in the host country language. Provision of multilanguage website information is another example of this kind of initiative; the effectiveness of dedicated web pages, however, is dependent on the degree of familiarity that the immigrant market segment has with personal computers and the internet.

Transparency and clarity of information in relations between the financial system and consumers are issues to which British and American authorities give particular importance. Their stated objectives include protection of consumer interests; the provision of multilanguage information and material can contribute to this.

7.6.2   Multilanguage staff

The use of multiethnic and multilanguage staff constitutes a second step towards the reduction of barriers separating banks from immigrant clients. The presence of staff who speak the same language as immigrants makes the above-mentioned measures (aimed at improving clarity and transparency) more effective and, in addition, it fosters a more welcoming environment. This second group of initiatives aimed at facilitating immigrant access to the banking system also includes the use of multilanguage staff in bank call centres. However, as with the provision of web pages, this service may not always be an effective means of reducing barriers, because call centre services are generally used by educated client segments that are more familiar with modern technologies. Nevertheless, this type of service may be of value in establishing customer fidelity among those who are already part of the banking system.

7.6.3   Dedicated branches

A more sophisticated initiative than those illustrated so far is the creation of dedicated immigrant branches. Creating a more immigrant-friendly environment is a means of sending clearly welcoming signals to immigrant customers, and thus of reducing barriers. Banks may also develop initiatives aimed at making dedicated branches more flexible and tailored to the needs of immigrants, such as for example greater flexibility in opening hours. However, the cost of setting up and running dedicated branches can be high compared to the amount of business coming from this market segment; this is a solution that is probably worthwhile only in specific areas of high immigrant population density. Moreover, the creation of branches totally dedicated to immigrants, generally to a specific community of immigrants, may be perceived as an obstacle to integration with local inhabitants and thus as a form of marginalization.

7.6.4   Community partnerships

Considerable benefits to the banking system may also come from alliance-building with community organizations. Firstly, partnerships with community groups are important in developing financial education; this facilitates trust-building and helps to bring immigrants into the mainstream financial system, thus creating formal market alternatives to informal products and services. Moreover, these partnerships facilitate a better understanding of immigrants' financial needs, thus making it possible to improve product offerings, broaden market penetration and develop business on a larger scale. Furthermore, community groups are important in providing technical assistance and support for immigrants within their institutions; in some cases they also provide guarantees. Community partnerships may include not only non-profit organizations but also banking associations and regulators.

The provision of multilanguage informational material and the use of multilanguage staff constitute fairly widespread strategies in the banking sectors of countries which have considerable immigrant populations. The opening of dedicated bank branches is still unusual, although some pilot-projects have already implemented this strategy.

In Italy, Banca Carige was in 1996 the first bank to open a dedicated immigrant customer branch. The bank opened the branch in the vicinity of the port of Genoa, with its high concentration of immigrants, in order to access a type of customer showing strong growth in terms of numbers, and also in demand for financial services. At the time, the press gave considerable publicity to the initiative; however, after ten years, it remains the only dedicated immigrant customer branch opened by the bank. The Sanpaolo Imi Group has also adopted a Multiethnic Point strategy, with branches located in areas with high immigrant density, employing mother-tongue speakers of French, English, Chinese, and Arabic, dedicated to a immigrant clientele. The Group, which is well-established at a local level and gives importance to client and local community relations, has established four Multiethnic Points in four cities where there is a strong immigrant presence: Turin, Padua, Naples, and Pescara. The aim is to encourage immigrant access to bank services, and to eliminate language and cultural difficulties. While providing better service to immigrants, the Multiethnic Points also enjoy the benefits resulting from links between the bank and representatives of the main local foreign communities. This has made it possible to combine a more immigrant friendly environment with a range of services which can satisfy the specific financial requirements of this client segment.

In the United States some banks are opening bank branches in high schools in order to reach the next generation of immigrants, which forms a large and growing segment of the population. The rationale behind this strategy is that young adults learn financial behaviour from their parents; when parents are unbanked, their children are likely to be unbanked as well. Moreover, contact with other members of immigrant households can be made through these young adults. Expanding the number of bank branches in high school could help to expand financial education opportunities and to bring immigrants into mainstream financial services. Mitchell Bank, an independently owned small-size bank mainly operating in the Southside of Milwaukee, Wisconsin, opened a bank branch in the local high school in Milwaukee, where over half the student body is of Hispanic origin. Students run the bank; they receive training in the skills required to manage the branch, which functions as a full-service branch subject to the same regulations as other branches. The students, in turn, then provide financial education to school employees and other students. The bank is also open during the evening when parents are at the school for various events.

In Spain there are many initiatives for facilitating access to the banking system. For example, Caja de Madrid has implemented a programme for hiring personnel of various nationalities (e.g., Chinese, Moroccan, Guinean);

they are employed in branch offices in the Madrid region, which has a large concentration of immigrants.

As regards community partnerships, a significant example of a partnership between regulators, financial institutions, and a community organization is the New Alliance Task Force (NATF). NAFT was launched in Chicago in 2003 by the FDIC Community Affairs Program and the Consulate General of Mexico. The purpose of NATF is to improve immigrant access to the US banking system by promoting financial education, support services, and the development of new financial products. NATF members are divided into four working groups focusing on four general areas: bank products and services, mortgage products, financial education, and social projects. They have collected data on the issuance of consumer, auto, and home equity loans, and studied the development of new remittance products and new mortgage products for immigrants. The involvement of high-profile institutions and regulatory agencies has given NAFT wide recognition and validity.

In the United Kingdom, Barclays Bank has developed many partnership programmes with non-profit organizations, which are designed to tackle financial exclusion. One of these projects aims to provide down-to-earth information and advice in order to make financial information more available and improve the overall level of financial literacy.

7.7 Product innovation

The second driver of financial innovation is product innovation: banks may offer products and services specifically designed to meet immigrant needs and interests.[41] In developing new financial products, banks must take into account the two following points:

1. the financial services that immigrants need change over time, as we have seen; this means there are opportunities to develop products that serve people differently at different points in their lives; and
2. customers are likely to move beyond basic transactional services to asset-building financial services.

For this reason, banks should offer a full range of financial services: basic products that meet simple financial needs and bring immigrants into the banking system, and more complex financial services designed to meet more sophisticated needs. As noted in Figure 7.3 there are three main drivers of product innovation, each related to a different life-cycle phase of immigrants. The products/services where innovation has been most apparent relate to:

- remittances
- mortgages
- pensions schemes.

7.7.1 Remittances

Various surveys in different countries prove evidence that remittances are largely made both through official non-banking channels and unofficial channels (Figures 7.4 and 7.5).[42] Remittances are generally made unofficially when money is physically transported from the host country to the country of origin by immigrants, by family members, and by friends or acquaintances. Sometimes they are made by unregistered operators that often provide services informally, collecting remittances through friends and 'chains of friends' and acting with a counterpart in the country of origin – generally they cover a limited geographical area – or relying on other informal networks for the effective transfer of funds. Another unofficial channel is use of non-official organizations such as 'hawala' for Muslims and Fei-Ch'ien for Chinese. Unofficial channels for remittances also include remittances in kind of high unit value goods (i.e., telephones, televisions, household appliances) which meet the needs of family members in the country of origin, or which, more commonly, are sold on the domestic market.

Remittances through official non-banking channels are generally made through operators such as Western Union and Money Gram: these are the best known, although in fact there are many others.[43] They manage international networks which guarantee rapid delivery of money, without the need for a bank account either in the country where money is sent from or in the country where money is received. Money transfer operators cover extensive geographic areas, using widespread networks that include, in addition to their own branches, distribution agreements with commercial operators

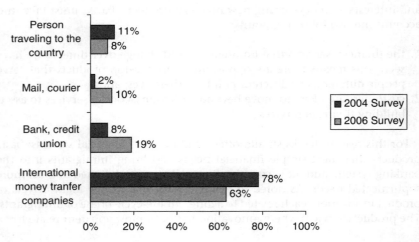

Figure 7.4 Type of channel used to remit money (United States)
Source: Inter-American Development Bank and Multilateral Investment Fund (2006b).

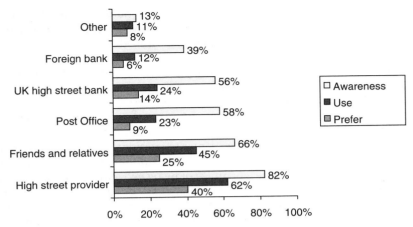

Figure 7.5 Awareness, preference and use of remittance services (United Kingdom)
Source: ICM (2006).

(such as phone centres, ethnic shops, and travel agencies) or with banks and post offices.

As shown in the previous figures, banks are increasing their share in the remittance business, first of all because it is an area that seems worthwhile developing in itself and, furthermore, because it represents an important opportunity to reach potential customers.[44] In order to become competitive, banks should work on:

- reducing upfront fees and exchange rate spreads
- guaranteeing delivery time
- guaranteeing access to a large network of pick-up locations.

For many immigrants, cost is not the main factor in deciding how to send remittances.[45] Rapid delivery time is more important because it gives a sense of security. When remittances are sent by international bank transfer, money transfer times depend largely on the wholesale payment system linking the sender bank to the receiver bank. In the last few years, changes at system level in clearing and settlement procedures have decreased the time required for processing operations, thus enabling transfers to be completed more rapidly.

In order to make money available rapidly and securely to family members in the country of origin, banks can also provide ATM access cards (debit cards or store value cards) that allow the recipient to access remitted funds at a local ATM in the country of origin. The bank issues two ATM cards to the customer, who sends one to a family member abroad. Unlike in bank transfers, in this case recipients do not need to have a bank account, because they withdraw money directly from the sender's account or from a dedicated sub-account. The delivery time problem is also solved because money is not actually transferred: the card recipient has immediate access to money deposited in the sender's account.

However, there is a further factor which effects a bank's ability to attract immigrants through the provision of remittance services: the distribution of payment locations in the receiving country, or in other words, the size of the network of pick-up locations. Many remittance recipients live far from bank branches or ATMs and this is especially true for families in rural areas. The largest money transfer operators have invested heavily in establishing extensive distribution networks that serve both rural and urban areas in receiving countries. Thus they have the advantage of being geographically well-placed in both sending and receiving locations. The lack of bank infrastructure in receiving countries is a significant barrier to the expansion of bank-based remittance products, particularly outside urban areas. At the same time the operating volumes of this business are still small and cannot cover the costs of setting up a whole network of branches. To overcome these problems, banks may establish partnerships with foreign banks and with money transfer operators. These agreements enable the bank to provide a service which is as rapid and as widespread as the networks of the largest specialist agencies, and at the same time acquire clients, who can then be offered other financial services. In this case, the degree of competitiveness of the product depends to a greater extent on the commission applied by the sender bank and those requested of the recipient by the domestic bank when the money is withdrawn. Many banks offer remittance services with innovative elements. Some examples are given below.

In the United States, Directo a Mexico is a Federal Reserve product launched in 2004. It is an automated clearing house money transmission option available to every depository institution in the United States; it charges banks a small fixed amount of money per transfer and guarantees a per cent exchange rate spread. The service provides direct access to all bank accounts in Mexico. It requires both remittance senders and recipients to have bank accounts. In a pilot programme begun in April 2006, Directo a Mexico is experimenting with allowing remittance senders to set up bank accounts for remittance recipients at participating bank branches in Mexico.

Bank of America offers a service, called SafeSend, which makes free money remittances to Mexico. The service is designed for customers with a bank account and a designated minimum balance in the account. Clients may make a total of three free remittances in a 30-day period, for up to three beneficiaries per remitter. In order to overcome problems arising from a lack of branches in the receiving country, Bank of America established partnerships with other institutions such as Banco Santander, Bansefi, La Red de la Gente, and Telecomm-Telégrafos. The strategy adopted by Bank of America shows that free remittances are a product that banks can provide if they take up the opportunity to acquire and keep clients, to create a long-term relationship, and to make the relationship profitable through cross-selling of other financial products.

In Italy a number of remittance services are beginning to appear with competitive costs and additional services aimed at improving services to customers and developing remittance products,[46] Banca Popolare di Milano, which is particularly active in Milan where there is a high concentration of immigrants, offers an 'Extraordinario' (Extraordinary) account which consists of a line of dedicated bank services for immigrants. The cost of remittances varies according to destination. Additional services are also offered, such as an assistance policy, which covers transmission of urgent messages to families, travel expenses for a family member if an immigrant who lives alone requires hospitalization, interpreter services, and return of the body to the country of origin in case of death. Monte Paschi has created 'Paschi senza frontiere' (Paschi without borders) an integrated package which offers current account, remittances, and bank transfers at no cost if sent to the country of origin. Credito Cooperativo Emiliano has produced the 'Radici' (Roots) Account, which offers tailored products such as remittances at pre-established costs and special insurance formulas to meet the needs of this type of clientele. BNL issues account holders with pre-paid cards which can be sent to family members and topped up as required by the account holder.

In Spain, BBVA offers a dedicated package of services to immigrants, 'Cuantas claras internacional', which includes remittances at no cost, the possibility of ordering operations not only from the bank branch, but also through ATMs, or by telephone, with money being immediately available for withdrawal at any branch of a large number of banks wiyh which BBVA has agreements.

7.7.2 Mortgages

Immigrant demand for mortgages to buy homes is growing. Banks have a competitive advantage here, in comparison to alternative finance providers such as investment or trust companies, because they have easy access to funding. Moreover, this is an area where banks have been active for decades and have acquired much experience and expertise.

Table 7.1 shows, for the UK market, the proportion of migrants remitters who own financial products; this proportion is lower than that found within the UK population as a whole.[47] As far as mortgages are concerned, it is 28 per cent against 41 per cent and this reveals that there is room for a further demand growth. However, at the same time, it is important to point out that the provision of mortgages to an immigrant clientele comes up against a series of specific difficulties.[48] Many immigrants have thin credit histories or none at all; they normally have no collateral; they do not always have income from a permanent job or documentable income (they may have no job security or work in the underground economy); they have difficulty saving the money

Table 7.1   Ownership of financial products (United Kingdom)

	Migrant remitters[1]	All people[2]
UK current account	78%	90%
Credit card	47%	65%
UK bank saving account	43%	64%
Mortgage	28%	41%
Household insurance	25%	78%
Life assurance	20%	–
Other bank account	19%	–
Private pension	10%	29%
Health insurance	9%	31%
National savings	6%	7%
Stocks and shares	5%	23%
None of these	6%	–

[1] Black and Minority Ethnic BME Remittance Survey (2006): Base all respondents (1778).
[2] ICM telephone omnibus – various dates in 2005. Nationally representative sample of all adults aged 18+.

Source: DFID-ICM (2006).

not covered by the mortgage because they may have no savings and high rental costs to meet while waiting to buy a house; they favour forms of flexible financing that take account of temporary moments of crisis.

In order to attract this demand, banks must act on a number of fronts:

- clear and transparent products
- relationship-building in the target community
- financial education
- flexible lending criteria
- flexible debt-to-income ratios
- full finance and flexible loan payment plans
- maintaining relationships with borrowers after loans are closed.

We have already discussed the benefits of the first three measures in the previous section. They enable banks to reach immigrant markets and develop closer relationships with potential customers. This helps to guarantee successful lending: immigrants can learn to manage their finances so that they can afford loan payments, and banks have the opportunity to work with them to help them reach the goal of home ownership, for example through asset-building programmes or offering flexible payment options. In order to overcome the problem of a lack of credit history, banks may add flexible lending criteria to their underwriting models. Common practice is to use non-conventional sources of information, which nevertheless enable evaluation of the creditworthiness of immigrants who apply for mortgages. These non-conventional sources, which indicate ability to make significant payments, include remittance history, utility payments, and regularity of housing and rental payments.

Providing flexibility in debt-to-income ratios to take into account the specific circumstances of the borrower also helps to reach immigrant markets. In this case, too, banks need to take a more flexible approach, recognizing, for example, that documented income does not usually provide the full picture of an immigrant family's finances. Most families have additional income which may include income from other working family members in the household or income from work with cash payments. Some lending programmes automatically provide a 25 per cent allowance for undocumented income in calculating the debt-to-income ratios.

Banks should also provide finance for 100 per cent of the value of the property, since immigrants often have difficulty accumulating the part of the money not covered by finance. In addition, banks should provide flexible loan payments in order to avoid problems with loan payments. In fact, the most common reasons for missing payments include temporary unemployment and illness. Banks could provide, for example, flexible instalments over a limited space of time, such as a three-month period.

Finally banks should maintain a closer relationship with the borrower after the loan is closed, in order to identify crisis situations and intervene promptly so as to overcome these temporary difficulties and ensure the loan has a good outcome. Wells Fargo & Company, the fourth US bank in terms of total assets, is one bank which offers a product with the above features. This bank offers a loan program suited for homebuyers with non-traditional credit histories, with high debt ratios and few savings, and with both documented and undocumented income. To better meet these customers needs, Wells Fargo offers a home mortgage that finances the entire purchase of the property and enables immigrants to use secondary stated income and non-occupant co-borrower income sources.

Nevertheless, it should be noted that, although these measures are able to meet the specific requirements of immigrant mortgage demand, the cost of these mortgages for the client may be too high, because of the difficulty of evaluating risk profile in the absence of traditional credit history, and because of the inclusion of flexibility clauses in loans.

As an alternative, or at the same time, banks could act to develop products aimed at building savings for buying a home.[49] These asset-building tools enable a number of objectives to be reached:

- the creation of a credit history that facilitates evaluation of immigrant creditworthiness or more generally that improves their credit-risk profiles, thus lowering the cost of payment services;

- building up funds needed to meet the expenses connected with starting a mortgage;
- financial education, since these programmes are usually accompanied by programmes of financial education; furthermore, asset-building programmes involve rigid saving plans and strong restrictions on withdrawing deposits, thus 'teaching' immigrants how to save, with positive effects on subsequently meeting deadlines in the mortgage repayment plan.

An important example of asset-building tools aimed at obtaining home mortgage loans[50] are the Individual Development Accounts (IDA) programmes in the United States[51]. IDAs are run by non-profit organizations in partnership with the financial institutions that hold the IDA accounts. The purpose of these programmes is to 'provide individuals and families with limited means an opportunity to accumulate assets and to enter the financial mainstream'. IDAs are restricted saving accounts that provide financial incentives for low-income individuals to save toward a particular set of approved purposes. Individuals make monthly deposits in their IDAs, over a specified time period; the deposits are matched on a one-for-one or higher basis[52] by outside contributors like local charities, foundations, and the federal Assets for Independence Program, a grant programme administered by the Office of Community Services in the US Department of Health and Human Services.[53] When the saving goal is reached, the full account balance of savings plus matching contributions becomes available.

7.7.3 Pension schemes

The third type of products with interesting growth potential are private pension schemes. Reductions in state pensions lead to increasing reliance on private provisions. However, the self-employed, those in low-paid and part-time jobs, and those not in the labour market at all, usually lack a private pension, and this is usually the case for immigrants. Financial intermediaries thus have a chance to acquire this market segment which represents a strong source for collecting funds that are modest in quantity for each individual, but which overall form a considerable amount.

To this end financial institutions should, firstly, stimulate demand for pension schemes by immigrants, and then propose retirement-focused asset-building savings able to meet immigrants' financial constraints. This is because the two most important reasons why immigrants do not have private pension schemes are:

1. Lack of knowledge; immigrants do not know about pension scheme opportunities or think these products are not suited with their profile.
2. Lack of disposable income: immigrants may be less able to sacrifice current income for future income.

Financial education, and accessible, transparent information, are important tools in helping immigrants to become aware of the importance of pension schemes and how they work: few people understand how personal pension contributions will translate into an income in old age and usually they are not in a position to calculate how much they need to contribute to a pension in order to secure an adequate income after retirement. To this end, it can be important for financial institutions to establish partnerships with ethnic associations because of their role as privileged channels of access with local communities. These agreements, by facilitating the spread of pension schemes in this market segment, would ultimately help banks to bring to scale their supply of these products.

Moreover, immigrants generally earn low to moderate incomes and this is why they lack disposable income to pay contributions to private pension schemes. For banks, facing the problem of lack of disposable income means providing savings plans which involve periodic payments by immigrants of modest sums. Moreover, since immigrants are more vulnerable to fluctuations in their income, these products should include the possibility of withdrawing money paid in or of closing the relationship, but without losing capital paid, as happens with many current pension plans if the subscriber ceases to make payments within the first two or three years of life of the product.

Financial institutions should thus provide products that are sufficiently portable and flexible to accommodate an insecure pattern of work that also involves frequent job changes and periods of unemployment, that are easy to understand, and that are low-cost, but that will provide a guaranteed retirement income.[54]

Finally, for people that remit money to overseas accounts with the intention of returning to their country of origin in their old age, banks should arrange products that provide retirement incomes in the currency of the country of origin, or, better still, in dollars, since savings in a strong currency are preferred.

Of course, there are doubts about whether the amounts immigrants can afford to put into a personal pension would be sufficient to provide an adequate retirement income, but this problem probably requires government intervention to be solved. Some retirement-focused asset-building schemes have been formulated with features similar to IDAs, aimed at building retirement savings for low-income earners. These initiatives are designed to include state intervention, and do not meet immigrant needs because they are directed at the local population. In 1999 US President Clinton announced a proposal to build retirement savings for low and moderate income workers.[55] Under the proposal the government was to match, on a dollar for dollar basis, voluntary contributions by low to moderate income earners. However, the proposal was never acted on. In Australia there is a product called Super Co-contribution.[56] It is a Government initiative that assists individuals to save for their retirement by similarly matching individual contributions with co-contribution on a 1.5 dollar for 1 dollar basis, up to a certain limits. However, eligibility criteria exclude people that do not hold a temporary resident visa; this excludes immigrants from participating in these programmes.

7.8 Conclusions and future perspectives

Theory and evidence suggest that it would be useful if the targeted response policies drafted by banks for migrants made reference to the needs expressed in the different phases of their life cycle. The aforementioned approach, which considers the development of needs over time, highlights the potential demand both from a qualitative and quantitative point of view and should make it easier to achieve a positive consideration of the potential represented by this market segment. The most far-sighted banks could become the first to occupy these new market niches, which in the long run could turn out to be highly profitable ventures.

A point that we suggest needs further analysis is that of the possible approaches to be adopted in addressing this market segment. The two alternative approaches are, on the one hand, the search for integration of the migrant population and, on the other, the highlighting of specific ethnic features. The first approach consists in a supply which is not differentiated, but associated with the services supplied to local market segments with similar economic resources and needs. Possible differences are found in specific services for fund transfers abroad related to remittances to the countries of origin. This still happens, as shown by the fact that the migrant population mainly resorts to agencies with specialized financial operators or to informal networks and circuits regarded as more efficient than banking networks. The second approach is based on a targeted offer; this means that dedicated counters are opened with suitably skilled staff and with *ad hoc* commercial and legal communications, but also that both specific products or product packages are prepared for the market target, and, in general, that the strategic orientation shifts towards a more specific customer segment. With this approach, the strategies might go so far as making agreements or alliances with ethnic organizations.

Each of these approaches has pros and cons; nevertheless, it is worth all banks to consider their possibilities. One of the attractions of the first approach is that it prevents the risk of creating ghettoes, and *de facto* discriminating against immigrant customers. As regards the second approach, the opposite may be the case – initiatives geared towards a specific ethnic segment may alienate other groups.

In this chapter, we suggest various types of financial innovations that can be targeted to migrants and we implicitly recommend that the second approach is preferable However, both the pros and cons of each approach should be carefully considered in elaborating strategies and offering policies: in all likelihood the above mentioned approaches will be differentiated according to the various stages of the migrant life cycle, moving from targeted offer to undifferentiated supply in order to promote migrants integration, with customized products for specific needs.

Notes

1. See OECD (2006).
2. An unusual, and in many ways unique, case is Luxembourg, where immigrants are mainly from other European countries (France, Portugal, Belgium, Germany, and Italy).
3. Part of this section was adapted from Anderloni and Carluccio (2006). See also Anderloni (2203a).
4. For a wide overview of this debate, see Goodhart (2004), Levine (1997, 2005). in which the main focus is on aggregate growth. They consider the impact on real economy, namely on the development of the country's economic activities in terms of several GNP configurations. The essential functions recognized by Levine for the financial system are described from a macroeconomic perspective and focus primarily on business activity. However, the most recent analysis and studies highlight new research perspectives on the relationship between finance, income distribution, and poverty. Furthermore, recent studies on the link between finance and growth in the developed countries have tended to address the question of whether bank-based systems are superior to the market-based ones.
5. In this respect, Sinclair (2001), p. 14 states that people facing difficulties accessing banking services can be prevented from being able 'to make an economic contribution to the community'.
6. See Kempson and Whyley (1999) and several other authors that have further studied and confirmed this nature.
7. A wider definition refers to low-income individuals as well as to socially disadvantaged people who face difficulties gaining access to the financial system in all its forms in order to meet their financial needs, e.g., to open a bank account, to have recourse to non-cash payment services, to have access to affordable credit, to build modest assets (savings and investment), taking into account uncertainties as regards length of holding and liquidity as well as forms of revenue with special regard for social security allowances and unstable work patterns. A more restrictive definition rather puts the emphasis on the fact that some specific types of financial services are absent: these specific services are sometimes defined as 'essential' and refer rather to a certain notion of universal service, that means 'services that do not have an impact on the households' budget, but they represent at the same time essential elements for the individual's life, subsistence, security and participation to the economic and social life'. See Anderloni and Carluccio (2006), pp. 5–11.
8. In this respect, Barr (2004) uses the term 'unbanked' to refer to 'individuals that do not have an account (savings, checking, or otherwise) at a depository institution' and refers to the 'underbanked' people as those with an account at a depository institute but who rely for their financial services providers (such as check cashers, pay-day lenders, auto title lenders, refund anticipation lenders, and rent-to-own companies) that largely serve low and moderate income neighborhoods. Barr observes that the problems faced by the 'unbanked' and 'underbanked' overlap significantly, but diverge in important aspects, which he further develops.

9. See Sinclair (2001). This notion is further accepted by Carbó, Gardener and Molyneux (2004). On the other hand, according to Gloukoviezoff G. (2004) financial exclusion is the process whereby people encounter such access and/or use difficulties in their financial practices that they can no longer lead a normal social life in the society in which they belong. In other terms, he links the notion with the social implications these difficulties imply and clearly underlines that the social consequences that constitute it vary depending on the society under consideration as well as the status of the person concerned.

10. See Connolly and Hajaj (2001).

11. This position is shared by Gloukoviezoff (2005) too. About this aspect, see also World Bank (2005) and the above-mentioned distinction between 'unbanked' and 'underbanked' proposed by Barr (2004).

12. This is especially the case for remittances made by migrants through money transfers and, also, by informal operators and networks. Evidence from the USA suggests that immigrants rely heavily on the alternative financial service sector not only to send remittances, but also for cashing cheques and paying bills. This is particularly true of immigrants with low incomes and low levels of education. See Dunham (2001).

13. An analysis of the main experiences worldwide is presented in Anderloni and Carluccio (2006), pp. 35–84.

14. See also § 7.4.2.

15. Part of this section was adopted from Anderloni (2006).

16. See Anderloni (2003a, 2003b).

17. See Sergi and Carchedi (1991), pp. 8–9 and Anderloni (2003b), pp. 163–4.

18. Actually, in most countries there are no legal restrictions because a valid passport suffices to open a bank account as a 'foreigner'. However, these accounts have very high fees and costs. For commercial reasons, i.e., for internal policy reasons, banks often do not publicize this.

19. In literature different theories have been developed explaining the reasons why a migrant makes remittances and according to these theories how – in principle – amount and frequency of flows will change during the life cycle. See Solimano (2003) who identifies four main approaches in literature: (i) the altruistic motive; (ii) the self-interest motive; (iii) implicit family contract: loan repayment; and (iv) implicit family contract: co-insurance.

20. Massey D.S. et al. (1993) and Schoorl J. (1995) show two different research approaches to international migration: studying why migration processes begin, and studying how the migration process continues over time.

21. See the later section on pension schemes.

22. When immigrants from the same country are concentrated in the same area, it is easier to provide them with information and to launch initiatives in their favour, even if there is no institutional organization to act in this capacity.

23. For instance they can promote bank initiatives on products, and other financial institutions, and they can refer their members to a specific bank. In some cases these associations have been targeted by banks or financial institutions wishing to reach their members.

24. Here different sources drive the process, such as the recommendations of the Bank of International Settlements and the World Bank, and also the OECD with the FATF-GAFI on Money Laundering and the European Commission.

25. See COM (2005), 600 final and Report A6 -0298/2006, Committee on Economic and Monetary Affairs. The objective of the proposed Directive is to create a Single

Payment Market where improved economies of scale and higher degree of competition would help to reduce the cost of payment systems. Therefore the Directive is aimed at establishing a common framework for the Community payment market creating the conditions for integration and rationalization of national payment systems through: (i) enhancing competition between national markets and ensuring a level-playing-field; (ii) increasing market transparency for both providers and users; and (iii) harmonizing rights and obligations of users and providers in Europe.

26. Aiming to remove legal barriers to market entry, establishing a single licence for all providers of payment services which are not connected to taking deposits or issuing e-money. See the mentioned proposal, point (8) of the introductory 'whereas'.

27. In principle those requirements should not be heavy due to the fact that these kinds of operators engage in more specialized and restricted activities. In fact, they generate risks that are narrower and easier to monitor and control than those that arise across the spectrum of credit institutions' activities.

28. In the Annex to the Directive, point (7) includes money remittances services, mentioned as follows: 'money remittances services where the cash, scriptural money or electronic-money is accepted by the payment service provider from the payment service user for the sole purpose of making a payment transaction and transferring the funds to the payee'.

29. Those cases should be subject to strict requirements related to the volume of transactions and importance of the public interest.

30. This is the case of the UK, where in 2001 the Government introduced a regime for the MSB sector, taking the approach of 'light touch' in line with the principle of 'starting low', and after five years is carrying out a structural assessment of the current regime in order to discover possible areas for reform. In Italy the anti-money laundering regulation was an occasion to regulate the activity of the agency of financial activities (in 1999) while money transfers where already subjected to a light regulation according to the Banking Law. In Spain, since 1996, enterprises specialized in the activity of money transfer are registered in the official register of foreign exchange institutions and money transfer agencies, i.e., 'establecimientos de cambio y transferencias de divisas al exterior', and they are submitted to the discipline regarding transparency and customer protection.

31. See CPSS-World Bank (2006).

32. It states that 'The market for remittance services should be transparent and have adequate consumer protection' with the aim of fostering a competitive and safe market for remittances.

33. It says that 'Improvements to payment system infrastructure that have the potential to increase the efficiency of remittance services should be encouraged.'

34. According to this principle: 'Remittance service should be supported by a sound, predictable, non-discriminatory and proportionate legal and regulatory framework in relevant jurisdictions.'

35. Here the principle is: 'Competitive market conditions, including appropriate access to domestic payment infrastructure, should be fostered in the remittance industry.'

36. 'Remittance services should be supported by appropriate governance and risk management practices', this principle states that these conditions can improve the safety and the soundness of remittance services and help protect consumers.

37. As previously stated, a number of studies, in a variety of contexts, have revealed that the immigrant population frequently meet their financial needs through informal channels or through alternative financial providers.

38. Hereinafter the term 'unbanked' describes people outside the mainstream financial system.
39. See Carbò, Gardener and Molyneux (2005), Federal Reserve Bank of Chicago and The Bookings Institutions (2006), FSA (2006), Milhaud (2006).
40. Language is a more or less serious problem according to context, that is to say according to immigrants' country of origin and host country. In countries like the UK and France, part of the immigrant population comes from countries which were once colonies, while Latin American immigrants in Spain come from Spanish-speaking countries. In these cases language is not a barrier to immigrant access to the banking system. However, in other countries, such as Italy and Germany, whose languages are spoken only in the country in question, the situation is different. In these cases immigrants are probably not familiar with the host country language, and language difficulties constitute a significant barrier to immigrants' access to the banking system. The same difficulties occur in all the above-mentioned countries, when immigrants are from countries with official languages that are different from the host country language, as in the case of immigrants from Eastern Europe.
41. See Carbò, Gardener and Molyneux (2005), Appleseed (2006b), Federal Reserve Bank of Chicago and The Brookings Institution (2006), ABA (2004).
42. See, in UK, ICM (2006) and, in the US, Inter-American Development Bank and Multilateral Investment Fund (2006b).
43. Other large MTO are: in the UK, Chequepoint, First Remit, Travelex and Express Funds; in Spain, Cabiosol, Ria Envia, and Unigiros e Mundoenvio; in Italy, Ria Envia, Money Express, Travelex, Unigiros, Go Money, and Euro Envios.
44. See Table 7.1.
45. See Paulson, Singer, Newberger and Smith (2006).
46. From an institutional perspective on the Italian debate about remittances, see Gaggi (2006) and Ministero dell'Economia e delle Finanze (2004).
47. For the USA, see Inter-American Development Bank and Multilateral Investment Fund (2006a): this survey describes which insurance and banking products are the most attractive for both senders and recipients and how these products may be acquired and applied in the remittance process.
48. See Nieri (2006).
49. See Braga (2006), Caskey (2000), Friedman and Boshara (2000), Kempson (2005) for further information on asset-building accounts and savings-building accounts.
50. It should be noted that home-ownership is only one of the possible aims of IDA programmes; the other two are education and small business development.
51. See Braga (2006) for critical analysis of the characteristics of IDAs.
52. All IDA programmes consists of two components for each participant: an Individual Development Account to which an individual contributes a predefined amount of cash and a parallel account in which all matched funds are deposited. For each dollar that the holder puts into the IDA, the programme will add a matching $1 or lessm, depending on the match rate, in the parallel account.
53. Normally the minimum amount is defined that must be deposited monthly by the participant; the participant may also deposit a higher amount, but in this case the part exceeding the agreed amount is not included when calculating the matched funds.
54. See FSA (2000).
55. See Friedman and Boshara (2000).
56. See Australian Taxation Office (2005).

Select bibliography

ABA (2004). *Best Practices in Immigrant Lending*, American Bankers Associations, May.

Anderloni, L. (2003a). *Il social banking in Italia. Un fenomeno da esplorare*, Milano: Giuffrè.

Anderloni, L. (2003b). 'Flussi migratori e flussi finanziari: il social banking', in *Secondo Rapporto Bocconi, DIA, DNA, UIC, Immigrazioni e flussi finanziari*, Milano: Egea.

Anderloni, L. (2005). 'L'exclusion financière en Italie: un phénomène encore diffus', in G. Gloukoviezoff (sous la direction de), *Rapport exclusion et liens financiers. L'exclusion bancaire des particuliers*, Rapport du Centre Walras 2004, Paris: Economica.

Anderloni, L. (2006). 'Migrants and remittances', in L. Anderloni, M. D. Braga and E. M. Carluccio, *New Frontiers in Banking Services. Emerging Needs and Tailored Products for Untapped Markets*, New York: Springer-Verlag, pp. 353–371.

Anderloni, L. and E. M. Carluccio (2006). 'Access to banking and payment services, in L. Anderloni, M. D. Braga and E. M. Carluccio, *New Frontiers in Banking Services. Emerging Needs and Tailored Products for Untapped Markets*, New York: Springer-Verlag, pp. 5–105.

Anderloni, L., E. Aro and P. Righetti (2005). 'Migrants and financial services in Spain', Mimeo.

Appleseed, (2006a). Expanding Immigrant Access to Mainstream Financial Services. Appleseed, Washington DC, www.appleseednetwork.org

Appleseed, (2006b). Expanding and Improving Financial Services for Low- and Moderate-Income Immigrant Communities Next Steps. Appleseed, Washington DC, www.appleseednetwork.org

Appleseed, (2006c). Banking Immigrant Communities. Appleseed, Washington DC, www.appleseednetwork.org

Atkinson, A. (2006). 'Migrants and financial services: A review of the situation in the UK', Working paper, PFRC, University of Bristol, March.

Australian Taxation Office (2005). 'Super Co-contribution: How it works', Canberra.

Barr, M. S. (2004). 'Banking the Poor', *Yale Journal on Regulation*, 21, Winter, 121–237.

Bauer, T. K., and M. Sinning (2005). 'The savings behaviour of temporary and permanent immigrants in Germany', IZA Discussion Papers, no.1632, June.

Braga, M. D. (2006). 'Access to investment and asset building for low income people', in L. Anderloni, M. D. Braga and E. M. Carluccio, *New Frontiers in Banking Services: Emerging Needs and Tailored Products for Untapped Markets*, New York: Springer-Verlag, pp. 141–181.

Carbó, S., E. P. M Gardener and P. Molyneux (2005). *Financial Exclusion*, Basingstoke: Palgrave Macmillan.

Caskey, J. P. (2000). 'Reaching out to the unbanked', Center for Social Development, Washington University in St Louis, Working Paper 00–15.

CECA (2002). 'Las remesas des emigrantes entre España y latinomérica', CECA, Caja Murcia, Caja de Ahorros El Monte de Se villa, SADAI, Noviembre.

Committee on Payment and Settlement System – The World Bank (2006). 'General principle for international remittance services', Consultative report, Bank for International Settlements – The World Bank, March.

Comptroller of the Currency (2006). 'Reaching minority markets: Community bank strategies, in *Community Developments – Insights*, November, pp. 1–14.

Connolly, C. and K. Hajaaj (2001). 'Financial services and social exclusion', Chifley research centre. Financial Services Consumer Policy Centre, University of New South Wales.

Dunham, C. R. (2001). 'The Role of Banks and Nonbanks in Serving Low- and Moderate- Income Communities', in J. L. Blanton, S. L. Rhine and A. Williams (eds), In Proceedings of the Changing Financial Markets and Community Development: A Federal Reserve System Research Conference, Federal Reserve Bank of Richmond, pp. 31–58.

Federal Reserve Bank of Chicago and The Brookings Institutions (2006). 'Financial access for immigrants: Lessons from diverse perspective, May.

Friedman, R. E. and Boshara R. (2000). 'Going to scale: Principles and policy options for an inclusive asset-building policy', Center for Social Development, Washington University in St. Louis, Policy Report.

FSA (2000). *In or Out? Financial Exclusion: A Literature and Research Review*, London: Financial Services Authority.

FSA (2006). *Financial Capability in the UK: Delivering Change*, London: Financial Services Authority.

Gaggi, P. (2006). 'Remittance services: The case of Italy', Conference on the CPSS-WB General Principles for International Remittance Services, The World Bank, Washington DC, May.

GES (2000). 'Bancos e Inmigrantes. Informe español', *Gabinet d'Estudis Socials*, August.

Gloukoviezoff, G. (2004). 'L'exclusion bancaire et financière des particuliers', in *L'Observatoire national de la pauvreté et de l'exclusion sociale, Les travaux de l'observatoire*, Paris: La Documentation Française, pp. 167–205.

Gloukoviezoff, G. (2005) (sous la direction de). *Rapport exclusion et liens financiers. L'exclusion bancaire des particuliers*, Rapport du Centre Walras 2004, Paris: Economica.

Goodhart, C.A.E. (ed.) (2004). *Financial Development and Economic Growth: Explaining the Links*, Basingstoke: Palgrave Macmillan.

HM TREASURY (2006). 'The regulation of money service business: A consultation', September.

HM TREASURY (2006). 'Implementing the third money laundering directive: A consultation document', July.

ICM (2006). 'BME remittance survey', Department for International Development Research Report, May.

IMF (2005). 'Two current issues facing developing countries', in *World Economic Outlook*, Cap. II, Avril 2005.

Institut Fur Finanzdienstleistungen (2000). 'Access to financial services: Strategies towards equitable provision', German National Report, Hamburg, August.

Inter-American Development Bank and Multilateral Investment Fund (2006a). 'Sending money home. Leveraging the development impact of remittances'.

Inter-American Development Bank and Multilateral Investment Fund (2006b). 'Public opinion research study of Latin American remittance senders in the United States', October.

Kempson, E. and C. Whyley (1999). *Kept In or Opted Out? Understanding and Combacting Financial Exclusion*, Bristol: Policy Press.

Kempson, E. and S. McKay and S. Collard (2005). 'Incentive to save: Encouraging saving among low-income households', Personal Finance Research Centre, University of Bristol, March.

Levine, R. (1997). 'Financial development and economic growth: Views and agenda', *Journal of Economic Literature*, 35(2).

Levine, R. (2005). 'Finance and growth: Theory and evidence', in P. Aghion and S. N. Durlauf, *Handbook of Economic Growth*, North Holland: Elsevier.

Massey, D. S., J. Arango, G. Hugo, A. Kouaouci, A. Pellegrino and J. E. Taylor (1993). 'Theories of international migration: A review and appraisal', in *Population & Development Review* 19, 431–466.

Milhaud, C. (2006). 'L'integration economique des migrants et la valorisation de leur epargne', *Caisse National des Caisses d'Epargne*, Paris, September.

Ministero dell'Economia e delle Finanze (2004). 'Italian action plan on remittances', available at: www.dt.tesoro.it

Nieri, L. (2006). 'Access to credit: The difficulties to households', in L. Anderloni, M. D. Braga and E. M. Carluccio, *New Frontiers in Banking Services: Emerging Needs and Tailored Products for Untapped Markets*, New York: Springer-Verlag, pp. 107–140.

OECD (2006). *International Migration Outlook*, Sopemi: OECD Publishing.

OECD (2005). *Migration, Remittances and Development*, OECD Publishing.

Orozco, M. (2005). 'Remittances, competition, and financial intermediation for unbanked immigrants', Paper presented before the Taskforce on Remittances and Development in the Inter-American Dialogue, 20 September.

Orozco, M. and E. Hamilton (2005). 'Remittances and MFI intermediation: Issues and lessons', Paper presented at the 2005 Financial Sector Development Conference on New Partnerships for Innovation In Microfinance, Franfurt, June.

Paulson, A., A. Singer, R. Newberger and J. Smith (2006). 'Financial access for immigrants: Lessons from diverse perspectives', Federal Reserve Bank of Chicago and the Brookings Institution, May.

Rapoport, H. and F. Docquier (2005). 'The economics of immigrants' remittances', ISA, Discussion Paper Series, DP no. 1531, March.

Sergi, N. and F. Carchedi (1991). 'L'immigrazione straniera in Italia. Il tempo dell'integrazione', *ISCOS*, Rome: Edizioni il Lavoro.

Sinclair, S. P. (2001). 'Financial exclusion: An introductory survey', Herriot Watt University, Scotland, Centre for Research into Socially Inclusive Services.

Schoorl, J. J. (1995). 'Determinants of international migration: Theoretical approaches and implications for survey research', In R. van der Erf and L. Heerings (eds), *Causes of International Migration*, Luxembourg: Office for Official Publications of the European Communities, pp. 3–14.

Solimano, A. (2003). 'Workers remittances to the Andean region: Mechanisms, costs and development impact', CEPAL.

Texas Appleseed, (2005). 'Building Texas communities. A guide for home mortgage lending to immigrant and low-income families', September.

World Bank (2005). 'Indicators of financial access – Household – Level Survey', September.

World Bank (2006). 'Global economic prospects. Economic implications of remittances and migration', The International Bank for Reconstruction and Development – The world Bank, Washington.

8
Deepening Banking Reforms of China to Ensure Sustainable Growth in a Global World

*René van der Linden**

8.1 Introduction

The Chinese authorities agreed upon a five year transition period provided by the WTO timetable to open its financial sector more fully to foreign investment by the end of 2006. Since the end of 2001, when the government began encouraging foreign companies to invest in local banks, many foreign players have invested in Chinese financial institutions. Foreign banks paid $18 billion for stakes in China's largest state-owned banks in 2005, in anticipation of selling products such as auto loans and credit cards through the banks' vast networks. This could be seen as a way to pressure the reforms of China's banking system, since the foreign investors will have an increasingly large stake in the success of China's financial system. Important steps have already been taken to push forward these reforms, for instance through the creation of a Central Banking Regulatory Commission (CBRC) and foreign listings.[1] However, foreign ownership stakes are still small, the banking reforms have not gone far enough and the state remains firmly in control. The ability of the banks to continue to extend credit to finance consumption and investments has clearly helped to sustain the economic growth, but rapid credit growth has also sparked new concerns about overheating and asset price inflation in the economy. The banking system has focused on financing the infrastructure, often encouraged by local authorities who are rewarded by the government for generating more growth. However, further

* Lecturer in Economics at the School of Economics (INHOLLAND), University of Amsterdam/Diemen in the Netherlands

consumption growth will need steady support from retail financing and it is in these areas that the inadequacies of the financial system are becoming more apparent. Mainly from a macro-economic perspective based on data from Western international institutions such as IMF and OECD, this paper will describe the further steps to be taken to modernize the Chinese banking sector in order to ensure sustainable economic growth in a global environment without digressing on successful banking strategies. The following research questions will be dealt with in order to explain the relation between reducing inefficiencies in China's banking system on the one hand and encouraging more sustainable growth on the other

- Why do banks continue to give a disproportionate share of funding to state-owned companies (SOEs)?
- How can China combine a high export- en input-led economic growth potential with an insolvent and vulnerable banking industry?
- To what extent does the weak financial sector contribute to the existence of overinvestments and overcapacity?
- How can the financial intermediation process be improved and finally lead to more market conforming interest rates, so that only profitable investments will be financed?
- Why do Chinese households save so much?
- To what extent will the injected capital by the government and the foreign investments be enough to end poor risk management in the current domestic banking industry?

In spite of the enormous economic development of the last 25 years, China has failed to handle the matter of inefficient State-owned banks (SOBs) with the risk of hard landing of the economy. In fact, China's macro-economic imbalances are related to the problems with its financial system. Firstly, the low return on savings deposits and the high risk associated with anything invested outside banks partly explains the high savings rate, consistently at 45% of GDP with a declining trend. With limited other financial options, it is understandable that there is a preference to invest in real estate, one of the few seemingly "safe" assets households can access. Secondly, a substantial part of corporate savings are re-invested in the real assets of the company itself. Furthermore, private firms know that financing from either the stock market or the SOBs is very uncertain. The Chinese banks have poured money into wasteful infrastructural projects and kept inefficient SOEs alive. This has not only created huge bad loans for the banks themselves, but also because China's investments are so unproductive, it has to transfer ever more money into its economy to maintain its current growth rate. With a fixed-asset investment ratio of 54% of GDP, no country can sustain having investment at more than it saves, which means that China has to raise the productivity of its economy. This leads to the following research questions:

- What kinds of restrictive economic policy measures can the government take in order to control growth in credit and investments?
- Why has the progress of the Chinese financial sector not matched to the rest of the real economy taking into consideration the relatively high credit to GDP ratio and the fact that the state-dominated banking system is weighed down by non-performing loans (NPLs) lending primarily to SOEs (the so called 'financial dependency triangle' between the Sate Council, SOBs and SOEs)?

Eventually we will have to take into consideration the fact that increasing integration with the global economy has made China more dependent on external demand and more vulnerable to external shocks and sudden fluctuations in the business cycle. The urgency of financial sector reforms has increased as domestic banks will need to be prepared to face intense competition when the financial sector is opened to foreign banks from the end of 2006. Banking reform in China is a race against time. Basically, the Chinese authorities have to implement a similar new Basel II (BIS) capital adequacy framework. This consists of regulatory capital requirements (pillar 1), an advanced way of reporting to the supervisory authorities (pillar 2), and the disclosure of information (pillar 3) based on a semi-planned economic environment in a Chinese context in order to improve the security and soundness of the financial system. A deepening of fast-paced banking reforms will be critical to sustaining China's economic success. The big dilemma remains: can China's banks be fully reformed while staying under government control?

This paper has the following structure: the first part about the real economy is a description of the current macro-economic situation of China, a diagnosis of its performance (in section 1.1), a description of the imbalances in the export- and investments-led economic growth (in 1.2), the restrictive economic policy measures taken since 2003 (in 1.3) and some future scenario's on the road to soft landing or hard landing (in 1.4).The second part will focus on the expanding bank-based financial system of China in order to understand the one-sided inadequate financial intermediation mechanism (in section 2.1), shortcomings of the dominant banking sector (in 2.2), a new WTO level playing field and the struggle for new customers (in 2.3) and finally this section will connect deepening banking reforms (in 2.4) with a future sustainable growth path for China (in 2.5). Finally, the paper highlights some concluding remarks and recommendations.

8.2 The current state of China's macro-economy

8.2.1 The main features of some macro-economic fundamentals

A change in the macro-economic situation appeared to have occurred near the end of 2002, which coincided with the transfer of the political leadership from Jiang Zemin and Zhu Rongji to Hu Jintao and Wen Jiabao. Since 2003 the positive inflation rate has turned out to be the beginning of a new trend. By July 2003, the Chinese economy was growing too fast and the key question is whether the overheating of the economy will lead to a 'soft or a hard landing'.[2] The more booming the economy gets, the greater the risk of a 'hard landing', and a repeat of 1994–1995 when a previous investment bubble occurred which had led to an excess capacity and a deflationary tendency for several years (1997–2003). After the bursting of the 1990s bubble, deflation set in, and staying for a long time, partly due to the trend slowdown of broad money growth. Recently, we see inflation is gradually coming back again and further price growth is expected due to the combination of declining saving rates, liberalisation of the external capital account, re-opening of the domestic equity IPO market and the coming corporate bond finance boom. These main drivers will reduce the pace of money demand growth and implies a gradual increase in trend inflation rates for the current monetary policy stance.[3]

However, the Chinese authorities are aiming at a 'soft landing' with a lower growth rate of GDP and the current macro-economic situation is quite different from a decade ago. The current policy makers have responded earlier with restrictive economic policy measures; the inflation in 1994–1995 was much higher than the inflation in 2003–2005 and the current money supply growth is much lower than ten years ago. In the early 90s the real lending interest rates were negative, while they are now low, but positive. Another difference in the current macro-economic situation compared with ten years ago is lower consumption in conjunction with higher national savings, which partly explains the surplus on the current account.

Since the outbreak of SARS, the economy has been booming again, mainly caused by increasing investments through the fast expansion of bank credits, increasing foreign direct investments (FDIs) and a rise in the investments in real estate. The services industry suffered the most from the outbreak of SARS, although within this services sector there was still some more growth, especially in the financial sector and the real estate market.[4] The real GDP growth remains around 9.5% in the period 2003–2005, but China faces increasing shortages of raw materials with increasing prices, increasing unemployment rates, overheating of the economy and an increasing gap between urban and rural areas. Severe difficulties in the banking sector need to be tackled if China is to maintain rapid growth through the next decade. If China fails, it could find itself going through the same experience as Japan in the 90s, when bad loans led to a credit crunch and a long economic slowdown. However, China's economy has a number of strengths beyond its rapid growth of GDP such as the return of government spending and the relatively high saving rates and foreign-exchange reserves.[5] However, China has been the most volatile economy in the Asian region, in particular this is true for inflation and real growth figures. As a result China goes through sharp boom/bust cycles. The first reason why the Chinese economy is so volatile is a historical lack of macro regulation. During the 80s and 90s the government removed most of its traditional socialist planning levers, but did not have functioning market institutions in place. Due to an absence of a modern banking system, this partly explains why the massive credit bubble of 1991–95 was able to last so long. In addition, the prevalence of the state-owned economy and the state monopoly in the banking system (the dominant role of the 'Big-4') partly explain the historical difficulties with fine-tuning in economic business cycles.[6]

Since 2004 the trade situation of China has strongly improved, partly supported by the undervaluation of the Chinese currency. This makes it easier for China to export more textiles to industrialized countries, sometimes causing significant unrest with some important trading partners such as Japan, US, Italy and France.[7] The increasing surplus on the current account of China rose in 2004 by 1.0% to 4.5% of GDP and increased even more in 2005 in spite of the revaluation of the RMB on the 21st July 2005. The large surplus on the current account and the many FDIs were responsible for the huge foreign exchange reserves in 2005. China has always had relatively balanced trade, until 2005, when the trade surplus suddenly jumped upwards, strengthened by the significantly undervalued currency. This is mainly caused by a collapse in import growth from heavy industrial products including metals, chemicals and machinery. China has "exported" abroad excess capacity pressures in the economy through lower import purchases and higher outward shipments. There are some signs that the capacity growth is fading, since fixed investment spending is already declining. By the end of the decade, growing commodity imports should keep the trade balance from increasing forward and of course a faster currency appreciation will have an important role to play in rebalancing the trade position again.[8]

8.2.2   Imbalances in the export- and investment-led economic growth

A number of factors can be identified as being responsible for propelling economic growth in China. Nowhere has this growing economic influence been more powerfully felt than in the world's commodity markets. The country's enormous appetite for base metals, minerals and fuels has pushed up their prices. Until now, China's increasing exports of manufactured goods have at least partly been balanced by its strong imports of raw materials. If it now starts to export both commodities and basic goods as well, trade tensions can only worsen and this imbalance will increase when not accompanied by a well-controlled financial system.[9] To a certain extent this remains a dilemma of the Chinese economy trying to achieve a sustainable growth path in the long run. The increasing exports caused a tremendous inflow of foreign exchange reserves. For a long time the authorities have protected their financial markets through a fixed exchange rate against the dollar, a partly convertible currency, and foreign capital restrictions in order to guarantee huge foreign capital inflows. Until the end of 2003, this capital inflow led to a rise in the money supply and more credit lending, mainly used for fixed investments. Although these investments can be considered as the engines of economic growth, it appeared that the authorities over-invest, for instance, in the car, steel, and real estate industry, which could bring the overall sustainability of the economy into danger.

Since the liberalization of the real estate market in 1998, an increasing imbalance in the economic growth path is the fast-rising property prices (in particular in Shanghai and some other coastal areas) due to speculation and rising incomes of a growing middle class.[10] Although the authorities have raised the mortgage and tax rate, prohibited selling of real estate too soon and selling "under construction" and issued directives aiming at cooling the market, property prices are still climbing rapidly. The interest rates are relatively low and the PBOC is reluctant to raise them sharply for fear of putting further pressure on the RMB to appreciate, which could dampen the exports and push up unemployment.[11]

Since WTO entry in 2001, most investments have been injected in the manufacturing and real estate sectors, because it was less attractive to invest in financial assets. This had some advantages for China, since these fixed investments in infrastructure are usually very illiquid, which prevents a sudden outflow of flash capital. China's economy has driven a boom in the commodity market and its growth is increasingly dependent on the use of more inputs (from abroad), rather than getting as much output and increased productivity as possible from existing inputs. A high level of investment has led to an increase in capital intensity of the economy. Since 1984 the growth of China's real capital stock has consistently been higher than real GDP growth and this growth model will inevitably reach its limits. Since 1995 the efficiency of China's investments is declining or its capital-output ratio (the inverse of the marginal productivity of capital) is rising from 4.6 in the period 1996–2000 to 4.9 in the period 2001–2003.[12]

8.2.3 Restrictive economic policy measures

Since inflation replaced deflation in 2003, the authorities have started implementing administrative measures like the closing down of investment projects in non-SEZs, implementing new guidelines requiring companies to use more of their own capital and less debt to fund steel, cement, aluminium and property projects, the sectors which show most signs of overheating.[13]

The PBOC increased the banks' reserve requirements and raised the base rate for re-lending among financial institutions in order to create a soft landing of the economy. The authorities have tried to reduce capital outflows through a rise in the interest rate (October 2004)[14] and have tried to restrain investment, prices, and lending through administrative directives under the guidance of the CBRC. The poor state that China's banks are currently in increases China's reliance on macroeconomic tools. This explains why the central bank raised its interest rates for the first time in 18 months, by 0.27% on 27 April 2006 and announced some new "guidelines" to control lending to many industries. Finally this brings the one-year interest rate to 5.85% from 5.56%, while keeping the savings deposit rate unchanged. The main objectives of this restrictive monetary policy by the PBOC since 2003 are to reduce overheating investments, to reach reasonable, not too high, asset pricing, and to rebalance consumption and investment targets. However, the task of China's policy-makers to fine-tune the economy is very limited because they do not have many tools at their disposal. Thousands of SOEs, as well as the banking system, do not respond very much to pricing signals or interest rates.[15] At the same time, with an increasing availability of financial means it becomes more difficult for the PBOC to intervene through open market operations. In this way the policy-makers lose a certain amount of control on the financial markets, necessary to reduce credit lending. The latest increase of the interest rate will very likely have the following effects. Firstly, it will increase the borrowing costs, which will be significant for highly coveraged companies such as airline operators, most of whose debt is denominated in foreign currencies. Secondly, the impact on demand will be very limited, since the interest rate responsiveness on the demand is very low. Since the consumption is not leveraged, the effect of the interest rate hike on consumer demand will be almost zero, while there might be a marginal impact on property demand, because the only highly leveraged demand in China is housing. Thirdly, the funding costs will change for capacity expansion. Probably the interest rate increase will scare off some low-return, mostly debt-funded projects.[16]

8.2.4   Future scenario's on the road to soft landing or hard landing

It is difficult to assess the extent to which China's economy is overheating, since China's boom is driven more by fixed investments than by household consumption, which dominates many Western market economies. This means that the macro-economic growth is especially vulnerable to any slowing of corporate investment or public spending on infrastructure. Since 2001 the overheating of the economy is not characterised by much price inflation, but relatively much more by asset price inflation or a rise of property prices with the risk of new bubbles as a consequence.[17] The challenge facing the policymakers is to slow down the economy enough to prevent overheating and ensure sustainable growth, but not too much to cause a hard landing as in 1989–90. A much slower growth scenario (hard landing) could pose a threat to social stability. But the authorities worry that the current high GDP rate is being sustained by irrational and resource-wasting investments. This could further weaken the bad debt burden of SOBs and eventually result in an abrupt and painful slowdown as credit dries up. So why is it proving so difficult to engineer the soft landing scenario that the government has been aiming at?

China's exchange rate policy is part of the problem. The trade surplus leads to large inflows of foreign exchange currencies, which are bought up by the central bank in order to hold down the exchange rate. But this boosts the supply of RMB deposited in banks. The PBOC usually curbs this money supply growth by borrowing back much of the excess RMB, but for a couple of months it relaxed these efforts to offset the potential impact of an upward revaluation of the RMB in July 2005. The result was a surge of cheap credit, which will inevitably mean bad news for banks when some of the loans eventually turn bad.

To help reduce net foreign currency inflows, the government announced plans that would make it possible for the first time, though still subject to quotas, for firms and households to invest in foreign security markets which might improve their security management. Still, with big events approaching such as the Beijing Olympic Games in 2008, Chinese policy makers are anxious that the economy keeps growing fast enough to ensure stability. This may make them reluctant to take the really tough measures necessary to ensure more rational growth: e.g. lifting controls on energy prices and removing restrictions on bank interest rates.[18] However, the new policy makers are eager to implement a more restrictive monetary policy in order to reduce the level of domestic demand. Since 2004 they began trying, with limited success, to put on the brakes in order to reduce fixed investments in infrastructure.

The new 11th five-year economic plan (2006–2010) gives little information about a fundamental shift in spending priorities and is modestly aiming at a mere doubling of GDP per person between 2000 and 2010. This means that the current GDP growth rate might slow down considerably to an average annual growth rate of 7.5% for the next few years. Because of the decentralized economic structure, the local authorities might have other, usually higher double-digit growth predictions, than the central government has in mind. Besides these growth prospects China calls for more environmentally friendly production combined with sustainable economic growth and a reduction of energy costs, in order to become less dependent upon foreign investments. In the absence of a comprehensive social-security system, the government should firstly increase its own consumption on health care, education and social-security in rural and urban areas taking the rapid ageing of the population into consideration.[19]

8.3   China's bank-based financial system

8.3.1   Inadequate financial intermediation mechanism

The financial intermediation process in China is characterized by several factors of which the following are the most important. Firstly, almost two-thirds of domestic savings continue to go to the public sector, mainly in the form of bank credits. Secondly, China's large pool of savings combined with a lack of alternative financial assets has been almost wholly intermediated through the domestic banking system.[20] Consumer households became the most important financial intermediation nexus for economic growth. Thirdly, financial intermediation is largely bank-based and dominated by the 'Big-4' with still relatively underdeveloped, but expanding financial markets. There is evidence that the resources intermediated through bank lending have been misallocated, which is reflected in the excess capacity built up in the 90s in the real estate and manufacturing sectors.[21]

China has a relatively high level of financial system depth[22] which grew from 11% of GDP in 1994 to 221% of GDP at the end of 2004. This indicates that a large portion of savings in the economy is intermediated by formal financial institutions (in particular by banks). This financial depth is explained mainly by China's high savings rate and closed capital account. Because China prohibits most capital outflows, this huge pool of savings is kept in the domestic financial system. It is augmented by a high level of foreign capital inflows, both directly into its equity markets and indirectly into the financial system through FDIs. However, two factors would likely lower China's financial depth. Firstly, the unusually high level of corporate deposits equivalent to 53% of GDP, partly because corporations are sometimes obliged to keep deposits as collateral against loans, inflate China's financial depth. Secondly, two-thirds of the shares issued on China's domestic exchanges are owned by the government, are legally non-tradable and cannot be exchanged. Excluding spare corporate deposits and the value of non-tradable equity shares lowers China's overall financial depth to 176% rather than 221% of GDP, which is still a relatively high percentage compared to other countries with similar levels of GDP per capita and explains how strong China's one-sided financial system is in mobilizing its savings.[23]

The most striking institutional feature of China's financial system is the dominance of its banking sector, which intermediates nearly 75% of the capital in the real economy (in the US only 19%). The Chinese banks' role is even larger if we take into account that they collect the bulk of household savings and have provided 95% of corporate funding in recent years. Chinese banks accept very few forms of collateral and since they are the major source of capital, the excess capital of some companies is kept in bank deposits because they cannot find suitable investment opportunities and its not common to pay out profits to shareholders. In addition, the high levels of bank deposits is caused by a lack of debt securities to fund their liquidity needs and because payment system inefficiencies prevent large companies with many branches from optimizing cash management nationally.[24]

8.3.2 Shortcomings of the dominant banking sector

The most obvious problem for China's banking system is its stock of non-performing or bad loans (NPLs). China's 'Big-4' have around 300 billion euro of outstanding bad loans. A lot of money has been put into real estate, which has not been very beneficial. In that sense the bad loans are three times as high as the official figures published by the authorities.[25] Significant progress has been made in reducing this stock of NPLs, from 31% of loan balances in 2001 to only 10% in 2005 for the large commercial banks. Since 1997, the government has injected new capital into China's banks and transferred a large proportion of NPLs to the state-owned Asset Management Companies (AMCs), set up in 1999. Since 2001, nearly 60% of the reduction of the NPLs has been due to the transfer to the four AMCs. However, private estimates[26] for recent years suggest the real value of NPLs may be twice as high as the official figures, because loan reissues could be masking the true extent of the problem, making banks technically insolvent. Although China has made some progress in shifting NPLs off the banks' balance sheets, there is little sign that the banks themselves have fundamentally changed their behavior and become more efficient lenders. The central authorities do not have enough grip on all kinds of provincial and local networks, due to the decentralized structure of the banking system. The huge amount of bad debts is the most visible sign of the persistent misallocation of capital. According to a McKinsey study China's GDP would be a staggering $320 billion, or 16%, higher if its lenders knew how to lend. Around $60 billion could be gained from raising the banks' operating efficiency by cutting costs, putting in proper electronic payment systems, and developing bond and equity trading. The rest would come from reallocate loans to more productive parts of the economy. The banks should switch funds from poorly run state-owned firms to private enterprises, which contribute 52% of GDP but account for only 27% of outstanding loans. This would both increase the efficiency of investment and raise the returns of many small savers.[27] The current legal framework is insufficiently developed. Current debtors can get away without paying loans, nobody needs to worry about bearing the legal consequences of default risks. There is a lack of transparency in the financial situation of debtors making it difficult to know whether or not they are truly unable to repay their loans. The market that handles NPLs is still inadequate and lacks a number of regulatory bodies and competition. Many enterprises want to avoid paying loans and are protected by the local government and there are no clear guidelines to properly assess the NPLs.[28]

Chinese banks need more effective performance-management systems. Loan officers face few consequences for issuing bad loans, particularly to SOEs, and little reward for taking a well-calculated risk in new segments.

Managers therefore have insufficient incentives to expand lending to household and SME loans, which typically have higher risks, but also potentially higher average returns, than loans to very large companies and SOEs. These weaknesses are barriers to expanding lending to SMEs. Banks continue to give a disproportionate share of funding to SOEs. From the banks' perspective, lending to SOEs is considered a "safe bet", as they are perceived to have an implicit guarantee by the government. The fast-growing private companies and SMEs contribute a lot to GDP, but receive a disproportionately small share of formal financing. SMEs funding is crowded out by lending to large companies, their access to credit is a significant obstacle and varies significantly in different regions. Banks are hampered by the limited coverage of independent credit agencies that assess the creditworthiness of companies, and by the absence of a consumer credit agency, which would allow SMEs to borrow funds directly. Because SMEs get little external finance, they must rely on informal lending, retained earnings, and private equity in order to finance their operations, which curbs China's economic growth. Better access to capital and connections with banks and regulatory bodies are the keys to success for a small business in China, regardless of the operational efficiency. SMEs use China's large, but high-cost, informal lending market from underground lending institutions and from family and friends as a last resort.[29] In more mature Western economies, banks mainly serve individuals and SMEs and take deposits from these segments, offer a variety of accounts, and provide debit and credit cards as well as mortgages and loans. The largest companies in Western economies seek funding not from banks, but from capital markets, where overheads are lower. In China, however, 10% of bank loans have gone to consumers and two-thirds of all China's bank lending goes to corporations, the bulk of it to large businesses that would and should normally raise their funding from capital markets. A disproportionately large share of funding goes to the SOEs, leaving smaller private companies credit constrained. Chinese banks also offer very few off-balance sheet services. The differences with the Western financial markets are explained by several factors, such as weak governance and a lack of commercial mindset due to the high level of state ownership of Chinese banks, operational weaknesses and a decentralized structure, which will make bank reforms more difficult to implement.

In contrast to the rest of China's economy, in which state ownership has declined greatly over the past ten years, the banking system remains firmly in government hands.[30] In the past year, the government has allowed "strategic" pre-IPO investments by foreign banks in several large banks. CBRC have decided to seek foreign financial investments in order to gain banking expertise. For example the Chinese Construction Bank, which went public in October 2005, listed on the Hong Kong exchange, rather than domestic stock markets and raised $18 billion. Although these foreign investments bring with them new management ideas and a position on the board, foreign ownership stakes are still small, and the state remains firmly in control.[31] China also has roughly 120 city commercial banks and joint stock banks, as well as more than 30,000 rural and urban credit cooperatives, most of which are controlled or influenced by various levels of government. As a group, these smaller institutions account for more than half of new lending, but they are more difficult to regulate and monitor. China has a history of strong provincial leaders and a relatively weak central control and because of this geographic dispersion, China's economy is often said to be a collection of provincial economies that are loosely integrated. The same holds true in the banking sector. A good deal of autonomy remains at the branch and regional levels in many places, with little direct control from the headquarters. Many local authorities work on the principle that as long as their areas achieve rapid economic growth with minimum unrest, then they have a considerable leeway to do as they want.[32] This decentralized structure makes introducing more market-oriented lending decisions more difficult, because lending decisions made at the local branch level are more susceptible to influence from local government to favor local SOEs. Their diffuse structure also makes it more difficult for banks to focus on particular customer segments. As a result, some corporate or consumer borrowers that default on a loan in one bank or region can still quite easily acquire a loan in another place.[33]

A key weakness of the current Chinese banking system is a lack of transparency. It is slow to meet the needs of current economic developments, and it lacks the products and services required to attract liquidity for redistribution, based on risk and return. The banking industry is built on shifting sands since they vastly overstate their profits because of the practice of capitalizing interest payments and accruing interest on NPLs and the absence of a deposit insurance scheme. In addition, in the absence of universally consolidated financial reporting, some banks continue to over report their profits if their subsidiaries have lost money.[34] Many banks have a lack of good internal credit assessment capabilities and there are no nationwide standards for collecting and sharing the necessary data. In addition, effective corporate governance is needed to manage the risks that banks undertake in their business. It is also necessary to avoid misappropriation and fraud, things which have plagued China's banking system for many years.[35]

8.3.3   A new WTO level playing field and the struggle for new customers

Although foreign banks are likely to compete only in coastal cities, at least in the initial period, the pressure on domestic banks can be high as the 'Big-4' extracts about 95% of their profits from many coastal cities. Chinese banks currently offer a limited range of undifferentiated products and services so foreign players will be able to attract new customers. Many foreign banks recognize the opportunities created by the opening of China's financial services sector, but they are uncertain about how or when their investments in the market will grow to become sustainable, successful operations. They assess the risk-return trade-off as far too high.[36] The key unknown is the speed of market deregulation, the lack of transparency in the regulators' decision-making processes. There is always another layer of decision-makers and an additional uncertainty surrounds the development of China's financial sector as a whole. In such a relatively immature market, foreign banks will need to invest time and money to fully understand their potential customers and the products and services that will appeal to them. For example, the typical credit-card customer segment in today's China is still difficult to penetrate, as the Chinese customers do not spend more than they have.

Because there is no 'lender of last resort' in China, the obvious question is whether depositors will believe that these foreign banks will drive the SOBs into open bankruptcy, and hence rush to withdraw their savings from SOBs, setting in motion the vicious downward spiral of credit contraction. The Chinese banking market has great growth potential, but high risks. That's why in conjunction with the new WTO accession China's opening to foreign bank investments is the acquisition of advanced banking expertise and technology, especially in the areas of risk control, a notorious weak spot for Chinese banks.[37] If the Chinese government decides to keep the SOBs as the dominant financial intermediation mechanism, then it could be argued that SOBs should not be recapitalized again. However, China's WTO accession has made recapitalization of the SOBs inevitable in the coming decade, because the large NPLs in the SOBs mean that they have much higher operating costs than the foreign banks. Since in the "new WTO level playing field" banks will not be allowed to have any NPLs, they can offer higher deposit rates and a lower lending rate than the "old" SOBs, and then capture both the deposit and lending business of the SOBs. A very important priority for the financial sector reform is the appearance and growth of more competitive domestic private banks. They might offer customers more choice and investment opportunities and lead to more competition within the banking industry, resulting in resources being more effectively allocated than those of the SOB's monopoly.

China has injected new capital into its biggest banks, set up corporate boards with independent directors and pushed them to list abroad. The big question is whether it will be enough to end the poor risk management. Currently, a few foreign banks focus on competition to build up a vast retail-banking network of their own from scratch. At the end of October 2005, the assets of foreign banks were just 2% of total banking assets in China. The lure for both domestic and foreign banks is China's underdeveloped retail market. In its WTO commitments, China promised to allow foreign banks to tap into China's local currency retail-lending market and its 1.3 billion consumers at the end of 2006. Foreign banks will be able to issue RMB-denominated deposits from Chinese individuals. But foreign banks focus primarily on investments rather than competition and on a "playing field with more levels". Only a few foreign banks have built a network with local-currency retail customers.[38]

Many shortcomings caused by the NPL-problem, operational weaknesses and banks' dependence on corporate lending put the banking system at risk for the future. Large banks' profitability would be significantly affected if affluent customers were to migrate to smaller local banks or to foreign banks following their entry into RMB-denominated products (end of 2006). Since 2% of the affluent customers produce more than half of the banks' profit, the existing banks could face a liquidity crisis if even a small number of these customers were to shift to foreign competitors. This means that the domestic banks should improve their operations now, taking into consideration their larger branch networks and the fact that Chinese consumers do not place a lot of value on foreign brands in the banking sector. Banks' dependence on corporate lending means they would be in trouble should large companies turn to bonds as their preferred form of debt, as they do normally in market-based economies. Moreover, when interest rates are further deregulated over the coming years as planned, bank margins will likely be squeezed and if banks move toward more fixed-rate or long-term products, they may be exposed to large Asset and Liability Management (ALM) risks on their balance sheets. Currently, Chinese banks do not have the sophisticated treasury and ALM capabilities they need to cope with this outcome of a deregulated interest rate environment. Increasingly, they accept real estate as collateral for corporate loans, but China's real estate market has grown rapidly in recent years. If the economic growth slows significantly and/or the property market slows down dramatically, the government's fear for hard landing, then NPLs could shoot upwards and as a consequence further deepening of banking reforms are needed as soon as possible.[39]

8.3.4 Deepening banking reforms

Banking reforms in China have been improved by stronger regulation as well as the upcoming privatization of leading banks, although the system remains weighed down by large NPLs and needs a privatization of property and land.[40] China's banking sector is not as weak as it might look, because it has little external debt and most of the banking obligations are local. In addition, China has huge foreign exchange reserves and the current policy makers are not reluctant to clean up the bad loans and are intensely aware that they need to maintain stable growth to prevent a decade-long economic slump as has happened in Japan. Led by the CBRC, the banking sector is undergoing a transformation through strengthened prudential standards, loan classification systems and governance requirements more or less in the line of the three pillars of the new Basel-II agreement (namely, enough capital adequacy requirements, a prudential supervision review and market discipline and transparency). According to the Boston Consulting Group[41] the following ten mega trends will transform banking in China:

1. Banks will shift from product silos to customer-based competition;
2. Fee-based income will increase as a proportion of total banking revenues;
3. The walls dividing banking, securities, and insurance will collapse;
4. Joint-stock banks will challenge the market position of the 'Big-4';
5. Foreign banks will cherry pick the most attractive customer, product, and geographic segments;
6. The gap will widen between China's developed East and its underdeveloped West;
7. Sophisticated players will spur growth in financing in SMEs;
8. The infrastructure supporting credit, information, and payments will improve dramatically;
9. The infrastructure will shift from primarily bank credit financing to financing from the capital markets;
10. Overcoming the scarcity of talent will become an increasingly important, and challenging factor for success.

Furthermore additional steps should be taken to improve the underdeveloped payment and customer-loan market system and the small and underdeveloped equity and bonds market. China's payment system is still heavily paper based for both wholesale and retail transactions, because of the slow adaption of electronic payments by consumers and retailers, and the reluctance of many bank branches to build links to the China National Automatic Payment System (CNAPS). Although the payments system is developing slowly, China is currently in the process of building a modern infrastructure for both wholesale and retail payments. Until a few years ago, interbank payment transactions across China were made using the "Electronic Interbank System" (EIS) that functioned on a gross, rather than net, settlement basis (each payment settled individually, even small ones). The CNAPS' success would create benefits for all financial system participants across the economy in terms of increased payment efficiency, security and treasury management, lower level of informality (less tax evasion) and better access to capital. Ultimately this will reduce financial risks and lead to higher and more sustainable economic growth. Since 2003, however, CNAPS has been put in place in some cities and offers both gross settlement for high-value payments and net end-of-day settlement for smaller-value payments. Still, CNAPS has a relatively low level of coverage in the economy today because of the high capital investments required by local banks to build links with CNAPS, and the decentralized structure of most banks is prohibiting more widespread adoption. For retail payments many consumers and businesses still prefer to use cash instead of electronic payments. Electronic payment systems are still in the infancy stage because the use of cash is an easier way to avoid taxes, the many small shops do not want to make the required initial investments and a large portion of China's population is still not using banks.

Lack of financial services for households lowers consumption and contributes to a higher household savings rate, which reflects a deficiency in the financial system, rather than a success for the banking sector.[42] The emphasis on lending to large corporations has left retail banking in China underdeveloped. Although the amount outstanding on mortgages and credit cards is still small, consumer credit is growing fast, due to rapid expansion in both the real estate and the credit card market. Households also lack diversified savings options because financial intermediaries are so scarce in the financial system. Over 80% of total household financial assets are kept in cash, bank deposits and savings accounts, which generally provide poor returns, but are the most attractive investments from a historical risk-return standpoint. China's high households savings rate has been driven mostly by strong economic growth and China's demographic profile. The precautionary motive for saving is also very strong in China, possibly because there are so few consumer financial products available, but Chinese households with life or health insurance do not save less. The very large flow of funding to the less productive SOEs has biased China's growth toward investment rather than consumption.[43]

The rather small and underdeveloped equity market suffers from poor selection of companies for IPOs and inadequate supervision and oversight of listed companies. In addition, the best Chinese companies list on overseas exchanges and a lack of institutional investors, hindered by restrictions on their investment portfolios, result in speculative trading and diminish market discipline. The stock market has consequently been more a vehicle for delivering government policy on privatization and recapitalisation, rather than a market where strongly performing companies seek to raise funds. Contrary to the equity market, China's bond markets, although very small in size, have performed relatively well. The corporate bond market is dominated by just a few large issuers, all companies in which the government is heavily involved.[44]

8.3.5   A future sustainable economic growth path

China's biggest economic challenge today is how to stimulate domestic demand, especially private consumption. The cheap labour is not China's advantage, but its problem because of a lack the purchasing power to consume. China has become the manufacturing floor of the world, not only because of cheap labour, but because China has the most open and flexible market. As China faces higher costs of production inputs, such as energy, the country is under pressure to increase productivity and innovation. This stampede leads to a new "two-way 21st-century gold rush": expectations of lucrative returns, competition for the best niches and plenty of risk. On the one hand, Chinese banks are spending a lot on research and development to go up into the value chain. On the other hand, foreign investors are rushing into China to take advantage of their low costs.[45]

Since the 90s the Chinese authorities have three pillars of their policy (in the line with the BIS-II accord), namely a reduction of the bad loans by strengthening the capital structure of banks with capital injections, introducing more prudential principles through credit lending and market liberalisation. Firstly, cheap credit to SOEs leads to overinvestments, while credit lending to profitable private companies has been reduced with some favourable consequences for the budget. Secondly, overinvestments lead to a larger cyclical volatility. According to the Keynesian 'accelerator theory', the level of investment depends on the rate of change of GDP, and as a result tends to be subject to substantial fluctuations. As long as the growth expectations are persistently high there is no problem, but if GDP declines, investments will decrease even more and, because of the enormous size of the investments, that might result in a hard landing of the economy. For a long time the export-led economic growth was financed by foreign capital. China has become less dependent upon foreign capital and has become more exposed to the whims of the business cycle. Thirdly, overheating might lead to a cyclical decline and another wave of investment injections is very unlikely taking into consideration a structural decline of the consumption rate. In the latest tenth National People's Congress of the Communist Party of China (CPC) more attention has been paid to an increase of private consumption. This will not be easy when it is combined with a restrictive monetary policy to dampen credit growth. This policy should be implemented in such a way that it discourages fixed-investments in certain faster growing areas and encourages private consumption. However, consumers have more reason to save in the absence of a social security net and rapidly increasing medical and education costs force people to arrange this for themselves. A cooling down of the global economy in combination with overinvestments on a macro-level and overheating in some parts of the economy might be the forerunner of a cyclical decline or hard landing in China.[46]

8.4   Concluding remarks and recommendations

The current state of China's macro-economy has to be changed and so has its bank-based financial system, which is still not sophisticated enough to compete on the world stage. The export- and investment-led economic growth imbalances expressed by over-capacity and risks of a property bubble in coastal China will have to be rebalanced. In the near future China should pay more attention to solving the one-sided inadequate financial intermediation mechanism, in order to absorb and allocate the national savings surplus in a more efficient way and raising domestic consumption and reducing the inefficient fixed investments in the infrastructure. We already can see the first signs into this direction. The establishment of improved channels to co-ordinate more private rather than public investments will be an effective way to recycle the pool of private savings back into the real economy. The domestic banks are likely to come under increasing competitive pressure, especially once foreign banks have entered the Chinese market completely under WTO accession commitments at the end of 2006. It is expected that China will have to import more resources from abroad if the authorities are aiming at a sustainable GDP growth rate of around 7.5% for the next few years. Currently, the economic development of China is at a stage where they no longer need so much foreign capital. Scarcity of talent will become increasingly important, so the policy makers are looking for foreign expertise in product development, design and marketing based on an old Chinese saying: "for reading scripture, a monk from outside is the best".[47] The party leaders still regard state ownership of the banks as a vital breakwater against financial instability. They know that it often leads to unproductive investments, but it also shores up public confidence in the banking system, which is essential for maintaining the flow of savings and foreign investments. Chinese banking officials admit that there is a need for foreign expertise, but fear that encouraging the development of privately controlled Chinese banks would worsen financial risks. With its huge foreign exchange reserves, strong revenues, and low budget deficit, China still has the means to prop up its banks. The savings rate is likely to remain high, given concerns about pensions and other social-security provisions and there are almost no alternatives for savers to put in their money: China's stock markets have been among the world's worst performers in the past five years, and controls on capital outflows remain relatively effective. The opening up of China's banking system to foreign competition at the end of this year, will have little effect in the short run because the banking regulatory commission (CBRC) makes the cost of setting up large branch networks prohibitively high.

China is struggling to retain its high volume of trade flows and reduce its unemployment rate, social unrest and corruption in spite of its successful macro-economic performance in terms of relatively low inflation rates, increasing surpluses on the current account, a relatively long-term external debt and an annual savings rate consistently at around 45%. Furthermore, it is very likely that the dominant role of the government has prevented the bad loans resulting in a credit crunch. However, the current policy makers are facing a dilemma when they fine-tune their macro-economy with restrictive monetary and fiscal policy measures, since they have far fewer policy tools at their disposal than their counterparts in predominantly Western market economies. Therefore China continuously has to reform its financial system. Although the central bank raised the interest rate several times in order to create a 'soft landing' of the overheating economy, it is not plausible that this will have a significant dampening effect on loan demands as long as the 'soft budget constraints' for the state-owned enterprises are kept alive. The greatest threat to the stability of China's financial system is fiscal sustainability and the biggest threat to fiscal sustainability is successive rounds of bank recapitalisation. Without solving this dilemma, the problem of non-performing loans cannot be solved and this probably requires some new rounds of bank recapitalisation plus a further deepening of banking reforms.

Far more costly than bank recapitalisation are the inefficiencies in China's financial system and its misallocation of capital. Consequently, the real growth engines of the economy are deprived of capital. The poor allocation of capital lowers productivity and investment efficiency and contributes to China's high savings rate, which raises questions about the sustainability of the growth path that China is pursuing. A rising capital-output ratio combined with a high but declining and inefficiently used savings rate are some signals for a 'hard landing' in the near future. In more mature financial systems, very large organisations like China's state-owned enterprises do not take bank loans, because they are a more expensive form of financing than corporate bonds and commercial paper, for instance. However, in China bank loans to state-owned enterprises are at surprisingly low interest rates and combined with the long and cumbersome issuance process of bonds, this explains why even large companies continue to seek funding from banks and not from bond markets. The low cost of bank debt encourages large companies to use banks as primary source of capital. Poor allocation of funding lowers China's overall productivity and promotes wasteful investments. In order to improve the allocation of capital, reforms that enable a larger share of funding to go to the more productive private enterprises would increase investment efficiency and raise GDP. While such reforms might result in job losses in the public sector that failed to improve their operations, many new jobs would be created in the private sector. The inefficiencies of China's banks, payment system, retail business, bond and equity markets significantly increase the cost of financial intermediation in China's economy. To cover these costs, the financial intermediaries must offer lower returns to savers, or raise the rates charged to borrowers, or both. Deeper banking reforms to improve the efficiency of the financial sector would reduce these costs, enabling it to provide the same services and functions as today, but at lower prices. As a result, fee-based income will increase and net interest margins (currently, with a spread of 3.3% points) will fall as a proportion of total banking revenues. Further reforms to improve the banking efficiency are focusing on a move from a paper-based payments system to an electronic one, developing a corporate bond and improving the equity market, replacing informal lending with formal banking services and diversifying the financial portfolio available to companies. Finally, Chinese households and firms could earn higher returns on financial assets against lower costs of capital.

Since many of the shortcomings in the bank-based financial system are interlinked, only a co-ordinated, transparent, system wide reform can shape the modern financial system China requires to support the country's rapid growth and shift the economy into a more sustainable growth path. The current priorities for banking reforms have focused mostly on the large commercial banks to prepare them for foreign equity listing. Since its creation in 2003, CBRC has focused on reducing and resolving the volume of bad loans and WTO conditions have also forced some specific reforms on the banking system. The problems studied in this paper on China's financial system are all characterized by cheap corporate bank loans. In addition, these problems are closely interlinked by an underdeveloped consumer loan market, a very small bond market, a lack of domestic institutional investors, a small underdeveloped equity market, inefficient bank operations and very limited access to capital for small businesses. Priorities for the reform agenda in order to improve the allocation of capital and create a more balanced, less bank-dominated, and more efficient financial system must address each of these interlinkages. Reforms primarily to improve allocation of capital by the banking system should focus on improvement of the corporate governance and more competition in the banking sector in order to strengthen bank lending decisions; change collateral requirements for small businesses to improve their access to bank credit; improve information and data availability to make good lending decisions and deregulate the corporate bond market so that the largest companies can seek funding outside the banking sector. Reforms to balance the financial system and reduce the dominance of the banking sector should focus on deregulation of bank interest rates; more growth of domestic institutional investors through deregulation; and the creation of more strategic relationships between the foreign (e.g., HKSE) and mainland equity markets to leverage the strengths of both. Finally, there will be a need for more capital account liberalisation and exchange rate flexibility since China will gradually become more exposed to the whims of the fluctuations in the business cycle. The more privatized the real economy becomes, the more it needs to rely on market-driven prices and interest rates.[48]

On the one hand the current authorities seem to have a more global market-driven mindset, however, on the other hand the decentralized structure of the overall economy makes introducing more market-oriented banking decisions more difficult. China's biggest dilemma is that orders issued in Zhongnanhai, the party headquarters in Beijing, sometimes never leave the compound, but China's local leaders know where to draw the line.[49] The "iron grip" of the central authorities does not make much impression on the local leaders. Central decisions on a macro-economic level do not match at all with many micro-economic decisions on a local level.

Terms and abbreviations

ABC   Agricultural Bank of China
ALM   Asset and Liability Management

AMCs	Asset Management Companies created in 1999 (Huarong, China Orient, Cinda and Great Wall)
'Big-4'	Four main state-owned commercial banks: ABC, BoC, ICBC and CCB (more than half of commercial lending is still provided by them)
BIS	Bank for International Settlements
BoC	Bank of China
BOCOM	Bank of Communications (fifth biggest lender after the 'Big-4')
CBRC	China Banking Regulatory Commission, set up in 2003 (formulate regulatory rules governing the banks; authorize the establishment, changes, termination and business scope of banks; monitor banks' operation and take enforcement actions against offence activities; conduct fit-and-proper tests on the senior bank executives)
CCB	China Construction Bank
CMB	China Merchants Bank or China Minsheng Bank (= private-owned bank)
CNAPS	China National Automatic Payment System
CPC	Communist Party of China
CPI	Consumer Price Index
EIB	Export and Import Bank of China
EIS	Electronic Interbank System
FDI	Foreign Direct Investment: represents the finance used either to purchase assets for setting up a new subsidiary or to acquire an existing business operation
HSBC	Hong Kong and Shanghai Banking Corporation
IAS	International Accounting Standard
ICBC	Industrial and Commercial Bank of China
IMF	International Monetary Fund
IPOs	Initial Public Offerings
NPLs	Non-Performing Loans: both bad loans inherited from the past and new loans that will deteriorate to become classified loans
OECD	Organisation for Economic Development and Reconstruction
PBOC	People's Bank of China central bank of PRC (initiate related laws and rules for financial institutions; formulate and implement monetary policy; supervise the inter-bank's lending, debt market, foreign exchange and gold markets; formulate RMB policies; circulate RMB)
PPI	Producer Price Index
PPP	Purchasing Power Parity: exchange rate corrected to take into account the purchasing power of a currency (price of a Big Mac is the Economist's guide to PPP-rates)
PRC	People's Republic of China (since 1949)
RMB	Ren Min Bi official currency of China nominated in Yuan (CNY)[50]
RPI	retail price index (excludes services and housing)
SARS	Severe Acute Respiratory Syndrome (broke out in the first half of 2003)
SEZs	Special Economic Zones
ShDB	Shenzhen Development Bank (Shenzhen is located near Guangzhou)
SHSE	Shanghai Stock Exchanges
SMEs	Small and Medium Enterprises
SOBs	State-Owned Banks
SOEs	State-Owned Enterprises
SZSE	Shenzhen Stock Exchanges
WTO	World Trade Organisation

Notes

1. For the first time ever, The Banker publishes in June 2006 a top 100 banks in China listing, demonstrating the country's growing financial sophistication.
2. In reality, the real economy is slowing more markedly than these (highly) suspect official figures suggest. China has an institutional bias to over-reporting growth at the bottom of a cycle and under-reporting it at the top, to reduce the volatility of the numbers. Actual inflation could be 1pp higher or so, but the official data do a good job of capturing inflation volatility. See: The Economist Newspaper, 21st July 2005, p. 2 and Anderson, March 2007, p. 23.
3. Anderson, J., March 2007, p. 22–24.
4. Services sectors are the engines of sustainable economic growth in most economies, while China's economy is weighted towards manufacturing and construction (46% of GDP in 2004, 13% agriculture and mining and 41% services) concentrated in the export zones and coastal areas. Since the services sector is more labour intensive and it will create more jobs, financial reforms could thus help to promote more employment.
5. The Economist, 8th October 2005, p. 77.
6. Anderson, J., March 2007, p. 5–6.
7. Around 57% of China's exports (2004) is still produced by foreign companies whether or not accompanied by a joint venture construction. In that sense 'Made in China' is not always the same as 'Made by China', by Daling, T. in FD, 2005.
8. Anderson, J., March 2007, p. 31–35.
9. The Economist, 8th October 2005, p. 77–78.
10. Although China is a vast and populous country, banking opportunities are highly concentrated. The wealthiest 0.4% of households in China own more than 60% of the country's personal wealth. The Boston Consulting Group, May 2006, p. 8.
11. The Economist, 3rd June 2006, p. 55.
12. McKinsey&Company, May 2006, p. 77–78.
13. Further steps in the reforms of the financial sector have been taken along the northcoast in the so called Binhai New Area zone in order to enhance the freedom of venture capitalists and private investment in banking.
14. The one-year deposit rate and the one-year base lending rate were both raised by 27 basis points to 2.25% and 5.58% respectively. PBOC also removed the ceiling on loan rates to soften the reduction of credit on private business. In Nov. 2004 PBOC followed up on the tightening by raising the reserve requirements on commercial bank foreign exchange deposits.
15. IMF, Rapport, People's republic of China, Staff report for the 2005 article IV consultation, Chapter 1A and 1B, David Burton en Carlos Muniz, 8 July 2005, p. 4–10 and Icard, A., BIS Papers No.15, 2002, p. 14–18.
16. Robin Zhou, KPMG Shanghai, 8th May 2006.
17. Many prosperous Chinese in the coastal areas are investing in real estate as a way to diversify their savings portfolios, since they cannot invest overseas. There has also been speculative buying by overseas Chinese investors. See The Economist, 15th May, 2004, p. 67.
18. The Economist, 29th April 2006, p. 59–60.
19. IMF, Rapport, People's republic of China, Staff report for the 2005 article IV consultation, Chapter 1C, David Burton en Carlos Muniz, 8th July 2005, p. 10.

20. Currently there are five main categories of banks in China, namely 4 state-owned commercial banks (the 'Big-4': ABC, BoC, ICBC and CCB), 3 policy banks, joint-stock commercial banks, local banks and foreign banks.
21. Aziz, Jahangir, and Christoph Deunwald, IMF Working Paper, 2002, p. 3–7.
22. Financial system depth is the ratio of a nation's stock of financial assets, divided by the size of the economy or GDP and measures the degree to which funding in a nation's economy is intermediated through the formal financial system. See: McKinsey&Company, May 2006, p. 26.
23. McKinsey&Company, May 2006, p. 27–29.
24. McKinsey&Company, May 2006, p. 29–30.
25. Currently Ernst & Young (2006) claimed that China's stock of NPLs added up to $911 billion. This is more 5.5 times the latest government estimate of $164 billion, published in March 2006. The Ernst & Young report was more than a compilation of historic NPLs, since it has also estimated new NPLs that will result from lending between 2002 and 2004, which account for most of the difference between Ernst & Young and the official figures. Bad loans are almost certainly greater than the official numbers say, even if they are less than the Ernst & Young estimate. The Economist, 20th May 2006, p. 82.
26. For instance, USB estimates the true value of NPLs is $500 billion, as opposed to the $300 billion official figure, Anderson, 2006.
27. The Economist, 29th April 2006, p. 74.
28. According to PBOC nearly 30% of NPLs are due to wrong decisions made by various local governments in their efforts to promote economic development; nearly 30% NPLs are due to SOEs that include ownership restructure and bad performance; nearly 10% are due to lack of laws and regulations and 10% are due to economic restructuring by the central government. Finally, another 20% are caused by the banks themselves, mainly due to the banks' lack of risk assessment in adapting to a market-oriented system.
29. McKinsey&Company, May 2006, p. 61–64.
30. This also stands in contrast to the experience of Eastern Europe's transitional economies and other emerging markets. State-controlled banks accounted for 83% of bank assets in China in 2004, compared with 33% in Brazil, 18% in South Korea and 20% in Poland.
31. There is only one bank in China that is run by foreign owners, the Shenzhen Development Bank.
32. The Economist, 3rd June 2006, p. 55.
33. McKinsey&Company, May 2006, p. 31–40.
34. BIS Policy Papers No.7, Lardy, N.R., p. 17–25.
35. According to CBRC, the 'Big-4' handled 98 criminal cases of fraud and money laundering last year.
36. Bank- en Effectenbedrijf, December 2005, p. 43.
37. The Banker, April 2006, p. 25.
38. Wall Street Journal, by Rick Carew, 25th January 2006, p. 1 and 14.
39. McKinsey&Company, May 2006, p. 41–42.
40. One of the most debated issues of China's current economic reforms is whether, and how, to turn rural land into marketable commodity (privatisation of land or "land administration"). See: The Economist, 24th June 2006, p. 60–61.
41. The Boston Consulting Group, May 2006, p. 20.
42. The Chinese households have 76% of their financial savings invested in bank deposits, even though these have yielded a return only slightly higher than inflation over the past ten years (real return on their financial assets of just 0.5% over

the past ten years). This weak performance has provided little incentive for savers to put their money into the financial system rather than keep it as cash. Moreover, it may contribute to China's high savings rate, because almost all wealth accumulation must come from new savings out of income rather than asset appreciation.

43. McKinsey&Company, May 2006, p. 65–76.
44. McKinsey&Company, May 2006, p. 53–54.
45. Finance and Investment Wharton, 14th December, 2005.
46. Kücükakin, S., ESB 2-6-2006, p. 256–257.
47. McKinsey&Company, May 2006, p. 80.
48. McKinsey&Company, May 2006, p. 88–94.
49. The Economist, 25th March 2006, p. 11–12.
50. Renminbi (RMB) is the name of the currency meaning 'the people's currency', whereas the yuan is the basic unit of account issued and administered by the PBOC. RMB is the exchange rate of the currency and has been fixed for most of the past half century with a few major discrete changes and remained at around 8.277 yuan/US dollar since 1994. Since 21st July 2005 the RMB has abandoned its currency's peg to the dollar and revalued by 2.1% to 8.11 yuan/US dollar and has been linked to a basket of currencies.

References

ABN AMRO Bank, Report, *Chinese growth scenario's: impact on industries*, Erik Brommer and Hyung-a de Zeeuw (Group Risk Management), April 2005, p. 1–30.
Anderson, Jonathan, *The New China – Back to the Real World*, UBS Investment Research, Asian Economic Perspectives, March 2007, p. 1–53.
Aziz, Jahangir and C. Duenwald, *Growth-Financial Intermediation Nexus in China*, IMF Working Paper 02/194, Nov. 2002.
Bank- en Effectenbedrijf, *Banking in China*, December 2005, p. 1–43.
BIS Policy Papers, No.7, The challenge of bank restructuring in China, N.R. Lardy, October 1999, p. 17–25.
BIS Policy Papers No.23, *Challenges to China's monetary policy*, PBOC, 2005.
Buitelaar, P., *China's growth is sustainable*, ESB (Economic Statistical Bulletin),10th March 2006, p. 113–115.
Financieele Dagblad, *Challenges and Opportunities of the enormous economic growth*, Tjabel Daling, 2005.
Finance and Investment Wharton, *Why China's Banking Sector Isn't as Weak as It Might Look and Other Myths*, 14th December, 2005.
Icard, A., *Capital account liberalisation in China: international perspectives*, BIS Papers No15, 2002, p. 14–18.
IMF, PRC Staff Report for the 2005 Article IV Consultation, approved by D. Burton and C. Muñiz.
Konijn, R.J. and S.M.Wiemers, *SARS casts a shadow over the future*, ESB, 13 June 2003.
Kücükakin, S., ESB 2-6-2006, p. 256–257.
McKinsey&Company, *Putting China's Capital to work: The Value of Financial System Reform*, May 2006, p. 1–123.
Roach, S., *China Policy Mismatch*, Morgan Stanley, 2005.
Sloman, J., *Economics*, Prentice Hall, fifth edition, 2003.
The Banker, *Winners and losers in the race to China*, April 2006, p. 24–27.
The Banker, *Chinese banks step up drive for modernization*, June 2006, p. 93–94.

The Boston Consulting Group, *Banking on China: Successful Strategies for Foreign Entrants*, May 2006, p. 1–31.

The Economist, China's economy: *The great fall of China?*, 15th May 2004, p. 1–2

The Economist, Special Report China's economy: *Time to hit the brakes*, 15th May 2004, p. 67–69.

The Economist, *China and commodity markets: from accelerator to brake*, 8th October 2005, p. 77–78.

The Economist, *Keep growing: easier said than done*, 25th March 2006, p. 11–12.

The Economist, *China: struggling to keep the lid on*, 29th April 2006, p. 59–60.

The Economist, *Drag on the dragon*, 29th April 2006, p. 74.

The Economist, *Chinese banks: a muffled report*, 20th May 2006, p. 82.

The Economist, *China: atomized*, 3rd June 2006, p. 55–56.

The Economist, *Building the nation*, 24th June 2006, 60–61.

The Economist Newspaper, *China lets the yuan rise*, An Economist Group business, 21st July 2005, p. 1–3.

Wall Street Journal, by Rick Carew, *China's banks defy prediction*, 25th January 2006, p. 1 and 14.

Wing Thye Woo, *The Structural Obstacles to Macroeconomic Control in China*, Economics Department, University of California, November 2004, p. 1–36.

9

Efficiency and Productivity Change in Greek Banking: Methods and Recent Evidence

Georgios E. Chortareas, Claudia Girardone and Alexia Ventouri

9.1 Introduction

This chapter examines the most recent developments pertaining to the efficiency and productivity of Greek banks. In this context we discuss some of the trends characterizing the Greek banking sector since the early 1990s and review the relevant empirical evidence. The Greek banking sector has recently undergone significant transformations that resulted in an extensive deregulation process and wide structural reforms. Over the 1990s the integration process in the context of the run up to the Economic and Monetary Union (EMU) and the increasingly competitive euro-area environment has contributed to raise banks' concerns about their overall performance, efficiency, and productivity. As in other European countries, Greek banks have responded to these exogenous pressures with a wave of consolidation and privatization: between 1996 and 2003, 16 mergers and acquisitions took place, and seven out of ten state-owned banks were privatized (Garganas, 2003). Furthermore, banks have strived to improve their customer base by looking for new markets (e.g., in the Balkans) and providing a range of new, non-traditional products and services, such as insurance, underwriting, asset management, and so on.

The literature on bank efficiency and, to a lesser extent productivity, is copious; the Greek banking sector has been investigated in several previous studies, mainly in the context of country-specific analyses, but only in relatively few pan-European ones. Typically EU cross-country studies tend to focus specifically on the five largest economies, namely France, Germany, Italy, Spain, and the United Kingdom, and even if they use enlarged samples they tend to exclude the smallest banking markets, such as Greece. There is no doubt that the Greek banking sector presents a relatively low number of banks: at present 21 commercial banks operate in Greece, of which the first three share 62.5 per cent of the market. Indeed these market features make the application of some sophisticated econometric techniques (such as the Stochastic Frontier Approach, see Section 9.2.1) difficult for modelling efficiency and productivity. This chapter also offers an overview of the different econometric techniques used to estimate cost and profit efficiency in banking and the main recent developments in efficiency and productivity analysis.

Many features of the period under examination render the experience of the Greek banking case interesting. In microeconomic terms, for example, the Greek banking system displays one of the highest concentration ratios in Europe. It has been expected that the catch-up process in the context of economic and financial integration with the other EMU countries will get entangled in a virtuous circle with financial liberalization. There is evidence that this was indeed the experience during the transition period.[1] Such developments have created euphoria and optimism. An authoritative analysis of the Greek banking system in 2001 suggested that in an environment of privatization, liberalization, and enhanced competition, the way of preserving the banks' profit rate would be through changes in their overall operating efficiency (Eichengreen and Gibson, 2001). Currently Greek banks enjoy a high degree of profitability as compared to that of the other European countries. In 2005, for example the ROA (Return On Assets) and ROE (Return On Equity) indices were at 0.9 and 16.2 respectively, figures that are only slightly surpassed by those of the Spanish and Portuguese banks. Whether the source of such performance is in efficiency or the imperfectly competitive conditions in the Greece banking industry remains to be investigated. While the typical concentration indices have been declining up to the mid-1990s and remained low up to the kick-off of the EMU, they have picked up again more recently displaying signs of an upward trend.[2] In 2005 the Greek banking sector's concentration index (CR5) was well above the average in the euro area.

The above considerations make apparent that accurate measurement of bank efficiency is crucial for a sober characterization of the banking system in Greece. While a number of indicators can be readily constructed, they are not free from a number of deficiencies. Traditionally, performance measurement relied on simple accounting ratios such as ROA or cost to income. Those indices, however, fail to capture the multi-dimensional character of the production process and under particular circumstances may convey misleading information. For instance, a high cost-income ratio may indicate cost inefficiency due to poor management skills or simply be the result of high competition that pushed marginal revenue close to marginal cost. Similarly, the ROA indicator cannot provide an indisputable picture either since earnings tend to be susceptible to management manipulation that can artificially inflate or deflate them.[3]

More recently the set of accounting ratios has been complemented by efficiency measures that address the above shortcomings. In this context, banks are now evaluated in terms of their ability to maximize output production with given inputs or minimize inputs usage given the level of output, relative to the performance of other banks. The aim of this chapter is to review and assess the empirical literature in the area of Greek bank efficiency. We also evaluate the current challenges for Greek banks and identify potential new areas of research. To our knowledge there are no studies that have reviewed the existing published research on the efficiency and productivity of Greek banks and therefore this review may be of interest not only to academics but practitioners as well.

9.2 A brief overview on the recent methods of frontier analysis

The vast majority of efficiency studies carried out over the last three decades or so have adopted frontier analysis to estimate alternative efficiency measures such as scale, scope, and, more recently, X-efficiencies. While scale advantages occur when a bank is able to reduce costs per unit of output as the bank gets bigger, scope economies refer to cost savings available through the joint production of financial services; on the other hand X-efficiencies (Leibenstein, 1966) relate to efficiencies brought about by superior management and technology.

The estimation of bank efficiency implies the explicit definition and measurement of banks' inputs and outputs. Two main approaches are generally used to measure the flow of services provided by financial institutions. In the 'production' approach banks are treated as firms that employ capital and labour to produce different types of deposit and loan accounts. Hence, their outputs are measured by the number of deposits and loan accounts or by the number of transactions performed on each type of product, whereas total costs are the operating costs used to produce these products. Under the alternative 'intermediation' approach, banks are considered as intermediaries between liability holders and those who receive bank funds, rather than producers of loan and deposit account services. As a consequence, the values of loans and other assets are defined as bank outputs, while deposits and other liabilities (capital and labour) are inputs to the production process. It follows that operating costs and financial expenses (interest on deposits) are the relevant components of total costs.[4]

9.2.1 Parametric and non-parametric methods for efficiency measurement

Typically two main methods of estimating bank cost efficiency can be used: a parametric approach that assumes an explicit functional form that presupposes the shape of the frontier for the production, cost or profit function; and a non-parametric approach that relies on linear programming techniques to identify a best-practice frontier.

The earliest bank efficiency studies focused mainly on analysing banks' cost structures and employed deterministic versions of parametric models, in which essentially all deviations from the frontier were assumed to be the result of inefficiency. Parametric frontiers were specified in the form of: Constant Elasticity of Substitution models (Arrow, Chenery et al., 1961) and Cobb Douglas (Aigner and Chu, 1968). Since the mid-1980s, applications of more flexible cost curves such us the U-shaped transcendental logarithmic (translog) became popular in the bank cost efficiency literature (Christensen, Jorgenson and Lau, 1973). One of the main criticisms of deterministic parametric frontier models is that no account is taken of the possible influence of measurement errors and other noise on the frontier.

In the 1990s bank efficiency studies began to rely on the Stochastic Frontier Approach (SFA) that assumes a two-component error term (i.e., random/statistical noise and possible inefficiency) and allows for the measurement of X-efficiency scores in addition to scale and scope economies. Other parametric techniques include: (i) the Thick Frontier Approach (TFA), that assumes that deviations from predicted costs within the lowest average-cost quartile of banks in a size class represent a random error, while deviations in predicted costs between the highest and the lowest quartiles represent inefficiency (Berger and Humphrey, 1991, 1992a, 1992b; Bauer, Berger and Humphrey, 1993; Berger, 1993); and (ii) the Distribution Free Approach (DFA); that assumes that the efficiency differences are stable over time, while random error averages out over time (Berger and Humphrey, 1992b; Berger, 1993).

As mentioned above, non-parametric techniques are also widely applied to banking data for the calculation of scale and X-efficiencies. With non-parametric models no functional form (other than linear interpolation between certain data points) is specified or estimated and the best-practice banks are actually positioned on the frontier, while the other banks are less efficient relative to them. These techniques use linear programming and include Data Envelopment Analysis (DEA) (Charnes, Cooper and Rhodes, 1978) and the Free Disposal Hull (FDH) approach (Déprins, Simar and Tulkens, 1984). The deterministic nature of DEA and FDH is often considered as a critical drawback of non-parametric methodologies. This is because while imposing less structure on the frontier, the non-parametric approach does not allow for random error. Finally, only a handful of stochastic non-parametric models have been applied to estimate X-efficiencies in the banking industry (see, e.g., Land, Lovell and Thore, 1993; Resti, 1997).

9.2.2   Recent developments in bank efficiency analysis

Recently the application of efficiency analysis in banking has produced contributions in a number of diverse directions:

1. In the context of parametric methodologies, McAllister and McManus (1993) suggested that most previous empirical literature on bank efficiency

might be biased because of problems related to the statistical techniques used. Berger and Humphrey (1997) later argued that since the parametric approach imposes functional forms that restrict the shape of the frontier, the solution lies in adding more flexibility by using a Fourier approximation that technically represents the unknown cost function using a Fourier series.

2. Berger and Humphrey (1997) stressed the limitations of non-parametric methodology, suggesting that it should consider using a resampling technique, such as *bootstrapping*, in order to accommodate random error in the efficiency estimates. This technique (e.g., Simar, 1992; Simar and Wilson, 1995) appears to be a way of obtaining an empirical approximation to the underlying sampling distribution of DEA and FDH efficiency estimates (see for an application to the EU banking sector, e.g., Caşu and Molyneux, 2003).

3. A typical criticism of bank efficiency studies relates to ignoring the revenue/profit side of banks' operations. Recently, studies employing profit functions or investigating both banks' cost and profit efficiency have gradually acquired greater importance. The rationale for these studies is that banks that show the highest inefficiency and incur the highest costs might be able to generate more profits than the more cost-efficient banks. Of the 130 studies on bank efficiency reviewed by Berger and Humphrey (1997) only nine analysed profit efficiency and, although there have been a number of recent additions to the list, e.g., Caşu and Girardone (2004); De Young and Hasan (1998); Maudos, Pastor and Perez (2002); Rogers (1998); Vander Vennet (2002). Studies that test the profit side are still relatively few.

4. The focus of banks on off-balance sheet (OBS) activities is a new development and a number of recent studies found that omitting OBS items like lines of credit, loan commitments, securitization, and derivatives in the estimation of bank efficiency may result in a misspecification of bank output and lead to incorrect conclusions. This is because the traditional business of financing loans by issuing deposits has declined in favour of a significant growth in activities that are not typically captured on banks' balance sheets (see Boyd and Gertler, 1994; Caşu and Girardone, 2005; Rime and Stiroh, 2003; Rogers and Sinkey, 1999; Siems and Clark, 1997; Tortosa-Ausina, 2003).

5. Bank efficiency studies have identified a few variables that should be added as arguments in the cost function to control for various environmental aspects on the grounds that unless they are accounted for in the cost function, bank levels of X-efficiencies and economies of scale may be miscalculated. The most relevant variables have been identified in the following: the level of capital to control for risk of default; and loan losses to control for output quality (see, e.g., Altunbaş, Goddard and Molyneux, 1999; Berger and Mester, 1997; Clark, 1996; Girardone, Molyneux and Gardener, 2004; Hughes and Mester, 1993; McAllister and McManus, 1993).

6. Recently, criticism has also been made to studies ignoring the level of productivity and its relationship with efficiency. Heshmati (2001) surveyed a number of contributions to, and developments of, the relationship between outsourcing, efficiency, and productivity growth in manufacturing and services. Different parametric and non-parametric approaches to the productivity measurement in the context of static, dynamic, and firm-specific modelling have been applied in the literature. The former typically include a time trend as a proxy for disembodied technical change, whereas the non-parametric approach involves the estimation of the Malmquist Total Factor Productivity (TFP) Index (see, e.g., Alam, 2001; Battese, Heshmati and Hjalmarsson, 2000; Berg, Claussen and Forsund, 1993; Grifell-Tatjé and Lovell, 1995 and 1996; Pastor, Perez and Quesada, 1997). Recently, Berger and Mester (1999, 2003) reinterpret the literature by proposing a parametric method to decompose total changes in cost over time into a portion due to changes in business conditions and a portion due to changes in bank productivity. Both the Malmquist index and the methodology suggested by Berger and Mester (2003) have been applied to a sample of European banks by Caşu, Girardone and Molyneux (2004), who also review the main literature.

9.3   Studies on bank efficiency and productivity in Greece

9.3.1   Scale and scope economies: recent studies

The first study to investigate economies of scale for a sample of 11 Greek commercial banks is by Karafolas and Mantakas (1996). Using a U-shaped translogarithmic (translog) cost function, they analyse economies of scale over the period 1980–89. On average, they do not find any significant total-cost scale economies, although operating-cost economies of scale are found to be statistically significant. The authors use pooled data for all Greek banks, and they also test the efficiency of large versus small banks. Overall, their findings indicate that on average, Greek banks should increase their size to be able to exploit fully the benefits of economies of scale.

More recently, in a cross-country study across European banking markets, Huizinga, Nelissen and Vander Vennet (2001) examine the performance effects of European banks' M&As (including operations that took place in Greece) over the 1990s. The sample consists of 52 EU bank mergers over the period 1994–98 and the methodology used is the translog cost function. Using a pooled sample over the studied period, their results indicate substantial unexploited economies of scale across different institutional types of credit institutions and for the largest banks. Overall, the results indicate the existence of economies of scale for commercial banks, cooperative and savings, mortgage banks with total assets up to 10 billion euro, and for 'other' banks (with the exception of one size group).

Athanasoglou and Brissimis (2004) examine the impact of M&As on Greek banking efficiency, by comparing operational costs for Greek banks of different sizes for the periods 1994–97 and 2000–02. Their results report scale economies for small and medium-size banks and scale diseconomies for large banks, over the period 1994–97. However, for the period 2000–02 scale economies are not found for any bank size. Similarly, Apergis and Rezitis (2004) examined alternative efficiency measures, including economies of scale. More specifically, they consider the long-run scale economies and they calculate it as one minus the cost elasticity along an output ray (as in Brown, Caves and Christensen, 1979). Their dataset consists of four state and two private Greek banks for the period 1982–97. Overall, their findings show significant economies of scale, implying that Greek banks could improve their cost efficiency levels by engaging in activities such as mergers and acquisitions. In particular, the values of scale economies in each year and in the whole studies period are relatively high and significant. These results remain unchanged after using both the intermediation and production approaches. Moreover, while economies of scale tend to increase over time using the intermediation approach, they do not seem to show any specific pattern in the production approach.

Kamberoglou and colleagues (2004) analyse cost efficiency in Greece using the SFA, and they measure scale economies by the ray scale elasticity. Their analysis is conducted using a panel of 20 Greek banks over 1993–99. Their results lead in general to the same conclusion that Greek banks experience economies of scale, however, these tend to decline throughout the studied period. Moreover, scale economies appear to be more important for small banks.

Overall, there are only a handful of studies measuring scale economies in the Greek banking sector. With the exception of Karafolas and Mantakas (1996), the general consensus is that in banking scale economies are soon exhausted and large banks sometimes even suffer from diseconomies. This is in line with the extant international literature that has often found that scale economies do not continue indefinitely with the expansion of size: as the scale of operation increases, there comes a point at which limitations to efficient management set in and long-run marginal costs tend to rise. This might also be evidence of the managerial theory of the firm, where managers pursue growth at the expense of efficiency and profitability.

On the other hand, no studies to our knowledge have attempted to measure the level of scope economies for the Greek banking sector. Indeed, the existing international literature on joint production economies is generally scarce, primarily due to the problems involved with their appropriate econometric estimations. Nonetheless, recent studies have pointed out that scale and scope economies in banking appear to be small compared with X-efficiencies levels. Berger, Hunter and Timme (1993) were among the first to emphasize that while scale and scope efficiencies account for nearly

5 per cent of bank costs, average X-inefficiencies account for approximately 20 per cent of costs as a result of the application of parametric approaches, and may range from less than 10 per cent to over 50 per cent in non-parametric approaches. In short, banking X-efficiencies may be over 400 per cent more significant than corresponding scale and scope efficiencies. The next section reviews the existing literature in this area.

9.3.2   X-efficiencies and productivity change

Since the early 1990s many researchers have focused their attention on modelling technical and allocative efficiencies of individual banking firms as opposed to scale and scope economies. This is because the rapid changes in the banking market and the effects of deregulation have increased the importance of differences in managerial ability to control costs or maximize revenues. As discussed in Section 9.2, the concept of X-inefficiency was first introduced by Leibenstein (1966) who noted that, for a number of different reasons, people and organizations generally work neither as hard nor as effectively as they could.

Most studies that investigate the efficiency and productivity of the Greek banking sector tend to favour the non-parametric approach for two main reasons. Firstly, the relatively small number of observations available excludes the possibility that a parametric frontier may be employed due to the considerable number of cross-products and transformations to the input/output variables needed to specify the functional form for the optimization process (e.g., in a translog or Fourier-Flexible frontier). Secondly, the Malmquist Index for estimating the evolution of productivity over time is conveniently implemented using DEA. Despite the recent proliferation of parametric versions of the Malmquist and other productivity indexes, the DEA Malmquist is still the most widely used Total Factor Productivity change measure in bank efficiency and productivity literature.

Over the 1990s a number of efficiency and productivity studies have been carried out on the Greek banking sector. As illustrated in Table 9.1 most studies tend to be country-specific and focus mainly on efficiency rather than productivity. Moreover, a few of them focus on bank branches.

Focusing on pan-European studies, most of the early empirical evidences suggest that the average cost efficiency ranges from 70 per cent (Ruthenber and Elias, 1996), to 80 per cent (Vander Vennet, 2002), which are roughly in line with the results from US studies (Burger and Humphrey, 1997). However, even recently, most European studies tend to focus on the largest EU countries and often neglect examination of the Greek banking industry.

Altunbaş and Chakravarty (1998) investigate the effect of the banking structure on the aggregate measure of the dispersion of X-inefficiency across Europe. In particular, this study evaluates the efficiency scores by estimating a Fourier Flexible function for all banks in Europe falling into four different types (i.e., commercial, savings, cooperatives, others) and taking an average

Table 9.1 Survey of Greek studies on bank X-efficiency and productivity change

Author (publication date)	Period under study	Institution type & number of sampled banks	Approach used		Methodology Efficiency[a]/ productivity	Main findings: averages for Greece (EU averages in brackets)[c]		Type of study (country specific vs. cross-country)
			Inputs (Levels or Prices)	Outputs		Overall efficiency	Productivity change	
Vassiloglou and Giokas (1990)	1987	20 commercial bank branches	Labour hours, supplies expenses, number of terminals	Number of transactions processed at each branch	DEA	90%	n.a.	Athens (Greece)
Giokas (1991)	1988	17 commercial bank branches	Labour hours, supplies expenses, number of terminals	Number of transactions processed at each branch	DEA, Log linear model	87%	n.a.	Athens (Greece)
Athanassopoulos (1997)	Data from field survey (1995)	68 commercial bank branches	Production approach: Number of employees, On-line and ATM, Number of computers Intermediation approach: Interest and non-interest expenses	Production approach: Number of deposits, credits, debits transactions, loan applications, and transactions involving commissions. Intermediation approach: Volume of Loans, Time deposit, saving deposit, and current deposit accounts, non-interest income	DEA	90%	n.a.	Athens (Greece)
Noulas (1997)	1991–1992	State and private (20 banks)	Capital, labour, deposits	Assets, loans and advances, investments	DEA / MALMQUIST	85%	8%	Greece
Ruthenberg and Elias (1996)	1989–1990	65 commercial large banks	Labour, fixed assets, loan shares	Total assets	TFA	n.a. (70%)	n.a.	EU-15

Continued

Table 9.1 Continued

Author (publication date)	Period under study	Institution type & number of sampled banks	Approach used — Inputs (Levels or Prices)	Approach used — Outputs	Methodology Efficiency[a]/ productivity	Main findings: averages for Greece (EU averages in brackets)[c] — Overall efficiency	Main findings — Productivity change	Type of study (country specific vs. cross-country)
Altunbaş and Chakranarty (1998)	1988–1995	Commercial, savings, cooperative and others (2,412 obs)	Labour, physical capital, deposits	Loans, securities and OBS activities	SFA	n.a. (75%)	n.a.	EU-15
Schure and Wagenvoort (1999)	1993–1997	Commercial, savings, cooperative, others (2,185 obs)	Price of labour, funds and buildings	Deposits, loans, equity investments OBS, other services	RTFA, Cobb-Douglas	36% (80%)	n.a.	EU-15
Gehrig and Sheldon (1999)	1993–1997	Commercial and savings (1,783 obs)	Interest costs, personnel costs, commission, fee and trading expenses, other operating and administrative expenses and probability of insolvency	Loans, other earning assets, OBS, deposits, interest, commission, fee, trading and other operating income	DEA	16.2 (45%)	n.a.	EU
Soteriou and Stavrinides (2000)	July–December 1994	26 bank branches	Labour hours, branch size, computer terminals, operating expenses	Employee service quality perceptions of branches	DEA	80%	n.a.	Greece
Athanassopoulos and Giokas (2000)	1988–1994	47 commercial bank branches	Production approach: labour hours, branch size, computer terminals, operating expenses	Production approach: Credit and deposit transactions, foreign receipts.	DEA	81%	n.a.	Athens (Greece)

			expenditure. Intermediation approach: Saving, current, demand and time deposits.	Intermediation approach: Volume of accounts, number of accounts, average account size				
Altunbaş et al. (2001)	1989–1997	4,104 bank observations	Labour, physical capital, deposits	Loans, securities and OBS activities	SFA	75% (75%)	n.a.	EU-15
Noulas (2001)	1993–1998	State and private (19 banks)	Interest and non-interest expenses	Interest and non-interest revenue	DEA	65%	n.a.	Greece
Huizinga et al. (2001)	1994–1998	Commercial, cooperative, mortgage and other banks (15,869 obs)	Deposits, labour	Loans, securities or other earning assets	SFA	82% (91%)	n.a.	EU
Christopolous and Tsionas (2001)	1993–1998	18 commercial banks	Labour, capital and deposits	Loans, investments and liquid assets	SFA	83%	n.a.	Greece
Christopoulos et al. (2002)	1993–1998	19 commercial banks	Labour, capital and deposits	Loans and advances investments, liquid assets	SFA	~90%	n.a.	Greece
Vander-Vennet (2002)	1995–1996	Conglomerates and Universal banks (2,375 banks)	Labour, fixed assets, deposits	Loans and securities (or interest and non-interest income)	SFA	n.a. (80%)	n.a.	EU-15
Weill (2003)	1996 and 2000	640 commercial banks	Personnel and other non-interest expense, interest paid	Loans, investment assets	SFA	62% (Western EU: 69% Eastern EU 54%)	n.a.	Western and Eastern EU
Tsionas et al. (2003)	1993–1998	19 commercial banks	Labour, capital and deposits	Loans, investments and liquid assets	DEA/ MALMQUIST	98%	3.80%	Greece

Continued

Table 9.1 Continued

Author (publication date)	Period under study	Institution type & number of sampled banks	Approach used		Methodology Efficiency[a]/ productivity	Main findings: averages for Greece (EU averages in brackets)[c]		Type of study (country specific vs. cross-country)
			Inputs (Levels or Prices)	Outputs		Overall efficiency	Productivity change	
Apergis and Rezitis (2004)	1982–1997	4 state and 2 private banks	Production approach: wage rate, price of capital. Intermediation approach: wage rate, price of capital, price of deposits.	Production approach: loans, investment assets, time and demand deposits. Intermediation approach: loans, investment assets.	Translog cost function and cost share equations/Total Factor Productivity	n.a.	−0.385%	Greece
Halkos and Salamouris (2004)	1997–1999	18 commercial banks	Financial efficiency ratios (Interest Expenses, total assets, number of employees, operating expenses)	Interest income, net profits	DEA	77%	n.a.	Greece
Kamberoglou et al. (2004)	1993–1999	20 commercial banks	Financial and interest expenses	Loans, securities and other income (fee)	DFA	67%	n.a.	Greece
Schure et al. (2004)	1993–1997	Commercial and savings banks (2,220 obs)	Interest, total operating and commissions expenses	Deposits, loans, equity investments, OBS, commission revenue, securities	RTFA	28% (77%)	n.a.	EU-15
Rezitis (2006)	1982–1997	State and Private (6 banks)	labour, capital and deposits	loans and investment assets	DEA/ MALMQUIST	91%	2.40%	Greece

over each category. On average, the inefficiency score for all banks (including Greek ones) is reported to be on the order of 75 per cent, whereas the variation in the inefficiency measures is largely explained by the differences within the four groups of banks.

Gehrig and Sheldon (1999) investigate the efficiency of a large sample of European banks for the period following the introduction of the Second Banking Directive, 1993–97. According to the results, average efficiency is relatively low, ranging from 45 per cent from a cost perspective to 65 per cent from a profit standpoint. Moreover, the efficiency scores vary more within European countries than across their national borders, implying that market convergence and increased competition would engender a major disequilibrium in the industry. Accordingly, the average cost efficiency of Greek banks relative to other European banks is reported to be very low, on the order of 16.2 per cent. Hence, this result seems to suggest that banks in Greece are among the least efficient in Europe. Moreover, the main findings indicate that large and/or specialized banks are more efficient since measured efficiency seems to increase with size and decrease with scope.

In line with the results of Gehrig and Sheldon (1999), Schure and Wagenvoort's (1999) findings on cost efficiency are also somehow 'extreme' for the Greek banking industry. That is, for their overall EU-15 sample, the reported findings show the existence of X-inefficiency, on the order of 20 per cent on average. However, the results for Greece indicate that although Greek commercial banks have improved their efficiency scores over the studied period (1993–97), their relative inefficiency levels are found to be very high, on the order of 64 per cent on average.

In an effort to measure and compare cost inefficiencies across European countries, Altunbaş and colleagues (2001) apply the Fourier Flexible functional form to estimate scale economies, X-inefficiencies, and technical change. The panel comprises data from the 15 EU countries over the period 1989–97. In line with previous research, evidence of large inefficiency measures ranging between 20 per cent and 25 per cent is found across the EU banks, whereas for the Greek banking sector the average inefficiency is reported to be around 25 per cent on average. As a concluding remark, Altunbaş and colleagues (2001) emphasize the potentially significant gains for the EU banking sector from improving their managerial inefficiencies rather than increasing size.

Huizinga, Nelissen and Vander Vennet (2001) examine the efficiency effects of European bank M&As over the period 1994–98, that is, the period immediately preceding the start of EMU. By employing the parametric SFA methodology for a sample of 14 European countries, the empirical results show large cross-sectional variations in the operational efficiency of European banks. That is, efficiency estimates across EU countries vary from 80 per cent to 95 per cent, with the Greek banking industry at around 82 per cent on average.

More recently, Weill (2003) compares the efficiency of banks from 11 Western and six Eastern European countries to assess the performance gap between both groups, testing also the possible influence of environmental variables and risk preferences on the efficiency gap. The results show, as expected, that there is a significant gap in bank efficiency between Eastern and Western European countries; however, the reported inefficiency level of the Greek banking sector is relatively high, on the order of 38 per cent on average.

Following the implementation of the Second Banking Directive of the European Union in 1992, Schure, Wagenvoort and O' Brien (2004) assess the efficiency of the European banking sector by using the recursive thick frontier approach (RTFA) in a large sample covering commercial and savings banks in the EU15. A surprising finding in this study is that while overall efficiency for European banks is on the order of 77 per cent on average, Greek banks experience high inefficiency levels, with the efficiency scores around 28 per cent.

Overall, it becomes apparent that in spite of a disparity in the efficiency estimates for the Greek banking sector in European cross-country studies, which could be due to differences in methodologies, years, and countries sampled, the Greek banking sector seems to perform relatively poorly in terms of cost efficiency when compared with its European counterparts.

Concerning the country-specific studies, Noulas (1997) measures technical efficiency for the Greek banking sector over the years 1991–92 and concentrates on the performance of state versus private banking institutions. The data are drawn from individual bank reports for 20 banks and the model is specified using banks deposits and other liabilities as inputs to the production process, while loans and other assets are considered outputs. The main conclusions are that efficiency is, on average, 85 per cent and decreases for both private and state banks over the years under study; yet state banks experienced technological progress while private banks did not. Turning to the results derived from the estimation of the Malmquist productivity index, the Greek banking sector seem to have experienced an increase of productivity by about 8 per cent, with state banks obtaining higher productivity growth than private banks.

Noulas (2001) uses the same non-parametric technique as well as traditional financial ratio analysis to extend the efficiency analysis to the following period (1993–98) with the aim of assessing the effects of deregulation on both private and public banks in Greece. Average efficiency levels are estimated at around 65 per cent and state banks are found to be less efficient than their private counterparts. However, the gap in the efficiency levels between the two groups is not found statistically significant, thereby indicating that, on average, the two groups of banks are on an 'equal footing' to compete in the deregulated banking environment.

Christopoulos and Tsionas (2001) estimate technical and allocative efficiency of the Greek banking sector using a sample of commercial banks over the deregulation period 1993–98. The main methodology is the parametric heteroscedastic SFA, and results indicate that Greek banks exhibit fairly high cost inefficiency levels ranging on the order of 20 per cent, while allocative inefficiency is found to be around 14 per cent, thereby suggesting that there is still plenty of room for further improvements in the Greek banking sector in terms of profitability and cost competitiveness. Focusing on the same period and similar method, Christopoulos, Lolos and Tsionas (2002) examine cost efficiency for the Greek banking system and find that small and medium-sized banks are almost fully efficient, while in large banks efficiency measures range from 60 per cent to 95 per cent.

By using the non-parametric DEA approach, Tsionas, Lolos and Tsionas (2003) estimate cost efficiencies of all Greek commercial banks (i.e., an unbalanced panel of an average of 18 observations per year) over 1993–98 focusing on differences in bank size rather than ownership. They use the intermediation approach and describe a 3-input/3-output model with labour, capital, and deposits as inputs; and loans, investments, and liquid assets as outputs. The data used are drawn from the Balance Sheet Accounts and Income Statements of the Greek banking system. The results indicate that the majority of Greek banks operate at relatively high levels of overall efficiency (around 98 per cent) and that larger banks seem to be more efficient relative to smaller institutions. Furthermore, results from the application of the Malmquist index indicate that an increase by 3.8 per cent in total factor productivity has occurred over the period, and it was mainly due to improvements gained in large banks' technical change.

More recently, several other papers also examine cost efficiency for the Greek banking sector. Apergis and Rezitis (2004) analyse the cost structure of the Greek banking sector and measure the rate of technical change and the rate of growth in total factor productivity, using a parametric translog cost function. In this study, both the intermediation and the production approaches are used to specify the production process of banks. As regards the dataset used, it consists four state and two private banks operating in Greece over 1982–97. Overall, the results obtained from both models show that Greek banks exhibit negative annual rates of growth in technical efficiency and in total factor productivity.

Halkos and Salamouris (2004) measure Greek banks' efficiency over the period 1997–99. In particular, the authors include a number of financial efficiency ratios as output measures in the DEA model to calculate the efficiency for a sample of Greek commercial banks. Overall, their findings reveal that the Greek banking sector exhibits relatively high cost inefficiency levels, on the order of 23 per cent. Moreover, the improved profitability of the Greek banking system is mainly attributed to the participation of various banking firms in the Athens Exchange Market, rather than to the increase of traditional banking activities.

Kamberoglou et al. (2004) applies the distribution-free approach to a sample of 18 banks for the period 1993–99 and find that Greek banks could achieve cost savings by improving their X-efficiency levels, currently at 70 per cent on average. Furthermore, this study investigates the correlation between various bank characteristics and cost inefficiency, and concludes that large, public and risk averse banks seem to be more efficient.

In a recent study Rezitis (2006) measures efficiency and productivity for the Greek banking sector over a relatively long time period: 1982–97. The data employed derive from the annual reports of six individual banks and the input/output approach is the same as in Noulas (1997). The author also attempts a comparison across the two periods 1982–92 and 1993–97 in order to test the effects, if any, of intense deregulation and liberalization after 1992. The results indicate average efficiency levels of 91.3 per cent and productivity growth of 2.4 per cent per year over the whole period. Rather surprisingly, the mean efficiency level does not seem to change in the two periods. However, after 1992 the TFP index increases considerably from 1.7 per cent to 4.4 per cent per year. Among the main reasons put forward for this positive change in productivity are the more intense competition and the internationalization process that has characterized the Greek banking sector over the second half of the 1990s.

Table 9.1 also reports a number of other Greek studies that have focused their attention on the assessment of productive efficiency of bank branches (namely Athanassopoulos, 1997; Athanassopoulos and Giokas, 2000; Giokas, 1991; Soteriou and Stavrinides, 2000; Vassiliglou and Giokas, 1990). These studies employ DEA methodology to evaluate the performance of commercial bank branches located in Athens. The reported results are similar in the sense that they all find relatively high efficiency scores for Greek bank branches (86 per cent efficiency on average). However, we should not compare these findings with the other country-specific or pan-European studies discussed above, given the different nature of bank branch studies.

Overall, taking into account all country-specific studies reported in Table 9.1, the average inefficiency level for Greek banks in the 1990s is found to be around 19 per cent and this is in line with the main evidence from the international literature. Moreover, the average inefficiency levels for Greek bank branches in the literature are reported to be on the order of 14 per cent. DEA studies seem to produce lower inefficiency levels compared with parametric approaches (15 per cent against 25 per cent respectively on average), as usually do country-specific studies relative to pan-European ones. Indeed, results for the Greek banking sector derived from international comparisons are mixed and should be interpreted with some caution given also the variation in the efficiency scores that ranges between 28 per cent and 90 per cent. On average, pan-European studies report lower efficiency levels for Greek banks, around 58 per cent. This could also help explain why European studies tend to exclude Greece from the analysis. On the other hand, with only one exception, the productivity growth has always been found positive and relatively high, with an average TFP of about 3.5 per cent in 1993–97.

The past and present Greek papers on bank efficiency suggest several important topics for future research. First, the variations in the efficiency scores across European countries suggest that further research should investigate in detail the reasons for the Greek banking sector's efficiency scores relative to the other European countries. This is crucial given the fact that Greece is a member of the Economic and Monetary Union (EMU), operating in the increasingly competitive and integrated euro-area environment. Second, additional research on parametric studies is needed given the relative small number of parametric studies compared to non-parametric ones (see Table 9.1) for the Greek banking industry. Moreover, the differences in efficiency levels among the various methodological approaches indicate that future research should focus on thoroughly investigating the Greek banking sector's efficiency by carrying out a methodological cross-checking, that is, using wherever possible (i.e., when data are available for a relatively long time span) both parametric and non-parametric approaches. Third, studies are needed focusing both on the cost and profit/ revenue side of banks' operations, because cost inefficient banks may be able to earn higher profits than cost efficient banks. This is of particular interest for the Greek banking sector given that, as discussed earlier, in recent years Greek banks have enjoyed relatively high profitability levels compared to their European counterparts. Fourth, following the most recent literature, researchers should test the significance of including off-balance sheet items in the banks' input/output definition. Such analysis is important because banks operating in most advanced economies have increasingly diversified their business towards OBS activities both for risk management purposes and as a result of their search for new sources of income. In Greece, for example, OBS business has increased by 45 per cent over 1997–2003. Fifth, according to our review, to date only four studies have investigated productivity change for the Greek banking sector up to 1998 and all of them have used the Malmquist Total Factor Productivity index. Including the most recent years and attempting the use of alternative productivity techniques would certainly add to the existing literature. Finally, more efficiency and productivity studies are needed to incorporate Greek banks in their samples, measuring and comparing the efficiency/productivity scores across-country and internationally, as today's financial markets are subject to greater integration, globalization, and competition and also in light of the strategies outlined in the recent EU Financial Services Policy.

9.4 Conclusions

This chapter reviews and assesses studies on Greek banking efficiency and productivity; and, where possible, suggests potential areas for future research. The banking sector in Greece has recently experienced major transformations that have resulted in extensive deregulation and widespread structural reforms. Over the 1990s the integration process in the context of the run-up to Economic and Monetary Union (EMU) and the increasingly competitive euro-area environment has contributed to raise banks' concerns about their overall performance, efficiency, and productivity. Following the recent developments, a number of efficiency and productivity studies have been carried out on the Greek banking sector. However, most of these studies tend to be country-specific and focus mainly on efficiency rather than productivity. Still, there is little or no information about several important issues that have already been addressed by other EU and international studies. Areas that potentially deserve greater research attention relate to further analysis of the determinants of Greek bank productivity and also more detailed study of factors that explain Greek profit performance and the link to efficiency and competition.

Notes

1. For example, see Stournaras (2006) for a summary.
2. See for example, Gibson (2005) who analyses concentration data for Greek banks (including the Herfindahl-Hirschmann index) up to 2003.
3. See, for example, Dechow, Sloan and Sweeney (1995).
4. Other approaches have also been used to define bank inputs and outputs. Some studies use the so-called value-added approach, where each category of assets or liabilities may be identified as an important output, intermediate product, or input, according to whether they generate or destroy value (Berger and Humphrey, 1991 and 1992a). In particular, Berger and Humphrey (1992a) found that deposits and loans should be considered as important outputs since they generate the largest share of value added. Other efficiency studies employ the user-cost approach, which determines whether a final product is an input or an output on the basis of its net contribution to bank revenue. This means that a transaction is defined as an output if the financial return (asset) exceeds the opportunity cost of the funds, or else if the financial cost (liability) is less than the opportunity cost of those funds (Berger and Humphrey, 1991).

References

Aigner, D. J. and S. F. Chu (1968). 'On estimating the industry production function', *American Economic Review* 58, 826–39.
Alam, I. M. S. (2001). 'A non-parametric approach for assessing productivity dynamics of large banks', *Journal of Money, Credit and Banking* 33, 121–39.
Altunbaş, Y. and S. P. Chakravarty (1998). 'Efficiency measures and the banking structure in Europe', *Economic Letters* 60, 205–8.
Altunbaş, Y., J. Goddard and P. Molyneux (1999). 'Technical change in banking', *Economic Letters* 64, 215–21.
Altunbaş, Y., E. P. M. Gardener, P. Molyneux and B. Moore (2001). 'Efficiency in European banking', *European Economic Review* 45, 1931–55.
Apergis, N. and A. Rezitis (2004). 'Cost structure, technological change, and productivity growth in the Greek banking sector', *International Advances in Economic Research* 10(1), 1–16.

Arrow, K. J., H. B. Chenery, B. S. Minhas and R. M. Solow (1961). 'Capital-labor substitution and economic efficiency', *Review of Economics and Statistics* 43(3), 225–47.

Athanasoglou, P. P. and S. N. Brissimis (2004). 'The effect of mergers and acquisitions on bank efficiency in Greece', *Economic Bulletin* 22, 7–30.

Athanassopoulos, A. D. (1997). 'Service quality and operating efficiency synergies for management control in the provision of financial services: Evidence from Greek bank branches', *European Journal of Operational Research* 98, 300–13.

Athanassopoulos, A. D. and D. Giokas (2000). 'The use of data envelopment analysis in banking institutions: Evidence from the Commercial Bank of Greece', *Interfaces* 30(2), 81–95.

Battese G. E., A. Heshmati and L. Hjalmarsson (2000). 'Efficiency of labour use in the Swedish banking industry: A stochastic frontier approach', *Empirical Economics* 25(4), 623–40.

Bauer, P., A. N. Berger and D. B. Humphrey (1993). 'Efficiency and productivity growth in US banking', in H. O. Fried, K. A. L. Lovell and S. S. Schmidt (eds), *The Measurement of Productive Efficiency: Techniques and Applications*, Oxford: Oxford University Press, 386–413.

Bauer, P., A. N. Berger, G. Ferrier and D. Humphrey (1998). 'Consistency conditions for regulatory analysis of financial institutions: A comparison of frontier efficiency methods', *Journal of Economics and Business* 50, 85–114.

Berg, S. A., C. A. Claussen and F. R. Forsund (1993). 'Banking efficiency in the Nordic countries: A multi-output analysis', Working Paper, Research Department, Norges Bank, Oslo, SAB/ 9, 1–35.

Berg, S. A., F. R. Forsund and E. S. Jansen (1992). 'Malmquist indices of productivity growth during the deregulation of Norwegian banking', *Scandinavian Journal of Economics* 94 (Supplement), 211–28.

Berger, A. N. (1993). 'Distribution-free estimates of efficiency in the US banking industry and tests of the standard distributional assumptions', *Journal of Productivity Analysis* 4, 261–92.

Berger, A. N. and D. Humphrey (1991). 'The dominance of inefficiencies over scale and product mix economies in banking', *Journal of Monetary Economics* 28, 117–48.

Berger, A. N. and D. B. Humphrey (1992a). 'Megamergers in banking and the use of cost efficiency as an antitrust defense', *Antitrust Bulletin* 37, 541–600.

Berger, A. N. and D. B. Humphrey (1992b). 'Measurement and efficiency issues in commercial banking', in Z. Griliches (ed.), *Measurement Issues in the Service Sectors*, National Bureau of Economic Research, University of Chicago Press, 245–79.

Berger, A. N. and D. B. Humphrey (1997). 'Efficiency of financial institutions: International survey and directions for further research', *European Journal of Operational Research* 98, 175–212.

Berger, A. N. and L. J. Mester (1997). 'Inside the black box: What explains differences in the efficiencies of financial institutions?', *Journal of Banking and Finance* 21, 895–947.

Berger, A. N. and L. J. Mester (1999). 'What explains the dramatic changes in cost and profit performance of the US banking industry', Working paper, no. 1, February, Federal Reserve Bank of Philadelphia.

Berger, A. N. and L. J. Mester (2003). 'Explaining the dramatic changes in performance of US banks: Technological change, deregulation and dynamic changes in competition', *Journal of Financial Intermediation* 12(1), 57.

Berger, A. N., G. A. Hanweck and D. B. Humphrey (1987). 'Competitive viability in banking: Scale, scope, and product mix economies', *Journal of Monetary Economics* 20, 501–20.

Berger, A. N., W. C. Hunter and S. G. Timme (1993). 'The efficiency of financial institutions: A review and preview of research past, present, and future', *Journal of Banking and Finance* 17, 221–49.

Bos, J. W. B. and H. Schmiedel (2003). 'Comparing efficiency in European banking: A meta frontier approach', De Nederlandsche Bank Research Papers, 57.

Boyd, J. H. and M. Gertler (1994). 'Are banks dead? Or are the reports greatly exaggerated?', *Quarterly Review*, Federal Reserve Bank of Minneapolis, issue Summer, 2–23.

Brown, R. S., D. W. Caves and L. R. Christensen (1979). 'Modelling the structure of cost and production for multiproduct firms', *Southern Economic Journal* 46(1), 256–73.

Caşu, B. and C. Girardone (2004). 'Financial conglomeration: Efficiency, productivity and startegic drive', *Applied Financial Economics* 14, 687–96.

Caşu, B. and C. Girardone (2005). 'An analysis of the relevance of OBS items in explaining productivity change in European banking', *Applied Financial Economics* 15, 1053–61.

Caşu, B. and P. Molyneux (2003). 'A comparative study of efficiency in European banking', *Applied Economics*, 35(17), 1865–76.

Caşu, B., C. Girardone and P. Molyneux (2004). 'Productivity change in European banking: A comparison of parametric and non-parametric approaches', *Journal of Banking and Finance* 28, 2521–40.

Cave, D. W., L. R. Christensen and W. E. Diewert (1982a). 'Multilateral comparisons of output, input and productivity using superlative index numbers', *Economic Journal* 92, 73–86.

Cave, D. W., L. R. Christensen and W. E. Diewert (1982b). 'The economic theory of index numbers and the measurement of input, output and productivity', *Econometrica*, 50, 1393–414.

Charnes, A., W. W. Cooper and E. Rhodes (1978). 'Measuring the efficiency of decision making units', *European Journal of Operational Research* 2(6), 429–44.

Christensen, L. R., D. W. Jorgenson and L. J. Lau (1973). 'Transcendental logarithmic production frontiers', *Review of Economics and Statistics* 55, 28–45.

Christopoulos, D. and E. G. Tsionas (2001). 'Banking efficiency in the deregulation period: Results from heteroscedastic stochastic frontier models', *The Manchester School* 69(6), 656–76.

Christopoulos, D. K., S. E. G. Lolos and E. G., Tsionas (2002). 'Efficiency of the Greek banking system in view of the EMU: A heteroscedastic stochastic frontier approach', *Journal of Policy Modelling* 24, 813–29.

Clark, J. (1996). 'Economic cost, scale efficiency, and competitive viability in banking', *Journal of Money, Credit and Banking* 28(3), 342–64.

Clark, J. A. and T. F. Siems (1997). 'Competitive viability in banking: Looking beyond the balance sheet', Federal Reserve Bank of Dallas, Financial Industry Studies Working Paper, 97–5.

Clark, J. A. and T. F. Siems (2002). 'X-efficiency in banking: Looking beyond the balance sheet', *Journal of Money, Credit and Banking* 34(4), November, 987–1013.

Dechow, P. M., R. G. Sloan and A. P. Sweeney (1995). 'Detecting earnings management', *The Accounting Review* 70, 193–226.

Déprins, D., L. Simar and H. Tulkens (1984). 'Measuring labour efficiency in post offices', in M. Marchand, P. Pestieau, and H. Tulkens (eds), *The Performance of Public Enterprises: Concepts and Measurements*, Oxford: North Holland, 345–67.

DeYoung, R. and I. Hasan (1998). 'The performance of de novo commercial banks: A profit efficiency approach', *Journal of Banking and Finance* 22(5), 565–87.

Dietsch, M. and A. Lozano-Vivas (2000). 'How the environment determines banking efficiency: A comparison between French and Spanish industries', *Journal of Banking and Finance* 24, 985–1004.

Eichengreen, B. and H. D. Gibson (2001). 'Greek banking at the dawn of the new millennium', Centre for Economic Policy Research Discussion Paper, no. 2791, May.

Färe, R., S. Grosskopf and W. L. Weber (2004). 'The effect of risk-based capital requirements on profit efficiency in banking', *Applied Economics* 36, 1731–43.

Färe, R., S. Grosskopf, M. Norris and Z. Zhang (1994b). 'Productivity growth, technical progress and efficiency changes in industrialised countries', *American Economic Review* 84, 66–83.

Farrell, M. J. (1957). 'The measurement of productive efficiency', *Journal of Royal Statistical Society*, series A, 120(3), 253–90.

Ferrier, G. and C. A. K. Lovell (1990). 'Measuring cost efficiency in banking: Econometric and linear programming evidence', *Journal of Econometrics* 46, 229–45.

Garganas, N. C. (2003). 'The changing structures of European banking: The Greek experience', speech of the Governor of the Bank of Greece at the Bulgarian Central Bank, 14 February.

Gehrig, T. and G. Sheldon (1999). 'Cost, competitiveness and the changing structure of European banking', Foundation Bank de Franc: Papers and Non-Technical Reports.

Gibson, H. (2005). 'Profitability of Greek banks: Recent developments,' *Bank of Greece Economic Bulletin* 24/1, 7–27 (in Greek).

Giokas, D. I. (1991). 'Bank branch operational efficiency: A comparative application of DEA and the loglinear model', *Omega International Journal of Management Science* 19, 549–57.

Girardone, C., P. Molyneux and E. P. M. Gardener (2004). 'Analyzing the determinants of bank efficiency: The case of Italian banks', *Applied Economics*, 36(3), 215–27.

Goddard, J. A., P. Molyneux and J. O. S. Wilson (2001). *European Banking: Efficiency, Technology, and Growth*, Chichester: John Wiley.

Grifell-Tatjé, E. and C. A. K. Lovell (1995). 'A note on the Malmquist productivity index', *Economics Letters* 47(2), 169–75.

Grifell-Tatjé, E. and C. A. K. Lovell (1996). 'Deregulation and productivity decline, The case of the Spanish saving banks', *Economic Letters* 40, 1281–303.

Grosskopf, S. (1993). 'Efficiency and productivity', in H. O. Fried, C. A. K. Lovell and S. S. Schmidt (eds), *The Measurement of Productive Efficiency: Techniques and Applications*, Oxford: Oxford University Press.

Halkos, G. E. and D. S. Salamouris (2004). 'Efficiency measurement of the Greek commercial banks with the use of financial ratios: A data envelopment analysis approach', *Management Accounting Research* 15, 201–24.

Heshmati, A. (2001). 'Productivity growth, efficiency and outsourcing in manufacturing and service industries', SSE/EFI Working Paper, no. 394, October.

Hughes, J. P. and L. J. Mester (1993). 'A quality and risk-adjusted cost function for banks: Evidence on the "Too-Big-To-Fail" Doctrine', *Journal of Productivity Analysis* 4, 293–315.

Huizinga, H. P., J. H. M. Nelissen and R. Vander Vennet (2001). 'Efficiency effects of bank mergers and acquisitions in Europe', Gent University Working Paper, no. 01/106.

Humphrey, D. B. (1990). 'Why do estimates of bank scale economies differ?', Federal Reserve Bank of Richmond, *Economic Review* 76, 38–50.

Humphrey, D. B. (1993). 'Cost and technological change: Effects from bank deregulation', *Journal of Productivity Analysis* 4, 9–34.

Kamberoglou, N. C., E. Liapis, G. T. Simigiannis and P. Tzamourani (2004). 'Cost efficiency in Greek banking', Bank of Greece Working Paper, no. 9, January.

Karafolas, S. and G. Mantakas (1996). 'A note on cost structure and economies of scale in Greek banking', *Journal of Banking and Finance* 20, 377–87.

Kumbhakar, S. C., A. Lozano-Vivas, C. A. K. Lovell and I. Hasan (2001). 'The effects of deregulation on the performance of financial institutions: The case of Spanish savings banks', *Journal of Money, Credit and Banking* 33, 101–20.

Koopmans, T. C. (1951). 'An analysis of production as an efficient combination of activities', in T. C. Koopmans (ed.), *Activity Analysis of Production and Allocation*, Cowles Commission for Research in Economics, Monograph no. 13, New York: Wiley.

Land, K. C., C. A. K Lovell and S. Thore (1993). 'Chance-constrained data envelopment analysis', *Managerial and Decision Economics* 14, 541–54.

Leibenstein, H. (1966). 'Allocative efficiency vs. "X-efficiency"', *American Economic Review* 56, 392–415.

Lozano-Vivas, A., J. T. Pastor and I. Hasan (2001). 'European bank performance beyond country borders: What really matters?', *European Finance Review* 5, 141–65.

Lozano-Vivas, A., J. T. Pastor and J. M. Pastor (2002). 'An efficiency comparison of European banking systems operating under different environmental conditions', *Journal of Productivity Analysis* 18, 59–78.

Malmquist, S. (1953). 'Index numbers and indifference surfaces', *Trabajos de Estatistica* 4, 209–42.

Maudos, J. and J. M. Pastor (2003). 'Cost and profit efficiency in the Spanish banking sector (1985–1996): A non-parametric approach', *Applied Financial Economics* 13, 1–12.

Maudos, J., J. M. Pastor and F. Perez (2002). 'Competition and efficiency in the Spanish anking sector: The importance of specialization', *Applied Financial Economics* 12, 505–16.

McAllister, P. H. and D. A. McManus (1993). 'Resolving the scale efficiency puzzle in banking', *Journal of Banking and Finance* 17, 389–405.

Mukherjee, K., S. C. Ray and S. M. Millar (2001). 'Productivity growth in large US banks: The initial post-deregulation experience', *Journal of Banking and Finance* 25(5), 913–39.

Noulas, A. G. (1997). 'Productivity growth in the Hellenic banking industry: State versus private banks', *Applied Financial Economics* 7, 223–8.

Noulas, A. G. (2001). 'Deregulation and operating efficiency: The case of the Greek banks', *Managerial Finance* 27(8), 35–47.

Ondrich, J. and J. Ruggiero (2001). 'Efficiency measurement in the stochastic frontier model', *European Journal of Operational Research* 129, 434–42.

Pastor, J. T., A. Lozano and J. M. Pastor (1997). 'Efficiency of European banking systems: A correction by environmental variables', Working Paper, IVIE WP-EC 97-12.

Pastor, J. T., F. Perez and J. Quesada (1997). 'Efficiency analysis in banking firms: An international comparison', *European Journal of Operational Research* 98(2), 395–407.

Resti, A. (1997). 'Evaluating the cost efficiency of the Italian banking market: What can be learned from the joint application of parametric and non-parametric techniques', *Journal of Banking and Finance* 21, 221–50.

Rezitis, A. N. (2006). 'Productivity growth in the Greek banking industry: A non-parametric approach', *Journal of Applied Economics* ix(1), May, 119–38.

Rime, B. and K. J. Stiroh (2003). 'The performance of universal banks: Evidence from Switzerland', *Journal of Banking and Finance* 27, 2121–50.

Rogers, K. E. (1998). 'Nontraditional activities and the efficiency of US commercial banks', *Journal of Banking and Finance* 22, 467–82.

Rogers, K. E. and J. F. Sinkey (1999). 'An analysis of nontraditional activities at US commercial banks', *Review of Financial Economics* 8(1), 25–39.

Ruthenberg, D. and R. Elias (1996). 'Cost economies and interest margins in a unified European banking market', *Journal of Economics and Business* 48, 231–49.

Schure, P. and R. Wagenvoort (1999). 'Economies of scale and efficiency in European banking: New evidence', European Investment bank: Economic and Financial Report, 1999/01.

Schure, P., R. Wagenvoort and D. O' Brien (2004). 'The efficiency and the conduct of European banks: Developments after 1992', *Review of Financial Economics* 13, 371–96.

Sealey, C. W. and J. T. Lindley (1977). 'Inputs, outputs and theory of production and costs at depository financial institutions', *Journal of Finance* 34, 1251–66.

Shephard R. W. (1970). *Theory of Cost and Production Functions*, Princeton, NJ, Princeton University Press.

Siems, T. F. and J. A. Clark (1997). 'Rethinking bank efficiency and regulation: How off-balance sheet activities make a difference', *Financial Industry Studies*, Federal Reserve Bank of Dallas, 1–11.

Simar, L. (1992). 'Estimating efficiencies from frontier models with panel data: A comparison of parametric, nonparametric and semiparametric methods with bootstrapping', *Journal of Productivity Analysis* 3, 171–203.

Simar, L. and P. W. Wilson (1995). 'Sensitivity analysis of efficiency scores: How to bootstrap in non-parametric frontier models', Papers 9543a, Catholique de Louvain – Centre for Operations Research and Economics.

Simar, L. and P. W. Wilson, 2007. 'Estimation and inference in two-stage, semi-parametric models of production processes', Forthcoming paper, *Journal of Econometrics*.

Soteriou, A. C. and Y. Stavrinides (2000). 'An internal customer service quality data envelopment analysis model for bank branches', *International Journal of Bank Marketing* 18(5), 246–52.

Stiroh, K. J. (2000). 'How did bank holding companies prosper in the 1990s?', *Journal of Banking and Finance* 24, 1703–45.

Stournaras, Y. (2006). 'Interactions between financial sector developments and the macroeconomic environment: The Greek experience,' mimeo, University of Athens.

Tortosa-Ausina, E. (2003). 'Nontraditional activities and bank efficiency revisited: A distributional analysis for Spanish financial institutions', *Journal of Economics and Business* 55, 371–95.

Tsionas, E. G., S. E. G. Lolos and D. K. Christopoulos (2003). 'The performance of the Greek banking system in view of the EMU: Results from a non-parametric approach', *Economic Modelling* 20, 571–92.

Vander Vennet, R. (2002). 'Cost and profit efficiency of financial conglomerates and universal banks in Europe', *Journal of Money, Credit and Banking* 34, 254–82.

Vassiloglou, M. and D. Giokas (1990). 'A study of the relative efficiency of bank branches', *The Journal of the Operational Research Society* 41(7), 591–7.

Weill, L. (2003). 'Is there a lasting gap in bank efficiency between Eastern and Western European countries?', paper presented at the 'Twentieth Symposium on Monetary and Financial Economics', The University of Birmingham, 5–6 June.

Wagenvoort, J. L. M., D. O'Brien and P. Schure (2001). 'The recursive thick frontier approach to estimating frontier production functions', University of Victoria Econometrics Working Papers, no. 0503.

Wheelock, D. C. and P. W. Wilson (1999). 'Technical progress, inefficiency and productivity change in US Banking (1984–1993)', *Journal of Money, Credit and Banking* 31, 213–34.

Williams, J. (2001). 'Financial deregulation and productivity change in European banking', *Revue Bancaire et Financiere* 8, 470–7.

10
Electronic Money Use: Evidence from Survey Data

David Pelilli[*]

10.1 Introduction

This chapter sets out to analyse the factors influencing cashless payment instrument use (i.e., e-money use), both by considering these instruments' specific attributes and by combining the assumptions of the Theory of Planned Behaviour (TPB) with Technology Acceptance Models (TAM). A survey on undergraduate students has been conducted in order to identify the personal, sociological, and technological variables involved in e-money use. The proposed model has been tested on students' payment habits in using credit, debit, and prepaid cards. Overall we found that personal and technological attitudes, social and control beliefs, and payment instruments features (in terms of perceived efficacy and efficiency) are linked with electronic money use. We note that the identification of variables affecting adoption by retail customers could be useful for both regulators and financial institutions. Regulators, usually concerned with the behaviour of the institutions under their jurisdiction, could use these findings when drafting prudential and supervision rules governing financial institutions offering payment services. By recognizing issues that affect the behaviour of their customer segments, financial intermediaries can take advantage of aspects that produce differences and changes in payment practices, developing their product range in response.

10.2 Payment instruments in Europe: a cross-country comparison

In the last few years, the various aspects of the European payment services industry have been the subject of analysis by financial and academic

[*] University of 'Rome III', Faculty of Economics and Management 'Federico Caffè', Department of Management, Business and Law, Via Silvio D'Amico, 111 – 00145 – Rome – Italy, Tel. +39 06 57114671 pelilli@uniroma3.it

communities alike. The reasons for this high level of interest seem to reflect a context and sector which have undergone profound changes. The design at the European level of a single system of payment (SEPA) has generated an increase in competition even in the basic financial services designed to meet payment needs. The introduction of EC Directive 2000/46 regarding the taking up, pursuit of, and prudential supervision of the business of electronic money institutions has established the possibility for these subjects, once authorized by their country of origin regulators, to operate on a pan-European base, offering their payment services even beyond their national boundaries, as has already occurred for credit institutions.

Competitive pressure, only partially explained by these changes, has encouraged a strong trend towards integration amongst the various market participants: in some cases it has been caused by the search for synergies between different players, while in others the main explanation lies in technological variables.

The products offered by financial institutions in the payment services sector have thus undergone radical change: in the case of both euro-area countries and new entrants, there has been a gradual shift from paper-based to virtual forms of payment (credit cards, debit cards, prepaid cards, and e-purses) (ECB, 2006). Although the promotion of innovative payment instruments can be explained through the need on the part of the financial institutions involved to raise their efficiency levels, the adoption of these forms of payment by the retail segment is neither certain nor immediate. In fact, the payments market is 'two-sided'; that is to say, it needs to attract two different categories of subjects – merchants and cardholders – through the simultaneous satisfaction of both groups' payment needs (Rochet and Tirole, 2004). This situation has been the subject of a large body of literature interested in evaluating the network effects deriving from the market structure of payments systems.

In fact, simply the enrolment of merchants, nationwide availability of ATMs and the generalized use of payment cards alone might be insufficient to provide a reasonable explanation for the purchasing and usage behaviour of the market's two sides, and the behaviour of cardholders in particular. From an initial analysis of data relating to payment system structures in the euro area countries, it emerges that there are two different groups of states, whose relative positions remain almost unchanged even over a five-year comparison (Figure 10.1a and b).

The first group has a system structure in line with the European average, but a low number of electronic money transactions. The second, although its payment card acceptance network is similar to that of countries in the first group, shows strong penetration in terms of the number of payment cards in relation to total population, and numerically higher per capita card use. A comparison of the 2000 and 2004 data reveals that the increased spread of payment cards among the public and structural change in the acceptance

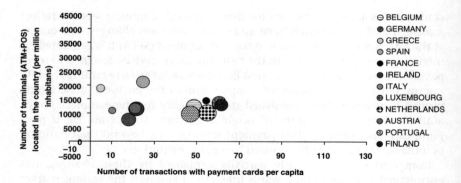

Figure 10.1a Payment system structure and card payment usage in the euro area, 2000

Source: ECB Bluebook, 2006. Size represents the penetration coefficient of cards on population. Belgium data are for year 2001. Spain data are for 2002. Austrian data are only for 2004. Data is transformed by David Pelilli. The information may be obtained free of charge from the ECB's web site.

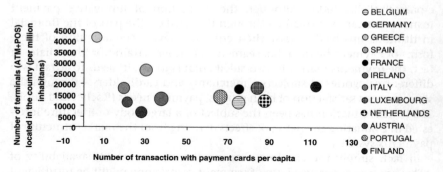

Figure 10.1b Payment system structure and card payment usage in the euro area, 2004

Source: ECB Bluebook, 2006. Size represents the penetration coefficient of cards on population. Data is transformed by David Pelilli. The information may be obtained free of charge from the ECB's web site.

network has not enabled any of the countries considered to significantly increase the use of payment cards.

Although in some European countries the introduction of innovative forms of payment has met with a favourable response from customers, in others this has happened only in part, because of the different features both of the structure of the payment system and of the customers in these geographical areas. The net result of the institutional, technological and sectoral stimuli can therefore be measured only in terms of the higher or lower rates of use of electronic money instruments: in both cases it is useful to understand the reasons and the causes which have created these differences. Therefore, when studying the characteristics of the demand side, it seems useful to adopt an approach which also considers the factors which encourage or restrict the adoption of innovative forms of payment.

10.3 Empirical studies on payment card usage: a review

Empirical studies related to payment card and electronic money use can be divided into two different groups. The first group consists of all the studies that have interpreted the phenomenon with an emphasis on the macroeconomic effects of the processes by which different types of instrument are chosen. Some authors (Humphrey, Pulley and Vesala, 1996) have analysed the phenomenon in relation to a number of economic (income per capita, ATM and POS availability) and institutional variables (crime rates, concentration of the banking system) that could be directly linked to the use of traditional and innovative payment instruments. The empirical analyses have measured both differences among countries and impacts on the payment system as a whole, in terms of operation pricing and differences in product ranges, in search of theoretical models capable of providing a general equilibrium (Shy and Tarkka, 2002).

In this first group of studies it is essential to remember the work of Humphrey, Kim and Vale (2001), with its important contribution of a model for consumers' choice of different payment instruments (cash, cheques, and debit cards) based on own price, cross prices, and payment substitution flexibility: the authors show that consumers are very sensitive to prices when it comes to making their choices. Other works aim to explain the network effects connected to a two-sided market like the payment instrument market, by empirically identifying some of the key characteristics of a market of this kind: in particular, analysis of the main payment circuit flows has revealed the existence of a 'single-homing effect', that is, the customer's preference for constant use of the most widely accepted card, showing a positive relationship between customer use and degree of merchant acceptance (Rysman, 2006). In other cases, the effects of innovation and competition in the card payment market have been measured, in order to explain and guide regulators' decisions (Mantel and McHugh, 2001).

The most useful inputs for this chapter come from a second group of studies based on surveys carried out to evaluate the relative importance of the explanatory variables linked to electronic money usage behaviour. Studies in this field (Hirschman, 1982) have considered customers' attitudes, evaluating the different occasions of use and the different characteristics of payment instruments (acceptance level, spending control, security), assuming that customers view different combinations of attributes as significant when judging the single payment instrument's suitability for use. In this context there have been several studies (Hayashi and Klee, 2003; Mantel, 2000; Stavins, 2001) which underline that social and demographic factors (Mantel, 2000; Stavins, 2001), such as wealth or personal preferences, can have a critical influence on e-money use. Another work (Oleson, 2004) focused on the relationship between individual attitudes towards money and different needs expressed on the basis of Maslow's theory (Maslow, 1954): the results show that when an individual moves on to the satisfaction of higher needs, the importance given to money is lower, although there may be some gender differences.

10.3.1   Technology acceptance models (TAM) and payment card usage

When analysing the factors which affect e-money usage behaviour, techno-logical aspects must also be considered. This has been the direction of study of a number of authors (Hayashi and Klee, 2003), who place more emphasis on the propensity to adopt technology as a factor which could affect the use of some electronic payment instruments: the results show that customers who use new technologies are also more willing to adopt electronic forms of payment. These studies derive from Technology Acceptance Models (TAM), which have already been usefully employed in the financial services sector to characterize the drivers connected with electronic banking use.

The TAMs most widely accepted in the literature consider factors such as ease of use and perceived usefulness as the main drivers behind acceptance of a new technology (Davis, 1989; Davis, Bagozzi and Warshaw, 1989). Other authors, using the same approach, develop a model also including individual and personal elements, referable to intrinsic and extrinsic motivational components in the adoption of new technology (Venkatesh, Speier and Morris 2002). Although not clearly backed up by empirical findings, these variables describe the enjoyment associated to use of a certain technology, apart from the positive results deriving from its adoption. Some of these factors will also be used to explain cashless payment instrument usage.

10.3.2   Electronic money and the theory of planned behaviour

The study of human behaviour has enjoyed much success over recent decades. This degree of attention has mainly been due to these theories' tan-gible applications in business management and marketing, in particular in the definition of target segment characteristics and the evaluation of market response to the introduction of new products. To identify the motivations that drive retail customers to use or reject electronic payment instruments, we will use the Theory of Planned Behaviour (TPB) (Ajzen, 1991) and its the-oretical bases to develop the empirical part of this study. This theory focuses on the intentions underlying the adoption of a specific form of behaviour. The TPB is a theoretical extension of the Theory of Reasoned Actions (TRA) (Fishbein and Ajzen, 1980) which starts from a very simple assumption – the stronger the intentions driving a person to behave in a particular way, the greater the probability that they will actually do so. Therefore the analysis of the intention's antecedents becomes of major significance when identifying the drivers influencing even the indirect adoption of a form of behaviour.

According to TPB, individual intentions to adopt certain behaviour derive from a combination of three factors:

- attitudes to the behaviour
- subjective norms
- perceived behavioural control.

The first derives from individual beliefs and is related to the degree to which a person takes a positive or negative view of the behaviour concerned. The second is connected to the perceived social pressure to adopt or reject the behaviour. The last factor regards the level of difficulties perceived by an individual in the adoption of the behaviour. This has recently been used in empirical studies of students' money management skills (Kidwell and Turrisi, 2004) because it not only provides a proxy for satisfaction obtained from past experiences, but often also incorporates the factors that facilitate or prevent the achievement of the results of the specific behaviour under consideration. In fact, ' ... because many behaviours pose difficulties of execution that may limit volitional control, it is useful to consider perceived behavioural control in addition to intention. It can serve as a proxy for actual control and contribute to the prediction of the behaviour in question' (Ajzen, 2002, p. 1). This theoretical statement not only allows identification of the motivational factors that can affect individual behaviour, but also makes it possible to measure the relative power these factors have in the adoption of a given behaviour. Some empirical works have applied TPB to the subject of payment cards (Furnham, 1984; Hayhoe, Leach and Turner, 1999; Xiao, Noring and Anderson, 1995), defining the hierarchical scales potentially capable of measuring the factors described above. One suggested measurement tool is a semantic Likert-scale (unfavourable/favourable) based on added scores, composed of a series of statements regarding personal attitudes to payment cards, with the statements subdivided into three different dimensions referring to affective, cognitive, and behavioural components (Xiao, Noring and Anderson, 1995; Rosenberg and Hoyland, 1960). This kind of measure will be applied later in this study.

10.4   The model

The model presented in this chapter aims to identify the factors capable of explaining the use of electronic money, with simultaneous reference to the motivational approach of TPB, the key characteristics of the technology acceptance models and the efficiency and efficacy characters typically ascribed to payment instruments (Ajzen, 1991; Hayhoe, Leach and Turner, 1999; Hirschman, 1982; Venkatesh, Speier and Morris 2002).

The TPB-related factors include the variables regarding attitudes to payment cards (affective, cognitive, behavioural), social pressures and the perceived behavioural control connected with the use of cashless instruments. The parameters used to establish the level of technological acceptance comprise five determinants: perceived ease of use (derived from TAM models), trust in technological devices, the familiarity and usefulness connected with technology devices use and, last but not least, the level of innovation-awareness, measured by the frequency with which these devices are changed during one year. Among the characteristics of payment instruments we considered their efficiency and efficacy factors: convenience of use, transaction speed, spending control, acceptance level, security, privacy, and economic benefits.

10.5 Research methodology

In the first part of the study, using a focus group of university students, we selected the semantic and content dimensions best suited to represent and describe the motivational and technological factors to be analysed in the next part. On the basis of these results and drawing on a comparison with the relative literature, an initial 35-point questionnaire was tested on a small sample of 12 students. The final version of the questionnaire, consisting of 29 questions, was distributed to a random sample of 62 University of 'Rome III' students.

This questionnaire was subdivided into five different parts:

* demographic characteristics
* levels of banking use and payment habits
* behaviours and attitudes towards cashless payment instruments
* perceptions of the characteristics of different payment instruments
* innovative technology adoption and perception of the importance of some of its characteristics.

For the study presented here, only the answers given to 16 questions, considered most significant for the research, were considered. We chose to carry out the analysis on a sample of Italian university students for two kinds of reasons. First of all, Italians have only recently begun to show significant interest in having and using payment cards, in contrast with the picture in other European countries (ECB, 2006); in fact, the per capita number of transactions performed with cashless instruments is lower than the European average.

Secondly, the literature studying this phenomenon has often used the student population as the sample of reference (Kidwell and Turrisi, 2004;

Hayhoe, Leach and Turner, 1999), whether focusing on students' ability to manage their financial budgets or analysing the personal and attitudinal characteristics of students with a large number of credit cards. This approach makes it particularly interesting to study the factors affecting cashless instrument payment use in the Italian student population, for both academics and practitioners; in fact, the latter may be keen to know the motivation underlying students' payments habits, because potentially they represent a very profitable market segment, in which the saturation of the card market is still close to zero.

10.6   The sample and variable measurement

The sample consisted of 33 males and 29 females over the age of 18: 73 per cent of those interviewed stated that they held at least one cashless payment instrument (credit cards, debit cards, prepaid cards), while 27 per cent did not have these instruments. Among cardholders, males accounted for 60 per cent and females the remaining 40 per cent; the majority of those who were not holders were female (65 per cent). Nevertheless, we must underline that 40 per cent of those who stated that they did not have cards had used a payment card held by someone else (typically their parents) at least once during the previous year. Thirty-three per cent of the sample held just one payment card while 40 per cent had two or more. Debit and prepaid cards were the instruments most commonly owned by students (57 per cent for both), while 44 per cent had credit cards in their names.

Variable measurement techniques were derived from previous studies (Ajzen, 1991; Filotto, 1998; Hayhoe, Leach and Turner, 1999; Xiao, Noring and Anderson, 1995). Possible answers relating to attitudes to electronic payment instruments were organized on a five-point semantic Likert-scale (strongly disagree/strongly agree) following the methodology used in other studies of attitudes to money and credit (Hayhoe, Leach and Turner, 1999; Xiao, Noring and Anderson, 1995). For the answers related to both attitudes to innovation and perception of payment instrument characteristics, we adopted a five-point semantic Likert-scale (Filotto, 1998), which also considered the results of previous focus group studies, as suggested by the literature (Ajzen, 2002). Attitudes to electronic forms of payment were measured using a narrower scale than in previous literature, adopting the general classification suggested by TPB (Ajzen, 1991). This scale comprises 23 items subdivided as follows:

- 10 regarding attitudes (3 affective, 4 cognitive, 3 behavioural)
- 7 related to subjective norms
- 6 regarding perceived behavioural control.

The variables assessing awareness of technological innovation (three items) were linked to the substitution frequency of high-tech devices (PC, mobile phone, and digital camera), while attitudes towards these devices (four items) were measured considering factors such as usefulness, ease of use, familiarity, and trust (Filotto, 1998). Moreover, participants were asked to express their level of agreement with statements about the typical characteristics of payment instruments, including both cash and payment cards.

The intrinsic characteristics of payment cards and cash were subdivided into two different groups, one related to efficacy and the other to efficiency (card/cash efficacy and card/cash efficiency). The first group contained the answers regarding spending control, acceptance level, security, and privacy, and the second those regarding the convenience, speed, and economic benefits associated to cash and payment card usage. Missing data were dealt with using one of the 'hot deck' non-parametric methods widely used in economic analysis: the Nearest Neighbour Donor (NND) (Cicchitelli, Herzel and Montanari, 1992), the methodological correctness of which has been confirmed by empirical findings (Chen and Shao, 2000; Little, 1998). The simple averages of all the variables previously described were calculated and were subsequently used to verify relationships with electronic money usage.

10.7   Results

10.7.1   Descriptive statistics

Table 10.1 illustrates the correlations with the predictive variables for electronic payment instrument usage, for the entire sample.

Table 10.1   Individual variables that differentiate between students with a cashless payment instrument and without

Two-tailed t-test results (only significant results are shown)		
	p values	t-statistic
Students with at least one cashless payment instrument compared to students without *(n = 62; d.f. = 60)*		
AFFECTIVE	0.0138	2.5359
BEHAVIOURAL	0.023	2.3333
SUBJECTIVE NORMS	0.0092	2.6912
CASHSPEED	0.0098	−2.6694
Students with credit card compared to students without credit card *(n = 62; d.f. = 60)*		
SUBJECTIVE NORMS	0.0198	2.3937
TECHCHANGE	0.0134	2.5479
Students that have used at least one time their card payment instrument compared to who have never used it *(n = 62; d.f. = 60)*		
AFFECTIVE	0.0067	2.8074
CARDSECURITY	0.0127	2.5699

An initial examination reveals that the relationships identified by TPB between attitudes (affective, cognitive, behavioural) and factors in the other two categories (subjective norms and perceived behavioural control) are confirmed (Ajzen, 1991). The mitigating function of perceived behavioural control compared with the other variables (except the behaviourals) also holds true, as indicated by previous literature (Kidwell and Turrisi, 2004). The results regarding attitudes towards technology are consistent with those of TAM models: the relationship between ease of use and perceived usefulness on the one hand, and the other variables, such as familiarity and perceived trust in technological devices on the other, is particularly significant. The results with regard to these last-named variables also show significant relationships to the degree of efficacy and efficiency attributed to the various payment instruments. In addition, there is a significant correlation between the efficacy and efficiency attributed to payment cards and perceived behavioural control. This relationship shows a link between the individual's perception of the potential of cashless payment instruments and the intrinsic characteristics of the instruments themselves.

Subsequently, in order to check for differences between holders of a cashless payment instrument and others, two-tailed t tests were performed on all the variables (Table 10.2).

The results show that students holding at least one cashless payment instrument (credit, debit or prepaid card) were the ones who expressed a favourable opinion regarding behavioural ($p < 0.03$) and affective attitudes ($p < 0.02$), and were more aware of social pressure concerning the use of payment cards ($p < 0.01$); moreover, they thought that cash transactions were slow ($p < 0.01$). Subdividing the sample on the base of credit card ownership, it is clear card holders are more aware of social pressure ($p < 0.02$) and technological innovations ($p < 0.02$). Finally, those who had used a cashless payment instrument at least once during the previous year, even if not card holders, not only expressed a positive opinion regarding affective attitude, but also showed particular awareness of the security item, giving it a positive evaluation ($p < 0.02$).

10.7.2   Linear regression results

Linear regressions were performed on the different types of payment instruments across the whole sample, using a stepwise selection of the predictive variables. The regressions examined credit, debit, and prepaid card frequency of use: a regression was also carried out regarding the average use of all the cashless instruments mentioned above. The F-statistic values were all significant ($p < 0.01$), although they varied from one regression to another. Average values of the Variance Inflation Factor (VIF) on all the regressions did not highlight any multi-colinearity problems: the average VIF regarding all cashless instruments was 1.06, on credit cards it was 1.62, on debit cards it was 1.18 and on prepaid cards it was 1.37. Furthermore, none of the VIF

Table 10.2 Pairwise correlations between predictors of cashless instruments use

		1	2	3	4	5	6	7	8
1	Credit card use	1							
2	Debit card use	0.2661**	1						
		(0.0366)							
3	Prepaid card use	−0.1324	−0.0055	1					
		(0.3049)	(0.9662)						
4	Owned cards	0.2283*	0.5071***	0.3770***	1				
		(0.0743)	(0.0000)	(0.0025)					
5	Affective	0.3601***	0.2800**	0.1552	0.1795	1			
		(0.004)	(0.0275)	(0.2285)	(0.1628)				
6	Cognitive	0.0694	0.0489	−0.0067	−0.0261	−0.0073	1		
		(0.5918)	(0.7056)	(0.9588)	(0.8406)	(0.9551)			
7	Behavioural	0.1163	0.2138*	0.1844	0.1813	0.3857***	0.0698	1	
		(0.3682)	(0.0952)	(0.1513)	(0.1584)	(0.002)	(0.5897)		
8	Subjective norm	0.3514***	0.0895	0.1977	0.2303*	0.4664***	−0.0953	0.3091**	1
		(0.0051)	(0.4889)	(0.1235)	(0.0717)	(0.0001)	(0.4613)	(0.0145)	
9	Perceived behavioural control	0.068	0.2459*	0.1214	0.2858**	0.3274***	0.3004**	0.0597	0.3313***
		(0.5993)	(0.054)	(0.3474)	(0.0244)	(0.0094)	(0.0177)	(0.645)	(0.0085)
10	Technological change	0.3788***	0.1631	−0.0774	0.2315*	0.0159	−0.1853	0.0629	0.2637**
		(0.0024)	(0.2054)	(0.5499)	(0.0703)	(0.9021)	(0.1494)	(0.627)	(0.0383)
11	Technological usefulness	0.2084	−0.0495	−0.0482	−0.1062	0.1933	0.0399	−0.0511	0.1873
		(0.1041)	(0.7023)	(0.71)	(0.4113)	(0.1322)	(0.7583)	(0.693)	(0.1449)
12	Technological ease of use	0.0446	−0.044	0.0149	−0.1887	−0.01	0.1048	0.0344	0.0745
		(0.7306)	(0.734)	(0.9083)	(0.1418)	(0.9385)	(0.4174)	(0.7908)	(0.565)
13	Technological familiarity	0.0204	0.0839	−0.1328	−0.1406	0.0737	0.2611**	−0.0839	0.0608
		(0.8749)	(0.5166)	(0.3036)	(0.2759)	(0.5693)	(0.0404)	(0.5168)	(0.6387)
14	Technological trust	0.0283	−0.0184	−0.0921	−0.1317	−0.0646	0.0122	−0.1638	−0.2220*
		(0.8269)	(0.8869)	(0.4766)	(0.3076)	(0.6177)	(0.9252)	(0.2034)	(0.0829)
15	Card efficacy	−0.1239	0.2221*	−0.0087	0.1362	0.0363	0.1677	0.0584	0.0711
		(0.3375)	(0.0828)	(0.9464)	(0.2912)	(0.7795)	(0.1927)	(0.6523)	(0.5831)
16	Card efficiency	0.1247	0.1338	0.0383	0.097	0.3630***	0.3036**	0.063	0.1815
		(0.3342)	(0.3)	(0.7676)	(0.4532)	(0.0037)	(0.0164)	(0.6266)	(0.158)
17	Cash efficacy	−0.0282	−0.0882	−0.0843	−0.1978	−0.1736	−0.259**	−0.0159	−0.0866
		(0.8276)	(0.4956)	(0.5145)	(0.1232)	(0.1773)	(0.0421)	(0.9022)	(0.5031)
18	Cash efficiency	0.0091	−0.2119*	0.0517	−0.1836	−0.1039	0.2360*	−0.2864**	−0.0696
		(0.9442)	(0.0982)	(0.6898)	(0.1532)	(0.4217)	(0.0648)	(0.024)	(0.591)

values for the predictive variables in any of the regressions exceeded 2. Finally, two kinds of test were performed to check for heteroscedasticity: the White test (White, 1980) and the Breusch-Pagan Lagrange multiplier test (Breusch and Pagan, 1979; Cook and Weisberg, 1983). The test results suggest the absence of heteroscedasticity in the regressions related to debit and prepaid cards; in the others (i.e., credit cards and overall cashless instruments), the tests results are conflicting: we therefore decided not to correct the regression for possible heteroscedasticity. The results of these regressions are shown below (Table 10.3).

If we consider overall cashless instrument use, only four out of a total of 15 predictive variables provide a satisfactory explanation of the phenomenon ($R^2 = 0.52$): two of these belong to the technology acceptance category (awareness of technological innovation and ease of use), while the most

9	10	11	12	13	14	15	16	17
1								
0.2373*	1							
(0.0633)								
−0.042	0.1153	1						
(0.7461)	(0.372)							
−0.2109*	−0.0667	0.3394***	1					
(0.1)	(0.6065)	(0.007)						
0.0811	0.0412	0.1643	0.4303***	1				
(0.531)	(0.7505)	(0.202)	(0.0005)					
−0.1408	−0.0326	0.2679**	0.3721***	0.1449	1			
(0.2752)	(0.8016)	(0.0353)	(0.0029)	(0.2613)				
0.2854**	−0.0365	−0.0019	−0.0062	−0.2463*	0.3193**	1		
(0.0426)	(0.7779)	(0.9885)	(0.9618)	(0.0536)	(0.0114)			
0.4663***	0.1578	0.1402	0.0747	0.1592	0.1186	0.2723**	1	
(0.0001)	(0.2205)	(0.2771)	(0.5638)	(0.2165)	(0.3584)	(0.0322)		
−0.1729	0.1589	−0.0776	−0.0789	0.1251	0.092	−0.2008	−0.1824	1
(0.1791)	(0.2174)	(0.5487)	(0.542)	(0.3326)	(0.4772)	(0.1176)	(0.1559)	
−0.0303	0.0481	0.1078	0.1084	0.2124*	0.2561**	−0.1791	−0.0046	0.2231*
(0.815)	(0.7103)	(0.4041)	(0.4015)	(0.0975)	(0.0445)	(0.1636)	(0.9718)	(0.0813)

significant are the number of cards owned and ($p < 0.01$) and the affective attitude ($p < 0.01$).

Looking at the results regarding credit card usage, 11 variables are significant ($R^2 = 0.54$). In particular, all the variables derived from TPB are significant: the cognitive ($p < 0.01$) and affective variables ($p < 0.01$), and those related to subjective norms ($p < 0.01$) are the most so. Perceived behavioural control is significant ($p < 0.05$) but with a negative sign, while the behavioural variable shows only a weak link to card use, in line with the results of previous studies (Hayhoe, Leach and Turner 1999). All the technology-related variables, except for perceived usefulness, are significant: the most significant and positively related to credit card usage are awareness of innovation ($p < 0.01$) and trust in technology devices; the others (ease of

Table 10.3 Linear regression on use of payment cards

Predictors	Overall cashless use	Credit card use	Debit card use	Prepaid card use
Personal attitudes				
Affective	0.328***	0.435***	0.486*	
Cognitive		0.481***		
Behavioural		−0.163		
Social and control beliefs				
Subjective norms		0.345***	−0.167	
Perceived behavioural control		−0.321**		
Perceptions and attitudes toward technology				
Technological change	0.120	0.460***		−0.221*
Technological usefulness				
Technological ease of use	0.213	−0.157		0.360**
Technological familiarity		−0.215*	0.218*	−0.182
Technological trust		0.356**		−0.253*
Payment instrument characteristics				
Card efficacy		−0.291**	0.191*	
Card efficiency				
Cash efficacy				0.159
Cash efficiency		−0.188	−0.122	0.193
Remaining predictors				
Owned cars	0.563***		0.486***	0.594***
Gender		−0.331***		0.360**
R^2	0.5249	0.5422	0.3838	0.3212
Adjusted R^2	0.4916	0.4301	0.3165	0.2187
F statistics	15.74***	4.84***	5.71***	3.13***
	n = 62	*$p < 0.10$	**$p < 0.05$	***$p < 0.01$

use and perceived familiarity) have a negative relationship and a lower significance level ($p < 0.05$).

The main characteristics of payment instruments have a negative relationship with the use of credit cards, in particular with regard to the efficacy of cards ($p < 0.05$) and the efficiency of cash. In the regression regarding debit cards there are six significant variables ($R^2 = 0.38$): the most significant, apart from the number of cards owned ($p < 0.01$), are affective attitudes ($p < 0.1$), perceived familiarity with technology devices ($p < 0.1$), and the efficacy of payment cards ($p < 0.1$), which all have a positive relationship to the phenomenon under analysis. Although less effective in providing explanations ($R^2 = 0.32$), the regression on prepaid cards reveals eight predictive variables. The most significant belong to the perception of technology category and are, in particular, ease of use (p < 0.05) and awareness of technological innovation (p < 0.1).

10.8   Conclusions and implications for further research

This chapter shows that payment card usage is linked not only with these instruments' typical characteristics, but also with some factors connected to motivational, social, and technological variables. An examination of the data related to average use of cashless instruments reveals that frequency of use is constantly correlated to the number of payment cards owned, in line with findings in the previous literature (Xiao, Noring and Anderson, 1995). The survey demonstrated that a higher awareness of technological innovation, measured by the frequency with which technological devices are upgraded, affects payment card use, in particular the use of credit cards. Furthermore, while the analysis of personal attitudes is significant in explaining credit card usage, technological factors have a clearer effect on prepaid cards.

Among personal attitudes, the affective component is more responsible than any other factors for credit and debit card use, confirming the results of previous studies (Hayhoe, Leach and Turner, 1999). Perceived behavioural control is only significant for credit cards, where it shows a negative correlation: this result can be explained considering that the influence of several factors beyond the individual's control may generate larger economic losses than in the use of other payment instruments, such as prepaid cards. This finding does not arise from a general lack of trust in technology, in view of the strong awareness of technological innovation typical of credit card customers; rather it is due to the difficulties that could occur in relation to the technology, or to the intrinsic characteristics of the instrument, which lead to doubts about its security or privacy. It is interesting to observe that these relationships have the opposite sign in the case of prepaid cards: their use, although not necessarily an absolute alternative to the use of credit cards, springs mainly from a lack of trust in technological devices and a low level of awareness of technological innovation. Even if these findings can be useful and effective for financial institutions offering payment services, the model presented in this chapter has some limitations. In particular, the phenomenon was analysed exclusively from the demand side, considering the ranges of products on offer as exogenous. This fails to consider that some payment systems offer customers only a limited choice of alternatives, both because financial institutions' product ranges do not envisage multiple forms of payment, and because merchants do not accept the payment instruments concerned. Furthermore, the model does not include variables regarding the moment of use (Hirschman, 1982): transaction characteristics, such as the value and the price paid for the payment service; or point of sale features, such as the level of contact with the vendor (online/offline) and the nature of the products bought.

Bringing them into the equation could be very useful, not only to broaden understanding of the variables which explain the exclusive or combined use of a specific instrument, but also to identify any substitution effects between instruments with different features.

References

Ajzen, I. (1991). 'The theory of planned behaviour', *Organizational Behavior and Human Decision Processes* 50, 179–211.

Ajzen, I. (2002). 'Constructing a TPB questionnaire: Conceptual and methodological considerations', Working Paper, University of Massachussets.

Breusch, T. S. and A. R. Pagan (1979). 'A simple test for heteroscedasticity and random coefficient variation', *Econometrica* 47, 1287–94.

Chen, J. and J. Shao (2000). 'Nearest neighbour imputation for survey data', *Journal of Official Statistics* 16, 113–31.

Cicchitelli, G., A. Herzel and G. E. Montanari (1992). 'Il Campionamento Statistico', *Il Mulino*, Bologna.

Cook, R. D. and S. Weisberg (1983). 'Diagnostics for heteroscedasticity in regression', *Biometrika* 70(1), 1–10.

Davis, F. (1989). 'Perceived usefulness, perceived ease of use and user acceptance of information technology', *MIS Quarterly* 13(3), 319–39.

Davis, F., R. Bagozzi and P. Warshaw (1989). 'User acceptance of computer technology: A comparison of two theoretical models', *Management Science* 35(8), 982–1002.

ECB (2006). 'Payment and securities settlement systems in the European Union and in the acceding countries', Bluebook, March 2006.

Filotto, U., (1998). 'Distribuzione e Tecnologia: la Banca del Domani', EGEA.

Fishbein, M. and I. Ajzen (1980). *Understanding Attitudes and Predicting Social Behaviour*, London: Prentice Hall.

Furnham, A., (1984). 'Many sides of the coin: The psychology of money usage', *Personality and Individual Differences* 5, 501–9.

Hayashi, F. and E. Klee (2003). 'Technology adoption and consumer payments: Evidence from survey data', *Review of Network Economics* 2(2), 175–90.

Hayhoe, C. R., L. Leach and P. R. Turner (1999). 'Discriminating the number of credit cards held by college students: Using credit and money attitudes', *Journal of Economic Psychology* 20, 643–56.

Hirschman, E., (1982). 'Consumer payment systems: The relationship of attribute structure to preference and usage', *Journal of Business* 55(4), 531–45.

Humphrey, D., M. Kim and B. Vale (2001). 'Realizing the gains from electronic payments: Costs, pricing and payment choice', *Journal of Money, Credit and Banking* 33(2), 216–34.

Humphrey, D., L. Pulley and J. Vesala (1996). 'Cash, paper and electronic payments: A cross-country analysis', *Journal of Money, Credit and Banking* 28(4), 914–39.

Kidwell, B. and R. Turrisi (2004). 'An examination of college students money management tendencies', *Journal of Economic Psychology* 25, 601–16.

Little, R. J. A. (1988). 'Missing data adjustment in large survey', *Journal of Business and Economics Statistics* 6, 287–95.

Mantel, B. (2000). 'Why do consumers pay bills electronically? An empirical analysis', *Economic Perspectives*, Federal Reserve Bank of Chicago, no. 24.

Mantel, B. and T. McHugh (2001). 'Competition and innovation in the consumer e-payments markets? Considering the demand, supply and public policy issues', *Emerging Payments Occasional Working Paper Series*, Federal Reserve Bank of Chicago.

Maslow, A. H. (1954). *Motivation and Personality*, New York: Harper & Row.

Oleson, M. (2004). 'Exploring the relationship between money attitudes and Maslow's hierarchy of needs', *International Journal of Consumer Studies* 28(1), 83–92.

Rochet, J.-C. and J. Tirole (2004). 'Two-sided markets: An overview', IDEI Working Paper, no. 258.

Rosenberg, M. J. and C. I. Hoyland (1960). 'Cognitive, affective and behavioural components of attitudes', in C. I. Hoyland and M. J. Rosenberg, *Attitudes, Organization and Change: An Analysis of Consistency among Attitude Components*, Connecticutt: Yale University Press.

Rysman, M. (2006). 'An empirical analysis of payment card usage', Working Paper, Boston University.

Shy, O. and J. Tarkka (2002). 'The market for electronic cash cards', *Journal of Money, Credit, and Banking* 34(2), 299–314.

Stavins, J. (2001). 'Effect of consumer characteristics on the use of payment instruments', *New England Economic Review* 3, 19–31.

Venkatesh, V., C. Speier and M. G. Morris (2002). 'User acceptance enablers in individual decision making about technology: Toward an integrated model', *Decision Sciences* 33(2), 297–316.

White, H. (1980). 'A heteroskedasticity-consistent covariance matrix estimator and a direct test for heteroskedasticity', *Econometrica* 48, 817–38.

Xiao, J. J., F. E. Noring and J. G. Anderson (1995). 'College students' attitudes toward credit cards', *Journal of Consumer Studies* 19, 155–74.

Index

Note: Page numbers in bold indicate material in tables.